INTRODUCTION

This Snapshot guide, excerpted from my guidebook *Rick Steves'* *Germany*, introduces you to Germany's cutest corner, Bavaria, and its showpiece city, Munich. Salzburg, just across the border in Austria, adds sparkle.

Munich—a thriving and livable city—entertains visitors with rollicking beer halls, excellent museums, an inviting traffic-free core filled with grand facades, and a relaxing park that tempts visitors to become temporary *Münchners*. Bavaria is home to Europe's most famous castles—"Mad" King Ludwig's Neuschwanstein and its cousins—and idyllic alpine scenery. Scream down a mountain slope on a luge, ogle the ornate Rococo curlicues of the Wieskirche, glide up a lift to a summit viewpoint, and explore medieval castle ruins on a desolate hilltop. Then dive into the lively, strollable, music-crazy city of Salzburg—home to Mozart and *The Sound of Music*. Just thinking about the attractions in this book makes me want to yodel.

To help you have the best trip possible, I've included the following topics in this book:

• **Planning Your Time,** with advice on how to make the most of your limited time

• **Orientation,** including tourist information (abbreviated as TI), tips on public transportation, local tour options, and helpful hints

• **Sights** with ratings:

▲▲▲—Don't miss

▲▲—Try hard to see

▲—Worthwhile if you can make it

No rating—Worth knowing about

INTRODUCTION

 • **Sleeping** and **Eating,** with good-value recommendations in every price range
 • **Connections,** with tips on trains, buses, and driving

Practicalities, near the end of this book, has information on money, phoning, hotel reservations, transportation, and more, plus German survival phrases.

To travel smartly, read this little book in its entirety before you go. It's my hope that this guide will make your trip more meaningful and rewarding. Traveling like a temporary local, you'll get the absolute most out of every mile, minute, and dollar.

Gute Reise!

Rick Steves

MUNICH

München

Munich, often called Germany's most livable city, is also one of its most historic, artistic, and entertaining. It's big and growing, with a population of 1.5 million. Until 1871, it was the capital of an independent Bavaria. Its imperial palaces, jewels, and grand boulevards constantly remind visitors that Munich has long been a political and cultural powerhouse. Meanwhile, the concentration camp in nearby Dachau reminds us that 80 years ago, it provided a springboard for Nazism.

Orient yourself in Munich's old center, with its colorful pedestrian zones. Immerse yourself in the city's art and history—crown jewels, Baroque theater, Wittelsbach palaces, great paintings, and beautiful parks. Spend your Munich evenings in a frothy beer hall or outdoor *Biergarten*, prying big pretzels from buxom, no-nonsense beer maids amidst an oompah, bunny-hopping, and belching Bavarian atmosphere.

Planning Your Time

Munich is worth two days, including a half-day side-trip to Dachau. But if all you have for Munich is one day, follow the self-guided walk laid out in this chapter (visiting museums along the way), tour one of the royal palaces (the Residenz or the Nymphenburg), and drink in the beer-hall culture for your evening's entertainment. With a second day, choose from the following: Tour the Dachau Concentration Camp Memorial, rent a bike to enjoy the English Garden, head out to the BMW-Welt and Museum, or—if you're into art—tour your choice of the city's many fine art museums (especially the Alte Pinakothek). With all these blockbuster sights and activities, the city could easily fill three days. And remember, many visitors spend an entire day side-tripping south to "Mad" King Ludwig's Castles (covered in the Bavaria and Tirol chapter). Austria's Salzburg (2 hours one-way by direct train) is also within day-tripping distance.

Orientation to Munich

The tourist's Munich is circled by a ring road (site of the old town wall) marked by four old gates: Karlstor (near the main train station—the Hauptbahnhof), Sendlinger Tor, Isartor (near the river), and Odeonsplatz (no surviving gate, near the palace). Marienplatz marks the city's center. A great pedestrian-only zone (Kaufinger-strasse and Neuhauser Strasse) cuts this circle in half, running neatly from the Karlstor and the train station through Marienplatz to the Isartor. Orient yourself along this east-west axis. Ninety percent of the sights and hotels I recommend are within a 20-minute walk of Marienplatz and each other.

Despite its large population, Munich feels small. This big-city elegance is possible because of its determination to be pedestrian- and bike-friendly, and because of a law that no building can be taller than the church spires. Despite ongoing debate about changing this policy, there are still no skyscrapers in downtown Munich.

Tourist Information

Munich has two helpful city-run TIs (www.muenchen.de). One is in front of the **main train station** (with your back to the tracks, walk through the central hall, step outside, and turn right; Mon-Sat 9:00-20:00, Sun 10:00-18:00, hotel reservations tel. 089/2339-6500—no info at this number). The other TI is on Munich's main square, **Marienplatz,** below the glockenspiel (Mon-Fri 9:00-19:00, Sat 9:00-16:00, Sun 10:00-14:00).

At either TI, pick up brochures and buy the city map (€0.40, better than the free map in hotel lobbies—especially for anyone using public transit), and confirm your sightseeing plans. Private Munich Ticket offices inside the TIs sell concert and event tickets. The free, twice-monthly magazine *In München* lists all movies and entertainment in town (in German, organized by date). The TI can book you a room (you'll pay about 10 percent here, then pay the rest at the hotel), but you'll get a better value by contacting my recommended hotels directly. If you're interested in a Gray Line tour of the city or to nearby castles, don't buy your ticket at the TI; instead, you can get discounted tickets for these same tours at EurAide. For advice on transport and sightseeing passes, see "Getting Around Munich," later in this section.

The Bavarian Palace Department offers a 14-day ticket (called Mehrtagesticket) that covers admission to Munich's Residenz and

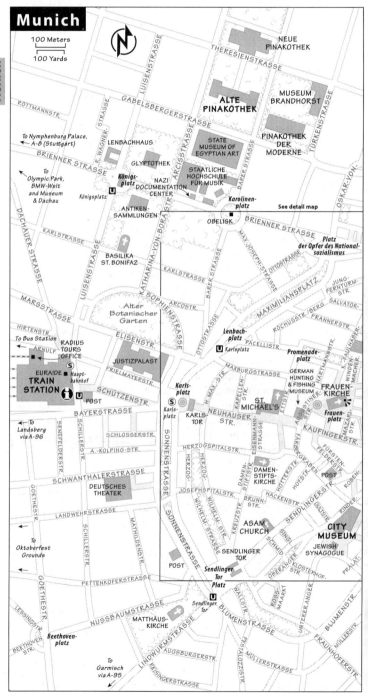

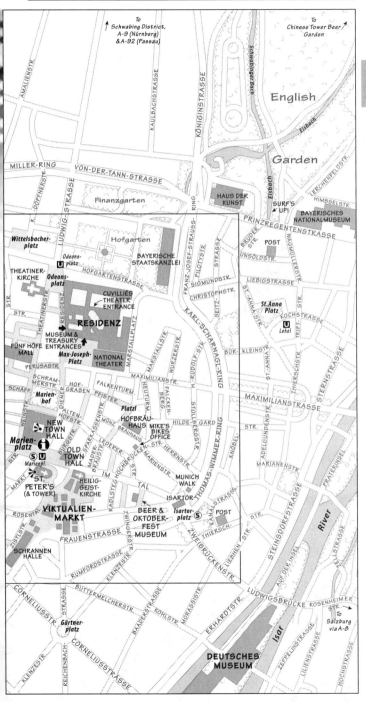

Nymphenburg Palace Complex, as well as other castles and palaces in Bavaria (€24, €40 family/partner pass, annual pass also available, not sold at TI—purchase at participating sights, www.schloesser.bayern.de). For avid castle-goers, this is a deal: Two people will save €5 with a family/partner pass even if only visiting the two Munich sights.

EurAide

At counter #1 in the train station's main *Reisezentrum* (travel center), the hardworking, eager-to-help EurAide desk is a godsend for

Eurailers and budget travelers. Alan Wissenberg and his EurAide staff can answer your train-travel and day-trip questions in clear American English. Paid by the German rail company to help you design your train travels, EurAide makes reservations and sells tickets, *couchettes,* and sleepers for the train at the same price you'd pay at the other counters (open March-Dec Mon-Fri 10:00-19:00, closed Sat-Sun and Jan-Feb, usually longer hours in summer). EurAide sells a €0.50 city map and offers a free, information-packed newsletter, *The Inside Track* (see www.euraide.com). As EurAide helps about 500 visitors per day in the summer, a line can build up; do your homework and have a list of questions ready. Chances are that your questions are already answered in *The Inside Track* newsletter—grab it and scan it first.

EurAide also sells cash-only tickets for Munich Walk city walking tours and Gray Line city bus tours, as well as for Gray Line tours to Neuschwanstein and Linderhof castles (all described later, under "Tours in Munich"). They offer a discount on these tickets to travelers with this book.

Arrival in Munich

By Train: Munich's main train station (München Hauptbahnhof) is a sight in itself—one of those places that can turn a homebody into a fancy-free vagabond.

Clean, high-tech **public toilets** are downstairs near track 26 (€1, showers-€7). For a quick rest stop, Burger King's toilets (upstairs,

€0.50 donation requested) are open to the public and as pleasant and accessible as its hamburgers.

Check out the bright and modern **food court** opposite track 14. For sandwiches and prepared meals to bring on board, I shop at **Yorma's** (two branches: one by track 26, another outside the station, next to the TI).

You'll find a city-run **TI** (out front of station and to the right) and **lockers** (€3-5, opposite track 26). The **k presse + buch** shop (across from track 23) is great for English-language books, newspapers, and magazines. **Radius Tours** (at track 32) rents bikes and organizes tours.

Up the stairs opposite track 21 are **car-rental agencies** (overlooking track 22), a quiet, non-smoking **waiting room** *(Warteraum)* that's open to anybody (overlooking track 23), and next door (opposite track 24) the plush **DB Lounge,** which is only for those with a first-class ticket issued by the Deutsche Bahn (German Railway; railpasses don't get you in).

Subway lines, trams, and buses connect the station to the rest of the city (though many of my recommended hotels are within walking distance of the station). If you get lost in the underground maze of subway corridors while you're simply trying to get to the train station, follow the signs for *DB* (Deutsche Bahn) to surface successfully. Watch out for the hallways with blue ticket-stamping machines in the middle—these lead to the subway, where you could be fined if nabbed without a validated ticket.

By Bus: Munich's central bus station, called the **ZOB,** is by the Hackerbrücke S-Bahn station (from the train station, it's one S-Bahn stop; www.muenchen-zob.de). The Romantic Road bus leaves from here, as do many buses to Eastern Europe and the Balkans.

By Plane: For airport information, see "Munich Connections" at the end of this chapter.

Helpful Hints

Museum Hours: Sights closed on Monday include the Alte Pinakothek, Munich City Museum, Jewish History Museum, Pinakothek der Moderne, Bavarian National Museum, Beer and Oktoberfest Museum, and the BMW Museum. The Neue Pinakothek closes on Tuesday. The art museums are generally open late one night a week. On Sunday, the Pinakotheks and Bavarian National Museum cost just €1 apiece, but you'll pay extra for the usually free audioguides.

Internet Access: There's free Wi-Fi on Marienplatz, courtesy of the city (connect to M-WLAN network, then click to accept terms). At the train station, you can get on Wi-Fi at Burger King, by the exit at the base of track 11 (buy an ice-cream cone for €0.80). If you need to use a computer, try the hole-in-the-wall call centers in the ethnic area near the train station.

Bookstore: The German bookstore **Hugendubel** towers above Marienplatz with a good selection of English guidebooks, comfy nooks for reading, and a view café (Mon-Sat 9:30-20:00, closed Sun, Marienplatz 22, tel. 089/3075-7575).

Need a Toilet? Munich had outdoor urinals until the 1972 Olympics and then decided to beautify the city by doing away with them. What about the people's needs? By law, any place serving beer must admit the public (whether or not they're customers) to use the toilets.

Pharmacy: Go out the front door of the train station, turn right, and walk past the TI to the corner of the building (Mon-Fri 7:00-20:00, Sat 8:30-20:00, closed Sun, Bahnhofplatz 2, tel. 089/5998-9040, www.hauptbahnhofapo.de); another one is just below Marienplatz at Im Tal 13 (Mon-Fri 8:30-19:30, Sat 8:30-18:00, closed Sun, tel. 089/292-760).

Laundry: A handy self-service **Waschcenter** is a 10-minute walk from the train station (€7/load, €12 for larger machines, drop-off service-€12/load; self-service daily 7:00-23:00, drop-off Mon-Sat 10:00-20:00, Sun 11:00-17:00; English instructions, Paul-Heyse-Strasse 21, near intersection with Landwehr-strasse, mobile 0171-734-2094). Theresienwiese is the closest U-Bahn station.

Bikes and Pedestrians: Signs painted on the sidewalk or blue-and-white street signs show which part of the sidewalk is designated for pedestrians and which is for cyclists. The strip of pathway closest to the street is usually reserved for bikes. Pedestrians wandering into the bike path may hear the cheery ding-ding of a cyclist's bell just before being knocked unconscious.

Taxi: Call 089/21610 for a taxi.

Private Driver: Johann Fayoumi is reliable and speaks English (€70/hour, mobile 0174-183-8473, www.firstclasslimousines.de, johannfayoumi@gmail.com).

Car Rental: Several car-rental agencies are located upstairs at the train station, opposite track 21 (open daily, hours vary).

The Inside Track **Train Travelers' Newsletter:** Anyone traveling by train should pick up this wonkish-yet-brilliant quarterly newsletter published by the wonkish-yet-brilliant Alan Wissenberg of EurAide (free, always available at the EurAide counter in the train station—described earlier, under "Tourist Information"). You'll find all the tedious but important details on getting to Neuschwanstein, Dachau, Nymphenburg, and Prague; the ins and outs of supplements and reservations necessary for railpass holders; a daily schedule of various tours in Munich;

and (of course) plenty of tips on how to take advantage of EurAide's services.

Great City Views: Downtown Munich's best city viewpoints (described in this chapter) are from the towers of St. Peter's Church (stairs only) and New Town Hall (elevator). Normally the Frauenkirche would make the list, but its towers are currently closed for renovation.

What's with Monaco? People walking around with guidebooks to Monaco aren't lost. "Monaco di Baviera" means "Munich" in *Italiano*.

Updates to this Book: For news about changes to this book's coverage since it was published, see www.ricksteves.com/update.

Getting Around Munich

Much of Munich is walkable. To reach sights away from the city center, use the efficient tram, bus, and subway systems. Taxis are honest and professional, but expensive and generally unnecessary.

By Public Transit

Subways are called U-Bahns and S-Bahns (S-Bahns are actually commuter railways that run underground through the city and are covered by Eurail Passes—but it's smarter to save your limited number of pass days for long-distance trips). Subway lines are numbered (for example, S-3 or U-5). The U-Bahn lines mainly run north-south, while the S-Bahn lines are generally east-west. The main S-Bahn lines (S-1 through S-8) converge on the central axis running from the Hauptbahnhof to Marienplatz. For a tourist, most of your public transit usage is along this corridor. Trams are more convenient than subways for some destinations (such as Nymphenburg Palace); one bus (#100) is useful for getting to the Alte Pinakothek and other major museums.

Ticket Options: The entire transit system (subway/bus/tram) works on the same tickets, sold at TIs, at booths in the subway, and at easy-to-use ticket machines marked *MVV* (which take coins and €5 and €10 bills; newer ones take PIN-enabled credit cards, too). There are four concentric zones—white, green, yellow, and orange. Almost everything described in this chapter is within the white/inner zone, except for Dachau (green zone) and the airport (orange zone).

• A one-zone **regular ticket** *(Einzelfahrkarte)* costs €2.60 and is good for three hours in one direction, including changes and stops. For short rides (four stops max, only two of which can be on the subway lines), buy the €1.30 *Kurzstrecke* ("short stretch") ticket. The €5.80 **all-day pass** *(Single-Tageskarte)* for the white/inner zone is a great deal for a single traveler. If you're going to Dachau, buy the *XXL* version of the *Single-Tageskarte*, which also includes

MUNICH

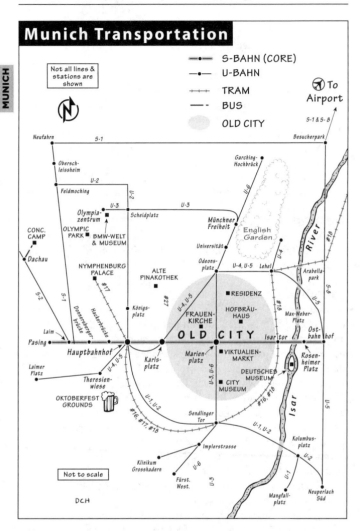

the green zone (€7.80); the **Gesamtnetz** version of the pass covers all four zones and gets you to the airport (€11.20).

• **All-day small-group passes** *(Partner-Tageskarte)* are an even better deal—they cover all public transportation for up to five adults and a dog (two kids count as one adult, so two adults, six kids, and a dog can travel with this ticket). A *Partner-Tageskarte* for the white/ inner zone costs €10.60. The **XXL** version, which includes Dachau, costs €13.60; and the **Gesamtnetz** version, including the airport, costs €20.40. These partner tickets—while seemingly impossibly cheap—are for real. Read it again and do the arithmetic. Even two people traveling together save money, and for groups, it's a real steal. The only catch is that you've got to stay together.

• For longer stays, consider a **three-day ticket** (€14.30/person, €24.60/partner ticket for the gang, white/inner zone only, does not include transportation to Dachau).

• The **City Tour Card,** which covers public transportation and adds stingy discounts on a few sights and tours, costs a little more than a transit pass (white/inner zone single traveler-€10/1 day, €20/3 days; white/inner zone partner ticket-€18/1 day, €31/3 days; discounts include the Residenz, BMW sights, and Nymphenburg Palace plus tours offered by Gray Line, Radius, and Munich Walks; details at www.citytourcard-muenchen.com). The partner tickets are the best value—three adults can save money with just one visit to the BMW Museum on public transit. For single travelers, the card usually isn't worth it. Students, seniors, and readers of this book qualify for many of the same discounts without having to buy the card.

Transit Tips: Maps of the transit system, available everywhere, help you navigate. To find the right platform, look for the name of the last station in the direction you want to travel. The name of this end-station is posted on trains and signs using the word *Richtung* ("direction"). Know where you're going relative to Marienplatz, the Hauptbahnhof, and Ostbahnhof, as these are so important to navigation that they are often referred to as end points.

In Munich, you must stamp all tickets with the date and time prior to using them (for an all-day or multi-day pass, you only have to stamp it the first time you use it). For the subway, punch your ticket in the blue machine *before* going down to the platform. For buses and trams, stamp your ticket once on board. Plainclothes ticket-checkers enforce this honor system, rewarding freeloaders with stiff €40 fines. All-day and multi-day passes are valid until 6:00 the following morning.

There's a transit customer-service center underground at Marienplatz (Mon-Fri 9:00-20:00, Sat 9:00-16:00, closed Sun, go down stairs by Beck's department store). For more transit info, call 0800/344-226-600 (Mon-Fri 8:00-20:00, not staffed Sat-Sun) or visit www.mvv-muenchen.de.

By Bike

Level, compact, and with plenty of bike paths, Munich feels made for those on two wheels. When biking in Munich, follow these simple rules: You must walk your bike through pedestrian zones; you can take your bike on the subway, but not during rush hour (Mon-Fri 6:00-9:00 & 16:00-18:00) and only if you buy a €2.50

bike day pass; and cyclists are expected to follow the rules of the road, just like drivers.

You can **rent bikes** quickly and easily from Radius Tours (in the train station), Mike's Bike Tours (near Marienplatz), and Munich Walk (by the Isartor). Each has an extensive selection of bikes; provides helmets, maps, and route advice; and offers bike tours. Radius and Mike's Bike both give a 10 percent discount with this book.

Radius Tours (*Rad* means "bike" in German) is in the train station in front of track 32 (3- to 7-speed city bikes-€3/hour, €14.50/day, €17/24 hours, €28/48 hours, fancier bikes cost more, give credit-card number as deposit, April-Oct daily 8:30-19:00, closed Nov-March, tel. 089/543-487-7730, www.radiustours.com).

Mike's Bike Tours is around the corner from the rear entrance to the Hofbräuhaus (€5 plus €2/hour, €15/day, daily mid-April-early Oct 10:00-20:00, March-mid-April and early Oct-mid-Nov 10:30-13:30 & 16:30-18:00, open by appointment mid-Nov-Feb, Bräuhausstrasse 10—enter around corner on Hochbrückenstrasse, tel. 089/2554-3987, www.mikesbiketours.com).

Munich Walk is just next to the Isartor, a short walk from Marienplatz (€10/4 hours, €18/24 hours, April-Oct Mon-Fri 11:00-18:00, Sat 9:00-18:00, Sun 10:00-15:00, Nov-March limited hours, Thomas-Wimmer-Ring 3, tel. 089/2423-1767, www.munichwalktours.de).

Suggested Ride: For a great city ride, consider this day on a bike: Rent from Radius at the train station, and take the bike path out Arnulfstrasse, pedaling along the canal out to Nymphenburg Palace. Ride around the palace grounds, then head to Olympic Park and BMW-Welt, and finish at the English Garden (for the late-afternoon or early-evening scene) before returning to the center. Or go for the Isar River bike ride.

Tours in Munich

Here's an overview of your tour options.

Munich's two largest conventional tour companies, Radius Tours and Munich Walk, both run bike tours, walking tours, and day trips to Dachau, Neuschwanstein Castle, and other places. Radius and Munich Walk compete directly with each other, and in my experience, they're comparable. Each company's website explains its ever-growing list of offerings (www.radiustours.com and www.munichwalktours.de). **Radius Tours** has a convenient office and meeting point in the main train station, in front of track 32 (run by Gabi Holder). **Munich Walk,** run by Ralph Lünstroth, uses Marienplatz as their meeting point. Both offer €2 off some of their tours with this book (described under "Walking Tours," below).

There's also **Gray Line,** which runs sightseeing buses around town and on day trips (tel. 089/5490-7560, www.sightseeing-munich.com), and a couple of bike tour companies. You can buy discounted cash-only tickets for Gray Line and Munich Walk tours at EurAide.

"Free" Tours: You'll encounter brochures advertising "free" walking and biking tours. These tours aren't really free—tipping is expected, and the guides actually have to pay the company for each person who takes the tour—so unless you tip more than they owe the company, they don't make a penny. The tours tend to be light on history, and the guides work hard to promote their company's other tours (which are not free).

Within Munich

Walking Tours

Munich Walk offers two daytime tours (€2 Rick Steves discount on each tour): a "City Walk" (€12, daily year-round at 10:45, April-Oct also daily at 14:45, 2.25 hours) and "Hitler's Munich" (€15, daily year-round at 10:15, 2.5 hours, extended €24 five-hour version Mon and Sat only). Their "Beer and Brewery" tour is more mature than your typical hard-partying pub crawl. You visit Paulaner, Munich's oldest brewery, to learn, eat, and drink in the city that made beer famous. The price includes three different beers in the brewery; afterward, the tour ends at the Hofbräuhaus (€22, May-mid-Sept daily at 18:15, fewer tours off-season, 3.5 hours). They also offer a Bavarian food-tasting tour, where you visit the Viktualienmarkt for lunch (€22 includes food). All Munich Walk tours depart from in front of the TI on Marienplatz. You don't need to reserve—just show up.

Radius Tours runs two city walking tours, both with reliably good guides: "Priceless Munich" (pay what you feel the guide is worth—not free, daily at 10:10, 2 hours) and "Birthplace of the Third Reich" (€15, €2 Rick Steves discount, April-mid-Oct daily at 15:00; mid-Oct-March Fri-Tue at 11:30; 2.5 hours). They also offer an educational "Bavarian Beer and Food" tour that includes a visit to the Beer and Oktoberfest Museum, samples of four varieties of beer, and regional food (€30, €2 Rick Steves discount; Tue, Thu, and Sat at 18:00; April-mid-Oct also Wed and Fri at 18:00; no tours during Oktoberfest; 3.5 hours). All tours depart from the Radius office in front of track 32 at the train station. No need to reserve; just show up.

The **Size Matters beer tour,** run by Kenyan-German-American Tim Muutuki, stops at the Augustiner Biergarten, Löwenbräu, and Park Café. Depart from Euro Youth Hotel, near the train station,

Munich at a Glance

In the Center

▲▲**Marienplatz** Munich's main square, at the heart of a lively pedestrian zone, watched over by New Town Hall (and its glockenspiel show). **Hours:** Always open; glockenspiel jousts daily at 11:00 and 12:00, plus 17:00 May-Oct; New Town Hall tower elevator runs May-Oct daily 10:00-19:00; Nov-April Mon-Fri 10:00-17:00, closed Sat-Sun. See page 19.

▲▲**Viktualienmarkt** Munich's "small-town" open-air market, perfect for a quick snack or meal. **Hours:** Beer garden open Mon-Sat until late, closed Sun. See page 24.

▲▲**Hofbräuhaus** World-famous beer hall, worth a visit even if you're not chugging. **Hours:** Daily 9:00-23:30. See page 34.

▲▲**The Residenz** Elegant family palace of the Wittelsbachs, awash in Bavarian opulence. Complex includes the Residenz Museum (private apartments), Residenz Treasury (housing Wittelsbach family crowns and royal knickknacks), and the impressive, heavily restored Cuvilliés Theater. **Hours:** Museum and treasury—daily April-mid-Oct 9:00-18:00, mid-Oct-March 10:00-17:00; theater—April-mid-Sept Mon-Sat 14:00-18:00, Sun 9:00-18:00; mid-Sept-March Mon-Sat 14:00-17:00, Sun 10:00-17:00. See page 40.

▲▲**Alte Pinakothek** Bavaria's best painting gallery, with a wonderful collection of European masters from the 14th through the 19th century. **Hours:** Wed-Sun 10:00-18:00, Tue 10:00-20:00, closed Mon. See page 46.

▲**Munich City Museum** The city's history in five floors. **Hours:** Tue-Sun 10:00-18:00, closed Mon. See page 25.

▲**Asam Church** Private church of the Asam brothers, dripping with Baroque. **Hours:** Sat-Thu 9:00-18:00, Fri 13:00-18:00. See page 28.

▲**Neue Pinakothek** The Alte's twin sister, with paintings from 1800 to 1920. **Hours:** Thu-Mon 10:00-18:00, Wed 10:00-20:00, closed Tue. See page 50.

▲**Pinakothek der Moderne** Munich's modern art museum with works by Picasso, Dalí, Miró, Magritte, and Ernst. **Hours:** Tue-Sun 10:00-18:00, Thu until 20:00, closed Mon. See page 51.

▲**English Garden** The largest city park on the Continent, packed with locals, tourists, surfers, and nude sunbathers. (On a bike, I'd rate this ▲▲.) **Hours:** Always open. See page 52.

▲**Deutsches Museum** Germany's version of our Smithsonian Institution, with 10 miles of science and technology exhibits. **Hours:** Daily 9:00-17:00. See page 53.

St. Peter's Church Munich's oldest church, packed with relics. **Hours:** Church—long hours daily; spire—Mon-Fri 9:00-18:30, Sat-Sun 10:00-18:30, off-season until 17:30. See page 22.

St. Michael's Church Renaissance church housing Baroque decor and a crypt of 40 Wittelsbachs. **Hours:** Church—Tue-Thu and Sat 8:00-19:00, Mon and Fri 10:00-19:00, Sun 7:00-22:15, open longer on summer evenings; crypt— Mon-Fri 9:30-16:30, Sat 9:30-14:30, closed Sun. See page 29.

Frauenkirche Huge, distinctive twin-domed church looming over the city center. **Hours:** Sat-Wed 7:00-19:00, Thu 7:00-20:30, Fri 7:00-18:00. See page 32.

Away from the Center

▲▲**Nymphenburg Palace** The Wittelsbachs' impressive summer palace, featuring a hunting lodge, coach museum, fine royal porcelain collection, and vast park. **Hours:** Park—daily 6:30-dusk, palace buildings—daily April-mid-Oct 9:00-18:00, mid-Oct-March 10:00-16:00. See page 57.

▲▲**BMW-Welt and Museum** The carmaker's futuristic museum and floating-cloud showroom shows you BMW past, present, and future in some unforgettable architecture. **Hours:** BMW-Welt—building 7:30-24:00, exhibits 9:00-18:00; museum—Tue-Sun 10:00-18:00, closed Mon. See page 62.

▲▲**Dachau Concentration Camp** Notorious Nazi camp on the outskirts of Munich, now a powerful museum and memorial. **Hours:** Daily 9:00-17:00. See page 64.

▲**Museum of Transportation** Deutsches Museum's cross-town annex devoted to travel. **Hours:** Daily 9:00-17:00. See page 55.

▲**Andechs Monastery** Baroque church, hearty food, and Bavaria's best brew, in the nearby countryside. **Hours:** Beer garden daily 10:00-20:00, church open until 18:00. See page 70.

at Senefelderstrasse 5 (€15, daily at 18:45, mobile 0176-7475-2100, www.sizemattersbeertour.de).

Local Guides

A guide can be a great value—especially if you assemble a small group. Six people splitting the cost can make the luxury of a private guide affordable. I've had great days with two good guides: **Georg Reichlmayr** (€160/3 hours, tel. 08131/86800, mobile 0170-341-6384, program explained on his website, www.muenchen-stadtfuehrung.de, info@muenchen-stadtfuehrung.de) and **Monika Hank** (€115/2 hours, €135/3 hours, tel. 089/311-4819, mobile 0175-923-2339, monika.hank@web.de). They've both helped me generously with much of the historical information in this chapter.

Bike Tours

Munich lends itself to bike touring, and four outfits fit the bill. You don't need to reserve for any of these—just show up—but do confirm times in advance online or by phone. Prices include bike rental (you'll pick up your bike after meeting your guide).

Munich Walk offers 3.5-hour bike tours around Munich (€20, €2 Rick Steves discount, June-Oct daily at 10:45, April-May Sat-Sun only at 10:45, no tours Nov-March, depart from Marienplatz TI). Confirm times at www.munichwalktours.de.

Radius Tours has similar 3.5-hour bike tours (€22, €2 Rick Steves discount, April-mid-Oct only, daily at 10:30). Tours leave from the Radius office at track 32 in the train station (confirm times at www.radiustours.com).

Mike's Bike Tours, in their 20th season, packs four hours of "edutainment" on wheels (€25, €3 Rick Steves discount, 1-hour break in Chinese Tower beer garden, daily mid-April-Aug at 11:30 and 16:30, March-mid-April and Sept-mid-Nov at 12:30, meet under tower of Old Town Hall at east end of Marienplatz; more options in summer, tel. 089/2554-3987, www.mikesbiketours.com).

Lenny's Bike Tours has a 3.5-hour tour that is pitched toward backpackers and is generally led by young Brits (€15 with request for tips at the end, 1-hour break in Chinese Tower beer garden, starts at fish fountain in Marienplatz, daily mid-April-Aug at 11:30 and 16:00, March-mid-April and Sept-mid-Nov at 12:30, www.discovermunichnow.com).

Hop-on, Hop-off Bus Tour

Gray Line Tours has hop-on, hop-off bus tours that leave from in front of the Karstadt department store at Bahnhofplatz, directly across from the train station. Choose from a basic, one-hour "Express Circle" that heads past the Pinakotheks, Marienplatz, and Karlsplatz (3/hour, 9:40-18:00); or the more extensive "Grand Circle" that lasts 2.5 hours and also includes the Nymphenburg

Palace and BMW-Welt/Museum (1/hour, 9:40-16:00). If you plan on visiting Nymphenburg and the BMW center, this is a very efficient way to see both—just plan your visits to these sights around the tour schedule (bus generally leaves from Nymphenburg at :30 past the hour, and from BMW at :45 past). This tour is actually well worthwhile—sitting upstairs on the topless double-decker bus, you'll see lots of things missed by the typical visitor wandering around the center. It complements the information in this book, though the live narration (in German and English) is delivered as stiffly as a tape recording. Just show up and pay the driver (€15 Express tour—valid all day, €20 Grand tour—valid 24 hours, daily in season, tel. 089/5490-7560, www.sightseeing-munich.com). You'll get a €1-2 discount by buying your ticket in advance on their website or (cash only) at EurAide.

Beyond Munich

While you can do all these day trips from Munich on your own by train, going as part of an organized group can be convenient—especially to Neuschwanstein.

"Mad" King Ludwig's Castle at Neuschwanstein

Choose between an escorted tour to Neuschwanstein by train and local bus, or guided private bus tours that include extras such as Linderhof Castle. Though they're a little more expensive, I prefer the bus tours—you're guaranteed a seat (public transport to Neuschwanstein is routinely standing-room only in summer), and you get to see more. All these tours can sell out, especially in summer, so it's wise to buy your ticket a day ahead (for information on visiting the castle on your own, see the next chapter).

Gray Line Tours offers rushed all-day bus tours of Neuschwanstein that also include Ludwig's Linderhof Castle and 30 minutes in Oberammergau (€51, €7 Rick Steves discount if you buy your ticket at EurAide—cash only, two castle admissions-€21 extra, daily all year, www.sightseeing-munich.com). Tours meet at 8:10 and depart at 8:30 from the Karstadt department store (across from the station). While tours are designed to be in both English and German, if groups are large they may split them up and you'll get only English. **Munich Walk** advertises a tour that sounds similar—because they're simply selling tickets for this Gray Line trip.

Bus Bavaria (run by Mike's Bike Tours) offers a similar private bus tour for English-speakers with an outdoor theme—a bike ride and short hike near Neuschwanstein are included (€49, €4 Rick Steves discount, Neuschwanstein admission-€11 extra; June-mid-Aug Mon-Tue and Thu-Sat; less frequent May and mid-Aug-Oktoberfest; daily during Oktoberfest; check web for departure times, meet at Mike's Bike Tours office near Hofbräuhaus,

Bräuhausstrasse 10—enter around corner on Hochbrückenstrasse, tel. 089/2554-3987, mobile 0172-852-0660, www.mikesbiketours. com).

Radius Tours runs all-day tours to Neuschwanstein Castle using public transportation. Your guide will escort you onto the train to Füssen and then the bus from there to the castle, give you some general information, and help you into the castle for the standard tour that's included with any admission ticket (€39, €32 with railpass, €2 Rick Steves discount, castle admission-€12 extra; daily April-mid-Oct at 9:30, back by 19:00; mid-Oct-March tours run Mon, Wed, and Fri-Sun at 9:30; smart to reconfirm times, departs from the Radius office near track 32 in the train station, www. radiustours.com).

Dachau Concentration Camp
The camp is easy to see on your own. But if you'd prefer a guided visit, Radius and Munich Walk tours are a great value, considering how good and passionate their guides are—and that you're only paying about €10 for the guiding, once you factor in transportation costs. Allow about five hours total. Both companies charge the same price (€22, includes €8 cost of public transportation, €2 Rick Steves discount). It's smart to reserve the day before, especially for the morning tours. Choose between **Radius** (April-mid-Oct daily at 9:15 and 12:15; mid-Oct-March daily at 10:00) and **Munich Walk** (April-Oct daily at 10:15 and 13:15; Nov-March daily at 10:15).

Nürnberg
Just an hour away by fast train, this makes a great day trip from Munich. Do it on your own using this book, or take the **Radius Tours** all-day excursion (see their website for details—www.radiustours.com).

Other Day Tours
Radius Tours also offers all-day trips to Salzburg and the castles at Herrenchiemsee (details at www.radiustours.com). Munich Walk does Salzburg tours (www.munichwalktours.de). These trips cost around €35-42 and include public transport there and back.

Self-Guided Walk

Munich City Walk
I've laced the top sights in the old town center into a ▲▲▲ walk, starting at Marienplatz and ending at the Hofgarten. You can do these sights in any order and take a break from the walk to tour the museums (details about visiting these sights are given later, under "Sights in Munich"), but if you want to cover the center in a logical way, this is a great template. I've included basic walking directions

linking the sights. You can also download this walk as a free Rick Steves audio tour.

• *Begin your walk at the heart of the old city, with a stroll through...*

▲▲Marienplatz

Riding the escalator out of the subway into sunlit Marienplatz (ma-RIEN-platz, "Mary's Square") gives you a fine first look at

the glory of Munich: great buildings, outdoor cafés, and people bustling and lingering like the birds and breeze with which they share this square. Most of the buildings around you were bombed in World War II and rebuilt—either matching their original design or in a modern, functional style. This place was a traffic mess until 1972 when—as part of the city's Olympics makeover—the subway was built, and the square was pe-destrianized. Take in the ornate facades of the gray, pointy Old Town Hall and the Neo-Gothic New Town Hall, with its beloved glockenspiel.

The **New Town Hall** (Neues Rathaus), built from 1867 until 1908, dominates Marienplatz. This very Neo-Gothic structure is a fine example of the same Historicism (mixing-and-matching of historical styles) that you see in nearby Neuschwanstein, London's Houses of Parliament, Budapest's Parliament, and other buildings of that era. Notice the politics of the statuary: The 40 statues—though sculpted only in 1900—decorate the New Town Hall not with civic leaders, but with royals and blue-blooded nobility. Be-cause this building survived the bombs and had a central location, it served as a US military headquarters in 1945.

The New Town Hall is famous for its **glockenspiel**—dating from 1908—which "jousts" daily at 11:00 and 12:00 all year (also

at 17:00 May-Oct). The *Spiel* has four parts: the wedding procession, the joust, the coopers' dance, and the rooster crowing. It recalls a noble wedding that actually took place here in 1568. The duke and his bride watch the action as the groom's Bavarian family (in Bavarian white and blue) joyfully jousts with the bride's French family (in red and white). Below, the barrel-makers—famous for being the first to dance in the streets after a deadly plague lift-ed—do their popular jig. Finally, the solitary cock crows.

At the very top of the New Town Hall is

MUNICH

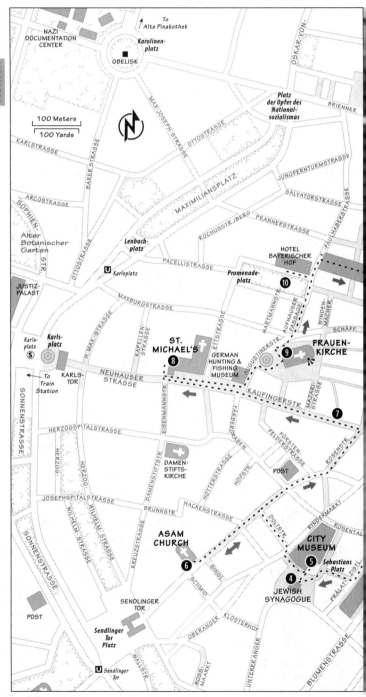

MUNICH

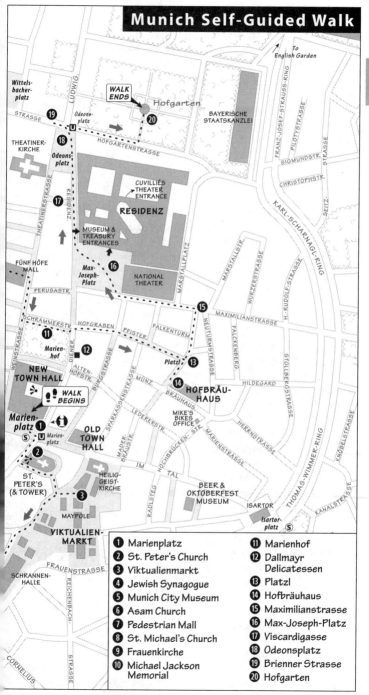

Munich Self-Guided Walk

1 Marienplatz
2 St. Peter's Church
3 Viktualienmarkt
4 Jewish Synagogue
5 Munich City Museum
6 Asam Church
7 Pedestrian Mall
8 St. Michael's Church
9 Frauenkirche
10 Michael Jackson Memorial

11 Marienhof
12 Dallmayr Delicatessen
13 Platzl
14 Hofbräuhaus
15 Maximilianstrasse
16 Max-Joseph-Platz
17 Viscardigasse
18 Odeonsplatz
19 Brienner Strasse
20 Hofgarten

a statue of a child with outstretched arms, dressed in monk's garb and holding a book in its left hand. This is the **Münchner Kindl,** the symbol of Munich (the city's name comes from *Kloster von Mönchen*—"cloister of monks"). You'll spot this mini-monk all over town, on everything from posters to tram cars (often holding other objects, like a bundle of radishes or a giant beer). Over the centuries, the monk has gone through several transformations. He started as a grown man, wearing a gold-lined black cloak and red shoes. Artists later represented him as a young boy, then a gender-neutral child, and, more recently, a young girl. Every year, a young woman dressed as the *Kindl* kicks off Oktoberfest by leading the opening parade on horseback, and then serves as the mascot throughout the festivities.

The New Town Hall tower offers **views** of the city (€2.50, elevator from under glockenspiel; May-Oct daily 10:00-19:00; Nov-April Mon-Fri 10:00-17:00, closed Sat-Sun).

Marienplatz is marked by a statue of the square's namesake, the **Virgin Mary,** moved here in 1638 from its original location in the Frauenkirche in thanks that the Swedes didn't sack the town during their occupation. It was also a rallying point for the struggle against the Protestants. The cherubs are fighting the four great biblical enemies of civilization: the dragon of war, the lion of hunger, the rooster-headed monster of plague and disease, and the serpent of heresy (Protestantism). The serpent that's being stepped upon represents the "wrong faith," a.k.a. Martin Luther. (In this bastion of Counter-Reformation Catholicism, Protestants were not allowed to worship openly until about 1800.)

The **Old Town Hall** (Altes Rathaus, the Disneyesque building at the right side of the square as you face New Town Hall) was completely destroyed by WWII bombs and later rebuilt. Ludwig IV, an early Wittelsbach who was Holy Roman Emperor back in the 14th century, stands in the center of the facade. He donated this great square to the people. On the bell tower, find the city seal with its Münchner Kindl and towers. Munich flourished because, in its early days, all salt trade had to stop here on Marienplatz.

• *Just beyond the southeast corner of Marienplatz, with its steeple poking up above a row of buildings, is...*

St. Peter's Church

The oldest church in town, St. Peter's overlooks Marienplatz from its perch near the Viktualienmarkt. It's built on the hill where

Munich's original monastic inhabitants probably settled. (Founded in 1158, the city celebrated its 850th birthday in 2008.) Outside, notice the 16th- and 17th-century tombstones plastered onto the wall—a reminder that in the Napoleonic age, the cemeteries surrounding most city churches were (for hygienic and practical space reasons) dug up and moved.

St. Peter's was badly damaged in World War II. Inside, photos show the bomb damage (near the entrance). As part of the soul of the city (according to a popular song, "Munich is not Munich without St. Peter's"), the church was lovingly rebuilt—half with Augustiner beer money, the rest with private donations—and the altar and ceiling frescoes were marvelously restored (possible with the help of Nazi catalog photos). After World War II, the bells played a popular tune that stopped before the last note, reminding locals that the church still needed money to rebuild.

Pop into the church. (If there's a Mass in progress, visitors are welcome in the back.) Apostles line the nave, leading up to St. Peter above the altar. On the ceiling, you'll see Peter crucified upside-down. The finely crafted, gray iron fences that line the nave were donated after World War II by the local blacksmiths of the national railway. The precious and fragile sandstone Gothic chapel altar (front left) survived the war only because it was buried in sandbags.

Munich has more relics than any city outside of Rome. For more than a hundred years, it was the pope's bastion against the rising tide of Protestantism in northern Europe during the Reformation. Favors done in the defense of Catholicism earned the Wittelsbachs neat relic treats. For instance, check out the tomb of Munditia (second side chapel on left as you enter). She's a third-century martyr (note the ancient Roman tombstone with red lettering), whose remains were given to Munich by Rome in thanks and as a vivid reminder that those who die for the cause of the Roman Church go directly to heaven without waiting for Judgment Day.

It's a long climb to the top of the **spire** (306 steps, no elevator)—much of it with two-way traffic on a one-lane staircase—but the view is dynamite (€1.50, Mon-Fri 9:00-18:30, Sat-Sun 10:00-18:30, off-season until 17:30, last exit 30 minutes after closing). Try to be two flights from the top when the bells ring at the top of the hour. Then, when your friends back home ask you about your trip, you'll say, "What?"

• Just behind and beyond (downhill from) St. Peter's, join the busy commotion of the...

MUNICH

▲▲Viktualienmarkt

Early in the morning, you can still feel small-town Munich here, long a favorite with locals for fresh produce and good service (open Mon-Sat, food stalls open late, closed Sun).

Such a market could never really afford the most expensive real estate in town, but Munich charges these old-time shops only a percentage of their gross income, enabling them to carry on (and keeping out fast-food chains). The city keeps an eye on what's being sold so the market stays classy and authentic. Wander around. Münchners consider the produce here to be top quality but expensive.

The beer garden, with its picnic tables filled with hungry and thirsty locals, seems to be the market's centerpiece. Notice the **beer counter.** Munich's breweries take turns here. Changing every so often, a sign *(Heute im Ausschank)* announces which of the seven brews is being served today. Here, under the standard beer-garden chestnut trees, you can order just half a liter—unlike at other *Biergartens* (handy for shoppers who want to have a quick sip and then keep on going). As is the tradition, picnickers are welcome at tables without tablecloths if they buy a drink. The Viktualienmarkt is ideal for a light meal.

The huge **maypole** is a tradition. Fifteenth-century town market squares posted a maypole as a practical information post—decorated with various symbols to explain which crafts and merchants were doing business in the market. Munich's maypole shows the city's seven great brews, and the crafts and festivities associated with brewing. You can't have a kegger without coopers—find the merry barrel-makers who are the four cute guys dancing. Today, barrel-making is coming back as top breweries like to have real wooden kegs to tap in their beer halls. The bottom of the pole celebrates the world's oldest food law: a beer-purity law signed in 1487 by Duke Albert IV of Bavaria (beer was liquid food in the Middle Ages).

• Leave the Viktualienmarkt from the far side. Behind the Pschorr beer hall stands a modern glass-and-iron building—the former grain exchange—called the Schrannenhalle. Wander through to enjoy a whiff of top-end edibles. Chocoholics can go downstairs into the Milka Coco World (tasty samples and a good WC). The Schrannenhalle spills out on the right into Sebastiansplatz (with a line of healthy eateries) leading to the synagogue. Walk two blocks (ask anyone: "Synagogue?") to find the...

Jewish Synagogue

Thanks to Germany's acceptance of religious refugees from former Soviet states, Munich's Jewish population has now reached its pre-Nazi size—10,000 people. The city's new synagogue and Jewish History Museum anchor a revitalized Jewish quarter, which includes a kindergarten and day school, children's play-

ground, fine kosher restaurant (at #18), and bookstore. Standing in the middle of the square, notice the low-key but efficient security.

While the **synagogue** is shut tight to non-worshippers, its architecture is striking from the outside. Lower stones of travertine evoke the Wailing Wall in Jerusalem, while an upper section represents the tent that held important religious wares during the 40 years of wandering through the desert until the Temple of Solomon was built, ending the Exodus. The synagogue's door features the first 10 letters of the Hebrew alphabet, symbolizing the Ten Commandments.

The cube-shaped **museum** (behind the cube-shaped synagogue) is stark, windowless, and as inviting as a bomb shelter. Its small permanent exhibit in the basement is disappointing. The two floors of temporary exhibits might justify the entry fee.

Cost and Hours: Museum-€6, discount with Munich City Museum, Tue-Sun 10:00-18:00, closed Mon, St.-Jakobs-Platz 16, tel. 089/2339-6096, www.juedisches-museum-muenchen.de.

• *Facing the synagogue, on the same square, is the...*

▲Munich City Museum (Münchner Stadtmuseum)

This museum's main draw is a big permanent exhibit on Munich's history, called "Typically Munich!" It tries to examine the various stereotypes—both positive and negative—that people around the world associate with this city. The recently redone exhibit feels fairly hip by city-museum standards. You'll start on the ground floor (medieval), and continue upstairs to the first floor (through 1850) and second floor (up to World War II) before ending back on the first floor in a kind of lounge which celebrates BMW, the 1972 Olympics, and the new Allianz Arena. Pick up the free, thick, small-print booklet with English translations of the exhibit's text, or pay for an audioguide.

The rest of the museum is skippable: marionettes and musical instruments from around the world (third and fourth floors, no

The History of Munich: Part 1
Monastic Beginnings to the Age of Kings

Born from Salt (1100-1500)

Munich began in the 12th century, when Henry the Lion (Heinrich der Löwe) muscled in on the lucrative salt trade, burning a rival's bridge over the Isar River and building his own near a monastery of "monks"—München. (The town's coat of arms features the Münchner Kindl, a child in monk's robes; see page 22.) Henry built walls and towers and opened a market, and peasants flocked in from the countryside. Marienplatz was the center of town and the crossroads of the Salzstrasse (Salt Road) from Salzburg to Augsburg. After Henry's death, the town was taken over by an ambitious merchant family, the Wittelsbachs (1240), and became the capital of the region (1255). Munich-born Louis IV (1282-1347) was elected king of Germany and Holy Roman Emperor, temporarily making Munich a major European capital.

By the 1400s, Munich's maypole-studded market bustled with trade. Besides salt, Munich gained a reputation for beer. More than 30 breweries pumped out the golden liquid that lubricated both trade and traders. The Bavarian Beer Purity Law assured quality control. Wealthy townspeople erected the twin-domed Frauenkirche and the Altes Rathaus on Marienplatz, and the Wittelsbachs built a stout castle that would eventually become the cushy Residenz. When the various regions of Bavaria united in 1506, Munich (pop. 14,000) was the natural capital.

Religious Wars, Plagues, Decline (1500-1800)

While Martin Luther and the Protestant Reformation raged in northern Germany, Munich became the ultra-Catholic heart of the Counter-Reformation. The devout citizens poured enormous funds into building the massive St. Michael's Church (1583) as a home for the Jesuits, and into the Residenz (early 1600s) as home of the Wittelsbachs. Both were showpieces of conservative power and the Baroque and Rococo styles.

During the Thirty Years' War, the Catholic city was surrounded by Protestants (1632). The Wittelsbachs surrendered quickly and paid a ransom, sparing the city from pillage, but it was soon hit by the bubonic plague. After that passed, the leaders erected the Virgin's column on Marienplatz to thank God for killing only 7,000 citizens. (Munich's many plagues are also remembered today when the glockenspiel's barrel-makers do their daily dance to ward off the plague.)

The double whammy of invasion and disease left Munich bankrupt and powerless, overshadowed by the more powerful Habsburgs of Austria. The Wittelsbachs took their cultural cues from France (Nymphenburg Palace is a mini-Versailles), England (the English Garden), and Italy (the Pitti Palace-inspired Residenz). While the rest of Europe modernized and headed toward democracy, Munich remained conservative and behind the times.

The Kings (1806-1918): Max I, Ludwig I, Max II, Ludwig II, Ludwig III

When Napoleon's army surrounded the city (1800), the Wittelsbachs again surrendered hospitably. Napoleon rewarded the Wittelsbach "duke" with more territory and a royal title: "king." Maximilian I (r. 1806-1825; see page 37), a.k.a. Max Joseph, now ruled the Kingdom of Bavaria, a nation bigger than Switzerland, with a constitution and parliament. When Max's popular son Ludwig married (Sept 1810), it touched off a two-week celebration that became an annual event: Oktoberfest.

As king, Ludwig I (r. 1825-1848) set about rebuilding the capital in the Neoclassical style we see today. Medieval walls and ramshackle houses were replaced with grand buildings of columns and arches (including the Residenz and Alte Pinakothek). Connecting these were broad boulevards and plazas for horse carriages and promenading citizens (Ludwigstrasse and Königsplatz). Ludwig established the university and built the first railway line, turning Munich (pop. 90,000) into a major transportation hub, budding industrial city, and fitting capital.

In 1846, the skirt-chasing King Ludwig (see Nymphenburg's Gallery of Beauties; page 60) was beguiled by a notorious Irish dancer named Lola Montez. She became his mistress, and he fawned over her in public, scandalizing Munich. The Münchners resented her spending their tax money and dominating their king (supposedly inspiring the phrase "Whatever Lola wants, Lola gets"). In 1848, as Europe was swept by a tide of revolution, the citizens rose up and forced Ludwig to abdicate. His son Maximilian II (r. 1848-1864) continued Ludwig's enlightened program of modernizing, while studiously avoiding dancers from Ireland.

In 1864, 18-year-old Ludwig II (r. 1864-1886) became king. He invited the composer Richard Wagner to Munich, planning a lavish new opera house to stage Wagner's operas. Munich didn't like the idea, and Ludwig didn't like Munich. For most of his reign, Ludwig avoided the Residenz and Nymphenburg, instead building castles in the Bavarian countryside at the expense of Munich taxpayers. (For more on the king, see page 117.)

In 1871, Bavaria became part of the newly united Germany, and overnight, Berlin overtook Munich as Germany's power center. Turn-of-the-century Munich was culturally rich, giving birth to the abstract art of Wassily Kandinsky, Paul Klee, and the Blue Rider group. But this artistic flourishing didn't last long. World War I devastated Munich. Poor, hungry, disillusioned, unemployed Münchners roamed the streets. Extremists from the left and right battled for power. In 1918, a huge mob marched to the gates of the Residenz and drove the forgettable King Ludwig III (r. 1913-1918)—the last Bavarian king—out of the city, ending nearly 700 years of continuous Wittelsbach rule.

For "The History of Munich: Part 2," see page 30.

English), a modest exhibit on the Nazi era in Munich (out back, limited English), and temporary exhibits which cost extra.

Cost and Hours: €4, audioguide-€3, Tue-Sun 10:00-18:00, closed Mon, no crowds, bored and playful guards, St.-Jakobs-Platz 1, tel. 089/2332-2370, www.stadtmuseum-online.de.

Shopping: The Servus Heimat souvenir shop in the courtyard is entertaining (Mon-Sat 10:00-22:00, Sun 10:00-18:00, tel. 089/2370-2380).

Eating: The museum's Stadt Café is handy for a good meal (listed under "Eating in Munich," later).

• *Continue through the synagogue's square, past the fountain, across the street, and one block further to the newly pedestrianized Sendlinger Strasse. Down the street 100 yards to the left, the fancy facade (at #62) marks the...*

▲Asam Church (Asamkirche)

The private church of the Asam brothers is a gooey, drippy Baroque-concentrate masterpiece by Bavaria's top two Rococonuts.

Just 30 feet wide, it was built in 1740 to fit within this row of homes. Originally, it was a private chapel where these two brother-architects could show off their work (on their own land, next to their home and business headquarters—to the left), but it's now a public place of worship.

Cost and Hours: Free, Sat-Thu 9:00-18:00, Fri 13:00-18:00, tel. 089/2368-7989. The church is small, so visitors are asked not to enter during Mass (held Tue and Thu-Fri 17:00-18:00, Wed 8:30-9:30, and Sun 10:00-11:00).

Visiting the Church: This place of worship served as a promotional brochure to woo clients, and is packed with every architectural trick in the books. Imagine approaching the church not as a worshipper, but as a shopper representing your church's building committee. First stand outside: Hmmm, the look of those foundation stones really packs a punch. And the legs hanging over the portico...nice effect. Those starbursts on the door would be a hit back home, too.

Then step inside: I'll take a set of those over-the-top golden capitals, please. We'd also like to order the gilded garlands draping the church in jubilation, and the twin cupids capping the confessional. Check out the illusion of a dome on the flat ceiling—that'll save us lots of money. The yellow glass above the altar has the effect of the thin-sliced alabaster at St. Peter's in Rome, but it's within our budget! And, tapping the "marble" pilasters to determine that they are just painted fakes, we decide to take that, too. Crammed between two buildings, light inside this narrow church is limited, so there's a big, clear window in the back for maximum illumination—we'll order one to cut back on our electricity bill.

Visiting the Asam Church, you can see why the Asam brothers were so prolific and successful. Speaking of the brothers, there are black-and-white portraits of the two Asams in oval frames flanking the altar. On the way out, say good-bye to the gilded grim reaper in the narthex (left side as we're leaving) as he cuts the thread of life—reminding all who visit of our mortality...and, by the way, that shrouds have no pockets.

• *Leaving the church, look to your right, noticing the Sendlinger Tor at the end of the street—part of the fortified town wall that circled Munich in the 14th century. Then turn left and walk straight up Sendlinger Strasse. Walk toward the Münchner Kindl, still capping the spire of the New Town Hall in the distance, and then up Rosenstrasse, until you hit Marienplatz and the big, busy...*

Pedestrian Mall

This car-free area (Kaufingerstrasse and Neuhauser Strasse) leads you through a great shopping district, past cheap department stores, carnivals of street entertainers, and good old-fashioned slicers and dicers. In the 12th century, this was the town's main commercial street. Traders from Salzburg and Augsburg would enter the town through the fortified Karlstor. This street led—past the Augustiner beer hall (opposite St. Michael's Church to this day)—right to the main square and cathedral.

Here, the commerce never stops. As one of Europe's first pedestrian zones, the mall enraged shopkeepers when it was built in 1972 for the Olympics. Today, it is Munich's living room. Nearly 9,000 shoppers pass through it each hour. The shopkeepers are happy...and merchants nearby are begging for their streets to become traffic-free. Imagine this street in Hometown, USA.

• *Stroll a few blocks away from Marienplatz toward the Karlstor, until you arrive at the big church on the right.*

St. Michael's Church

One of the first great Renaissance buildings north of the Alps, this church has a brilliantly decorated interior. Inspired by the Gesù (the Jesuits' main church in Rome), it was built in the late 1500s as a home to Bavaria's Jesuits (and rebuilt after WWII bombing—see photos in the back). The statue of Michael fighting a Protestant demon (on the front facade) is a reminder that this leader of heaven's army invited the Jesuits to literally counter the Reformation from here. Note the ornate pulpit, mid-nave, where Jesuit priests

The History of Munich: Part 2 Troubled 20th Century and Today's Revitalization

This picks up where "Part 1" leaves off (see page 26).

Nazis, World War II, and Munich Bombed (1918-1945)

Germany after World War I was in chaos. In quick succession, the prime minister was gunned down, Communists took power, and the army restored the old government. In the hubbub, one fringe group emerged—the Nazi party, headed by the charismatic war veteran Adolf Hitler.

Hitler—an Austrian who'd settled in Munich—made stirring speeches in Munich's beer halls (including the Hofbräuhaus) and galvanized the city's disaffected. On November 8-9, 1923, the Nazis launched a coup d'état known as the Beer Hall Putsch. They kidnapped the mayor, and Hitler led a mob to overthrow the German government in Berlin. The march got as far as Odeonsplatz before Hitler was arrested and sent to prison in nearby Landsberg. Though the Nazis eventually gained power in Berlin, they remembered their roots, dubbing Munich "Capital of the Movement." The Nazi headquarters stood near today's obelisk on Brienner Strasse, Dachau was chosen as the regime's first concentration camp, and Odeonsplatz was designated as a place where all who passed by were required to perform the Nazi salute.

As World War II drew to a close, it was clear that Munich would be destroyed. Hitler did not allow the evacuation of much of the town's portable art treasures and heritage—a mass emptying of churches and civil buildings would have caused hysteria and been a statement of no confidence in his leadership. While museums were closed (and could be systematically emptied over the war years), public buildings were not. Rather than save the treasures, the Nazis photographed everything.

Munich was indeed pummeled mercilessly by air raids, leveling nearly half the city. What the bombs didn't get was destroyed by 10 years of rain and freezing winters.

would hammer away at Reformation heresy. The interior is striking for its barrel vault, the largest of its day. The acoustics are spectacular, and the choir—famous in Munich—sounds heavenly singing from the organ loft high in the rear.

The **crypt** (*Fürstengruft*, down the stairs by the altar) contains 40 stark, somewhat forlorn Wittelsbach royal tombs, including the more ornate resting place of King Ludwig II. The flowers around

Munich Rebuilds (1945-Present)

After the war, with generous American aid, Münchners set to re-constructing their city. During this time, many German cities established commissions to debate their rebuilding strategy: They could restore the old towns, or bulldoze and go modern. While Frankfurt decided to start from scratch (hence its Manhattan-like feel today), Munich voted—by a close margin—to rebuild its old town.

Münchners took care to preserve the original street plan and re-create the medieval steeples, Neo-Gothic facades, and Neo-classical buildings. They blocked off the city center to cars, built the people-friendly U-Bahn system, and opened up Europe's first pedestrian-only zone (Kaufingerstrasse and Neuhauser Strasse). Only now, more than 65 years after the last bombs fell, are the restorations—based on those Nazi photographs—finally being wrapped up. And those postwar decisions still shape the city: Buildings cannot exceed the height of the church spires.

The 1972 Olympic Games, featuring a futuristic stadium, a sleek new subway system, and radical-at-the-time pedestrian zones, were to be Munich's postwar statement that it had arrived. However, the Games turned tragic when a Palestinian terrorist group stormed a dormitory and kidnapped (and eventually killed) 11 Israeli athletes. In 1989, when Germany reunited, Berlin once again became the focal point of the country, relegating Munich to the role of sleepy Second City.

These days, Munich seems to be comfortable just being itself rather than trying to keep up with Berlin. In fact, the city seems to be on a natural high, especially since the ascension of Joseph Ratzinger (the local archbishop) to the papacy in 2005, his wildly successful homecoming visit in 2006, and Munich hosting the World Cup soccer tournament that same year.

Today's Munich is rich—home to BMW and Siemens, and a producer of software, books, movies, and the latest fashions. It's consistently voted one of Germany's most livable cities—safe, clean, cultured, a university town, built on a human scale, and close to the beauties of nature. Though it's the capital of Bavaria and a major metropolis, Munich's low-key atmosphere has led Germans to dub it *Millionendorf*—the "village of a million people."

Ludwig's tomb aren't placed by the church, but by private individuals—romantics still mad about their "mad" king.

Cost and Hours: Church entry free, open Tue-Thu and Sat 8:00-19:00, Mon and Fri 10:00-19:00, Sun 7:00-22:15, open longer on summer evenings; crypt-€2, Mon-Fri 9:30-16:30, Sat 9:30-14:30, closed Sun; frequent concerts—check the schedule outside; tel. 089/231-7060, www.st-michael-muenchen.de.

• *Backtrack a couple blocks on the pedestrian mall, then turn left, swinging* *past the wild boar statue which marks the **German Hunting and Fishing Museum**. This place has outdoorsy regalia, kid-friendly exhibits, and the infamous Wolpertinger—a German "jackalope" created by very creative local taxidermists. When you reach Augustinerstrasse, you'll find Munich's towering, twin-domed cathedral.*

Frauenkirche

These twin onion domes are the symbol of the city. Some say Crusaders, inspired by the Dome of the Rock in Jerusalem, brought

home the idea. Others say these domes are the inspiration for the characteristic domed church spires marking villages throughout Bavaria.

Cost and Hours: Free, Sat-Wed 7:00-19:00, Thu 7:00-20:30, Fri 7:00-18:00, tel. 089/290-0820, www.muenchner-dom.de.

Visiting the Church: While much of the church was destroyed during World War II (see photos just inside the entrance, on the right), the towers survived, and the rest has been gloriously restored.

Built in Gothic style in the late 1400s, the Frauenkirche (Church of Our Lady) has been the city's cathedral since 1821. Construction was funded with the sale of indulgences, but money problems meant the domes weren't added until Renaissance times. Late-Gothic buildings in Munich were generally built of brick—easy to make locally and cheaper and faster to build than stone. This church was constructed in a remarkable 20 years (1468-1488). It's located on the grave of Ludwig the Bavarian (who died in 1347). His big, black, ornate, tomb-like monument (now in the back) was originally in front at the high altar. Standing in the back of the nave, notice how your eyes go right to the altar...Christ...and (until recently) the tomb of Ludwig. Those Wittelsbachs—always trying to be associated with God. In fact, this alliance was instilled in people through the prayers they were forced to recite: "Virgin Mary, mother of our duke, please protect us."

A plaque over the last pew on the left recalls the life story of Joseph Ratzinger, who occupied the archbishop's seat in this very church from 1977 until 1982, when he moved into Pope John Paul II's inner circle in the Vatican, and ultimately became Pope Benedict XVI in 2005.

Walk slowly up the main aisle, enjoying modern stained glass right and left. At the high altar, under a huge hanging crucifix and before the seat of the local bishop (once warmed by the man who became Pope Benedict XVI), look up and notice the tiny painted portraits of craftsmen who helped construct the church in the mid-15th century decorating the tops of the columns. Walk around behind the altar to the apse where three tall windows still have their original 15th-century glass. Each pane was painstakingly taken out and stored safely to survive the bombs of 1944.

• *Leaving the church, turn right, walk 50 yards and take the well-signed Aufhauser Passage through a modern building—it leads to Promenadeplatz. Before continuing straight down Kardinal Faulhaber Strasse, detour a few steps left. Opposite the huge Hotel Bayerischer Hof is a park with a colorful modern memorial.*

Michael Jackson Memorial

When Michael Jackson was in town, like many VIPs, he'd stay at the Hotel Bayerischer Hof. Fans would gather in the park waiting for him to appear at his window. He'd sometimes oblige, but his infamous baby-dangling incident happened in Berlin, not here. When he died in 2009, devotees created this memorial below a statue of composer Orlando di Lasso. They still visit daily and keep it tidy.

• *Now return to Kardinal Faulhaber Strasse. Continue walking on this street lined with 18th-century mansions of leading Bavarian families; their homes eventually became offices and bank buildings. At #11, turn right and walk through the Fünf Höfe Passage—a series of courtyards, exclusive shops, galleries, and restaurants—with a hanging garden dangling above the main hall. Emerging on a busy pedestrian street, head right, noticing the Münchner Kindl again high above, to a big green square.*

Marienhof

This square, tucked behind the New Town Hall, was left as a green island after the 1945 bombings. The square will be dug up for years while Munich builds an additional subway tunnel here. With virtually the entire underground system converging on nearby Marienplatz, this new tunnel will provide a huge relief to the city's congested subterranean infrastructure.

• *On the far side of Marienhof is the most aristocratic grocery store in all of Germany…*

Dallmayr Delicatessen

When the king called out for dinner, he called Alois Dallmayr. This place became famous for its exotic and luxurious food items: tropical fruits, seafood, chocolates, fine wines, and coffee (there are meat and cheese counters, too). As you enter, read the black plaque with the

MUNICH

royal seal by the door: *Königlich Bayerischer Hof-Lieferant* ("Deliverer for the King of Bavaria and his Court"). Catering to royal and aristocratic tastes (and budgets), it's still the choice of Munich's old rich. Today, it's most famous for its sweets, chocolates, and coffee—dispensed from fine hand-painted Nymphenburg porcelain jugs.

Hours: Mon-Sat 9:30-19:00, closed Sun; Dienerstrasse 13-15, www.dallmayr.de.

• *Reliquary Room (Leaving Dallmayr, turn right and right again. Hofgraben (which becomes Pfisterstrasse) leads three blocks east, going gently downhill and directly to Platzl—"small square." (If you get turned around, just ask any local to point you toward the Hofbräuhaus.)*

Platzl

As you stand here—in the heart of medieval Munich—recall that everything around you was flattened in 1945, and appreciate the facades. Imagine the work that went into rebuilding after World War II. The reconstruction happened in stages: From 1945 to 1950, they removed 12 million tons of bricks and replaced roofs to make buildings weather tight. From 1950 to 1972, they redid the exteriors. From 1972 to 2000, they refurbished the interiors. Today, Platzl hosts a lively mix of places to eat and drink—pop-culture chains like Starbucks and Hard Rock Café alongside top-end restaurants like the recommended Wirtshaus Ayinger and Schuhbecks (Schuhbecks Eis is a favorite for ice cream; Pfisterstrasse 9-11, tel. 089/2166-90430).

• *At the bottom of the square (#9), you can experience the venerable...*

▲▲Hofbräuhaus

Whether or not you slide your lederhosen on its polished benches, it's a great experience just to walk through the world's most famous beer hall in all its rowdy glory (and with its own gift shop).

Cost and Hours: Free to enter, daily 9:00-23:30, live oompah music during lunch and dinner; a 5-minute walk northeast of Marienplatz at Platzl 9, tel. 089/290-136-100, www.hofbraeuhaus.de.

Visiting the Hofbräuhaus: Standing outside, notice the structure from 1880. This is Historicism with huge arches. When the brewery moved out, this 5,000-seat food-and-beer palace was built in its place. Hofbräu remains one of the seven beers of Munich. The name means it's the beer of the royal court—the Wittelsbach choice (see the crown on the logo hanging outside the entry).

Before going into the actual beer hall, explore the building. Enter through the middle arch and climb to the top floor. Don't be shy. It's a people's place. You belong. As you climb the stone stairs, enjoy the historical photos showing what people ate, drank,

Oktoberfest

The 1810 marriage reception of King Ludwig I was such a success that it turned into an annual bash. These days, the Oktoberfest lasts just over two weeks (Sept 20-Oct 5 in 2014), starting on the third Saturday in September and usually ending on the first Sunday in October (www.oktoberfest.de).

Oktoberfest kicks things off with an opening parade of more than 6,000 participants. Every night, eight huge beer tents each fill with about 6,000 people. A million gallons of beer later, they roast the last ox.

It's best to reserve a room early, but if you arrive in the morning (except Fri or Sat) and haven't called ahead, the TI can usually help. The Theresienwiese fairground (south of the main train station), known as the "Wies'n" (VEE-zehn), erupts in a frenzy of rides, dancing, and strangers strolling arm-in-arm down rows of picnic tables while the beer god stirs tons of brew, pretzels, and wurst in a bubbling cauldron of fun. The triple-loop roller coaster must be the wildest on earth (best before the beer-drinking). During the fair, the city functions even better than normal, but is admittedly more expensive and crowded. It's a good time to sightsee, even if beer-hall rowdiness isn't your cup of tea.

If you're not visiting while the party's on, don't worry: You can still dance to oompah bands, munch huge pretzels, and show off your stein-hoisting skills any time of year at Munich's classic beer halls, including the venerable Hofbräuhaus (for descriptions of my favorite beer halls, see page 81).

The Theresienwiese fairgrounds also host a **Spring Festival** (*Frühlingsfestival*, two weeks in late April-early May, www.fruehlingsfest-muenchen.de) as well as Tollwood, an artsy, multicultural, alternative **Christmas market** (late Nov-Dec, www.tollwood.de). These fairs come with more locals, the same beer, music, and amusements, but no sky-high hotel prices or hour-long waits for the Ferris wheel.

In the city center, check out the humble **Beer and Oktoberfest Museum** (Bier- und Oktoberfestmuseum), which offers a low-tech and underwhelming take on history. Exhibits and artifacts outline the centuries-old quest for the perfect beer (apparently achieved in Munich) and the origins of the city's Oktoberfest celebration. The oldest house in the city center, the museum's home is noteworthy in itself (€4, Tue-Sat 13:00-18:00, closed Sun-Mon, between the Isartor and Viktualienmarkt at Sterneckerstrasse 2, tel. 089/2423-1607, www.bier-und-oktoberfestmuseum.de).

and wore a century ago. Check out the menus from 1911, 1955, and 1970. Skip the first floor, go to the top, open the door, and enter the huge hall. At the far end, in the loft above the stage, is an exhibit offering a fun photo op of a traditional table and a great look at Munich beer culture circa 1900.

OK, now go downstairs to the ground floor and dive headlong into the sudsy Hofbräu mosh pit. As you wander, look for the various *Stammtisch* signs (meaning "reserved" for regulars), hanging above tables where different clubs meet regularly; don't sit here unless you're specifically invited. Racks of locked steins, made of pottery and metal, are for regulars. You'll see locals stuffed into lederhosen and dirndls; giant gingerbread cookies that sport romantic messages; and postcards of the German (and apparently beer-drinking) pope.

After being bombed in World War II, this palace of beer was quickly rebuilt (reflecting the durability of traditional German priorities) and was back in business within a few years. Notice the quirky 1950s-style painted ceiling, with Bavarian colors, grapes, chestnuts, and fun "eat, drink, and be merry" themes. A slogan on the ceiling above the band reads, *Durst ist schlimmer als Heimweh* ("Thirst is worse than homesickness").

• *Leaving the Hofbräuhaus, turn right and walk two blocks up to the street called...*

Maximilianstrasse

This boulevard is known as the home of Munich's most exclusive shops. In 1816, King Ludwig I commissioned a stately boulevard with uniform facades in a Neo-Gothic style—Ludwigstrasse—which we'll see later. At the beginning of the 1850s, his son, Maximilian II, commissioned this more-engaging street designed for people and for shopping—not military parades. It leads from the National Theater, over the Isar River, to the Maximilianeum (home of the Bavarian parliament), which you can see at the end of the street.

Maximilianstrasse is busy with shoppers from places like Dubai and the United Arab Emirates. Walking here, you'll see wealthy, conservative Muslim families—casually dressed men, happy children, and women covered in black burkas. Locals explain that these families come here for medical treatment—usually operations, especially for the eyes and heart. And they make a vacation out of it, bringing the whole family and often their own car and driver. The shopping is great, there's no stress (like they might feel in London), security is excellent, and the weather is cool. Coming from a world with controls and constraints, being here—free and financially able to do what they like, has great appeal. Germans just politely provide the services, happy to make back some of what pours eastward every time they visit a gas station.

• *Walk left on Maximilianstrasse to the big square facing both the Residenz and the National Theater.*

Max-Joseph-Platz

The giant building wrapping around the square is the **Residenz,** the winter palace of the Wittelsbach royal family. Munich's best palace interior to tour, it features a museum (including some of the complex's most sumptuous staterooms), an impressive treasury, and the fine Cuvilliés Theater (all described later).

The centerpiece of the square is a grand statue of King Maximilian I, a.k.a. **Max Joseph,** who was installed as Bavaria's king in 1806 by Napoleon. Because Napoleon was desperate to establish his family as royal, Max Joseph was crowned on one condition: that his daughter marry Napoleon's stepson.

Later, with the Holy Roman Empire gone and Napoleon history, modern 19th-century kings had little choice but to embrace

constitutions that limited their power. (Remember that the country of Germany was only created in 1871. Until then, Bavaria was a middle-sized, independent power.) Max Joseph liberalized his realm with a constitution, emancipated Protestants and Jews, and established the Viktualienmarkt. He was a particularly popular king, and both his reign and his son Ludwig's were full of grand building projects designed to show that Bavaria was an enlightened state, Munich was a worthy capital, and the king was an equal with Europe's other royalty.

The **National Theater** (fronting this square), which opened in 1818, celebrated Bavaria's strong culture, roots, and legitimacy. The Roman numerals MCMLXIII (1963) mark the year the theater reopened after WWII bombing restoration.

• *Leave Max-Joseph-Platz opposite where you entered, walking alongside the Residenz on Residenzstrasse for about 100 yards to the next grand square. But before you get to Odeonsplatz, pause at the first corner on the left and look down Viscardigasse at the gold-cobbled swoosh in the pavement.*

Viscardigasse

In 1923 Hitler staged his failed coup, the Beer Hall Putsch, here in Munich. He riled up his followers and was leading them to Odeonsplatz to bring revolution to Germany. His angry parade was stopped by government forces at the square. Sixteen of his followers were killed (along with four policemen), and Hitler was sent to jail, where he wrote down his twisted ideas in *Mein Kampf*. Ten years later, when Hitler came to power, he made a memorial at Odeonsplatz to "the first martyrs of the Third Reich." Germans were required to raise their arms for the *Sieg Heil* salute as they passed. People wanting to skirt the indignity of saluting Nazism avoided the monument by detouring down Viscardigasse instead. Today the stream of shiny cobbles recalls their bypass route down this lane.

• *But now that Hitler's odious memorial in Odeonsplatz is long gone, you can continue to...*

Odeonsplatz

This square is another part of the royal family's grand imperial Munich vision. The church (Theatinerkirche) contains about half of the Wittelsbach tombs. The loggia (honoring Bavarian generals) is modeled after the famous Renaissance-style loggia in Florence. And two grand boulevards, Ludwigstrasse and Brienner Strasse, lead away from there.

Ludwigstrasse—used for big parades and processions—leads to a Roman-type triumphal arch that hovers in the distance. Though Max Joseph was himself a busy and visionary leader, it was his son and successor, the builder-king Ludwig I, who made Munich into a grand capital. His street, Ludwigstrasse, remains an impressive boulevard, with 60-foot-tall buildings stretching a mile from Odeonsplatz to the Arch of Victory. (The arch is capped with a figure of Bavaria riding a lion-drawn chariot; she's looking out to welcome home returning soldiers.)

• *From Odeonsplatz, face west, and look (or wander) down the grand...*

Brienner Strasse

This street gives you a taste of the Wittelsbachs' ambitious city planning. In the distance, and just out of sight on Karolinenplatz, the black obelisk commemorates the 30,000 Bavarians who marched with Napoleon to Moscow and never returned. Beyond that is the grand Königsplatz, or "King's Square," with its stern Neoclassicism, evocative of ancient Greece (and home to Munich's cluster of art museums).

Between here and the obelisk, Brienner Strasse goes through a square called **Platz der Opfer des Nationalsozialismus** ("Square of the Victims of Nazism"). It's the site of Himmler's Gestapo headquarters for the entire Third Reich, now entirely gone. If you went farther along, past the obelisk toward Königsplatz, you'd find two former Nazi administration buildings; one, with recognizably fascist architecture, was Hitler's main residence while in Munich (it's now the music academy; a plaque in the street explains the buildings' history). A big **Nazi Documentation Center** is scheduled to open here in 2014 (Brienner Strasse 34, www.ns-dokumentationszentrum-muenchen.de). Like documentation centers in Berlin, Köln, and Nürnberg, it will examine the reasons behind the Nazis' rise to power in Munich.

• *Backtrack to Odeonsplatz, then finish your walk just beyond Ludwigstrasse in the royal gardens or the genteel Café Tambosi, described next. The formal gate to the court garden is flanked by U-Bahn entries. Step through it and enter the...*

Hofgarten

The elegant court garden *(Hofgarten)* is a delight on a sunny afternoon. Just inside the gate is an arcade decorated with murals

Ludwig I painted in the early 1800s, telling the glorious story of Bavaria from 1155 to 1688. The garden's 400-year-old centerpiece is a Renaissance-style temple with great acoustics. (There's often a musician performing here for tips.) It's decorated with the same shell decor as was popular inside the Residenz.

For a good antidote to all the beer halls, try the venerable **Café Tambosi,** with its chairs lined up facing the boulevard as if to watch a parade. It has an Italian-influenced menu, Viennese elegance inside, and a relaxing garden setting out back (daily 8:00-24:00, €13-18 main courses, Odeonsplatz 18, tel. 089/298-322). In the garden beyond the café tables is a gravel *boules* court.

• *With this city walk completed, you've seen the essential Munich. Continuing on from here, a path leads to a building that houses the government offices of Bavaria, the Bayerischen Staatskanzlei. Look for the war memorial in front which honors the fallen heroes of World War I, but only the fallen of World War II. Beyond this point is the stern Haus der Kunst (a rare fascist building surviving in Munich) and a happy place where locals surf in the river—the gateway into Munich's sprawling English Garden, described later.*

If you're not tired, you can backtrack and tour the museum and treasury at the Residenz; or descend into the U-Bahn from the Odeonsplatz stop for points elsewhere. These—and many other—sights are described in the next section. If you're ready to eat, you have several choices. Café Tambosi (described above) and the elegant, recommended Spatenhaus are nearby, and there are more options if you head toward Marienplatz (see "Eating in Munich," later).

Sights in Munich

Most of the top sights in the city center are covered on my self-guided walk. But there's much more to see in this city.

The Residenz

For a long hike through corridors of gilded royal Bavarian grandeur, tour the Wittelsbachs' downtown palace. The sprawling Residenz, with a facade modeled after the Medici's Pitti Palace in Florence, evolved from the 14th through the 19th century—as you'll see on the charts near the entrance—and was largely rebuilt after World War II.

If you're torn about which of Munich's top two palaces to visit, the Residenz interior is best. Nymphenburg has the finest garden, grounds, and outdoor views.

Orientation: Within the Residenz complex are four sights: the 90-room Residenz Museum, the eight-room Residenz Treasury, the Halls of the Nibelungen (currently closed for renovation), and the Cuvilliés Theater. To reach the first three, enter the complex from the main entrance on Max-Joseph-Platz (at the corner of the palace nearest Marienplatz); there's also a side entrance on Residenzstrasse. Inside the main entrance, past the Halls of the Nibelungen, you'll find the ticket office and the entrances to the museum and treasury. The separate entrance to the Cuvilliés Theater is a little way up Residenzstrasse—ask staff to help if you can't find it.

Cost and Hours: €7 each to visit the Residenz Museum (palace apartments) and the treasury, including audioguides; €11 combo-ticket covers both; €13 version also covers Cuvilliés Theater; covered by Bavaria's 14-day ticket (Mehrtagesticket). The Halls of the Nibelungen are closed for renovation until at least late 2015. All parts of the palace are open daily April-mid-Oct 9:00-18:00, mid-Oct-March 10:00-17:00, last entry one hour before closing. The complex is located three blocks north of Marienplatz. Tel. 089/290-671, www.residenz-muenchen.de.

Halls of the Nibelungen (Nibelungensäle)

The mythological scenes in these halls—currently closed for renovation—were the basis of Wagner's *Der Ring des Nibelungen*. Wagner and "Mad" King Ludwig were friends and spent time hanging out here (c. 1864). The images in this hall could well have inspired Wagner to write his *Ring* and Ludwig to build his "fairy-tale castle," Neuschwanstein.

▲▲Residenz Museum (Residenzmuzeum)

Though called a "museum," what's really on display here are the best parts of the Residenz itself: the palace's spectacular banquet and reception halls, and the Wittelsbachs' lavish private apartments. It's the best place to get a glimpse of the opulent lifestyle of Bavaria's late, great royal family. (Whatever happened to the Wittelsbachs, the longest continuously ruling family in European history? They're still around, but they're no longer royalty, so most of them have real jobs now—you may well have just passed one on the street.)

❸ Self-Guided Tour: Leave the ticket office and pick up the free audioguide; later, if you visit the treasury, you'll need to stop by the desk again to have the guide switched over. Ask for a map of the museum (in English, often stacked up in the museum's first room or two).

You're about to walk through a 90-room residence, including three private chapels and several still-in-use banquet halls. Follow the red arrows along a one-way route made meaningful by the fine—if ponderous—audioguide and the English descriptions in each room. The rooms are numbered (in black on the bilingual information boards; these numbers are on the map too), and you'll also see red signs with numbers that you can punch into the audioguide. This tour just covers the highlights of the route, in the order you'll see them—use the audioguide to learn more about the rooms you find most compelling. Mercifully, you'll find chairs and benches in many rooms, as well as two WCs along the way.

• *One of the first rooms you'll come to is the...*

Shell Grotto (Room 6, actually outside, facing a courtyard, ground floor): The whole wall in front of you is made from Bavarian freshwater shells. This artificial grotto was an exercise in man controlling nature—a celebration of humanism. Renaissance humanism was a big deal when this was built in the 1550s. Imagine the ambience here during that time, with Mercury—the pre-Christian god of trade and business—overseeing the action, and red wine spurting from the mermaid's breasts and dripping from Medusa's head in the courtyard. Like the  rest of the palace, the grotto was destroyed by Allied bombs. After World War II, Germans had no money to contribute to the reconstruction—but they could gather shells. All the shells you see here were donated by small-town Bavarians, as the grotto was rebuilt according to Nazi photos (see "The History of Munich: Part 2" sidebar). To the right of the shells, the door marked *OO* leads to handy WCs.

• *The next room is the...*

Antiquarium (Room 7, ground floor): In the mid-16th century, Europe's royal families (such as the Wittelsbachs) collected

and displayed busts of emperors—implying a connection between themselves and the ancient Roman rulers. Due to the huge demand for these classical statues in the courts of Europe, many of the "ancient busts" were fakes cranked out by crooked Romans. Still, a third of the statuary you see here is original. This was, and still is, a festival banquet hall. Two hundred dignitaries can dine here, surrounded by allegories of the goodness of just rule on the ceiling. Check out the small paintings around the room—these survived the bombs because they were painted in arches. Of great historic interest, these paintings show 120 Bavarian villages as they looked in 1550. Even today, when a Bavarian historian wants a record of how his village once looked, he comes here. Notice the town of Dachau in 1550 (above the door on the left as you enter).

• *Keep going through a few more rooms, then up a stairway to the upper floor. Now the tour winds through a couple dozen small rooms on either side of a large courtyard—many of them the private apartments of the prince and his consort. In Room 32, detour to the right to see the...*

All Saints' Chapel (Room 32, upper floor): This early-19th-century chapel, commissioned by King Ludwig I, was severely damaged in World War II—and didn't reopen until 2003. It still hasn't been fully decorated and outfitted; photos by the entrance show how it used to look.

• *Keep going along the other side of the courtyard until you come to Room 45, where you'll have a choice between "short" and "long" routes. Unless you're in a real hurry and want to skip some of the best parts of the palace, choose the long route and turn right. You'll wind around through the large Imperial Hall (Room 111) and then through several small rooms, where the centerpiece painting on the ceiling is just blank black, as no copy of the original survived World War II. A little farther on, peek into the...*

Reliquary Room (Room 95, upper floor): This room harbors a collection of gruesome Christian relics (bones, skulls, and even several mummified hands) in ornate golden cases.

• *A few more steps brings you to the balcony of the...*

Chapel (Hofkapelle; the balcony is Room 96, and the chapel itself is Room 89): Dedicated to Mary, this late-Renaissance/early-Baroque gem was the site of "Mad" King Ludwig's funeral after his mysterious murder—or suicide—in 1886. (He's buried in St. Michael's Church.) Though Ludwig II was not popular in political circles, he was beloved by his people, and his funeral drew huge crowds. About 75 years earlier, in 1810, his grandfather and namesake (Ludwig I) was married here. After the wedding ceremony, carriages rolled his guests to a rollicking reception, which turned out to be such a hit that it became an annual tradition—Oktoberfest.

• *A couple rooms ahead is the...*

Private Chapel of Maximilian I (Room 98, upper floor): Duke Maximilian I, the dominant Bavarian figure in the Thirty Years' War, built one of the most precious rooms in the palace. The miniature pipe organ (from about 1600) still works. The room is sumptuous, from the gold leaf and the fancy hinges to the miniature dome and the walls made of stucco marble. (Stucco marble is fake marble—a special mix of stucco, applied and polished. Designers liked it because it was less expensive than real marble and the color could be controlled.) Note the post-Renaissance perspective tricks decorating the walls; they were popular in the 17th century. The case (on the right wall as you enter) supposedly contains skeletons of three babies from the Massacre of the Innocents in Bethlehem (where Herod, in an attempt to murder the baby Jesus, ordered all sons of a certain age killed).

• *Now you'll enter a set of rooms (#55-62) known as the Ornate Rooms (Reiche Zimmer), which were used for official business. The Wittelsbachs were always trying to keep up with the Habsburgs, and this long string of ceremonial rooms was all for show. The decor and furniture are Rococo—over-the-top Baroque. The family art collection, now in the Alte Pinakothek, once decorated these walls. The most lavish of these rooms is the...*

Red Room (Room 62, upper floor): The ultimate room is at the end of the corridor—the coral red room from 1740. (Coral red was *the* most royal of colors in Germany.) Imagine visiting the duke and having him take you here to ogle miniature copies of the most famous paintings of the day, composed with one-haired brushes. Notice the fun

effect of the mirrors around you—the corner mirrors make things go forever and ever.

• *From the Red Room, you'll circle around to a stairway that brings you back down to the ground floor, where you'll soon reach the long Ancestral Gallery (Room #4). Before walking down it, detour to the right, into the...*

Porcelain Cabinet (Room 5, ground floor): In the 18th century, the royal family bolstered their status with an in-house porcelain works (just like the one the Wettins, the ruling family of Saxony, had at Meissen, near Dresden). The Wittelsbach family had their own Nymphenburg porcelain made for the palace. See how the mirrors and porcelain vases give the effect of infinite pedestals. If this inspires you to own some pieces of your own, head to the Nymphenburg Porcelain Store at Odeonsplatz (see "Shopping in Munich," later).

• *Now go back into the...*

Ancestral Gallery of the Wittelsbach Family (Room 4, ground floor): This room is from the 1740s (about 200 years younger than the Antiquarium). All official guests had to pass through here to meet the duke (and his 100 Wittelsbach relatives). The family tree in the center is labeled "genealogy of an imperial family." Notice how the tree is shown being actually planted by Hercules, to boost their royal street cred. The big Wittelsbach/Habsburg rivalry was worked out through 500 years of marriages and battles—when they failed to sort out a problem through strategic weddings, they had a war. Opposite the tree are portraits of Charlemagne and Ludwig IV, each a Holy Roman Emperor and each wearing the same crown (now in Vienna). Ludwig IV was the first Wittelsbach HRE—an honor used for hundreds of years to substantiate the family's claim to power. You are surrounded by a scrapbook covering centuries of Wittelsbach family history.

Allied bombs took their toll on this hall. Above, the central ceiling painting has been restored, but since there were no photos of the other two ceiling paintings, those spots remain empty. Looking at the walls, you can see how each painting was hastily cut out of its frame. Museums were closed in 1939, then gradually evacuated in anticipation of bombings. But public buildings like this palace, which remained open to instill confidence in local people, could not prepare for the worst. It wasn't until 1944, when bombs were imminent, that the last-minute order was given to slice all portraits out of their frames and hide them away.

• *The doorway at the end of the hall deposits you back at the museum entrance. If you're also visiting the treasury, go to the audioguide desk to have them reset your guide.*

▲▲Residenz Treasury (Schatzkammer)

The treasury, next door to the Residenz Museum, shows off a thousand years of Wittelsbach crowns and knickknacks. Vienna's jewels are better, but this is the best treasury in Bavaria, with fine 13th- and 14th-century crowns and delicately carved ivory and glass.

Visiting the Treasury: A clockwise circle through the eight rooms takes you chronologically through a thousand years of royal treasure. (You can't get lost, as there aren't any side rooms.) You'll see little signs with a headphone icon and black-and-white numbers—punch these into your audioguide for full explanations.

The oldest jewels in the first room are 200 years older than Munich itself. Many of these came from various prince-bishop collections when they were secularized (and their realms came under the rule of the Bavarian king from Munich) in the Napoleonic Era

(c. 1800). The tiny mobile altar allowed a Carolingian king (from Charlemagne's family of kings) to pack light in 890—and still have a little Mass while on the road.

In Room 3, study the reliquary with St. George killing the dragon—sparkling with more than 2,000 precious stones. Get up close (it's OK to walk around the rope posts)...you can almost hear the dragon hissing. It was made to contain the relics of St. George, who never existed (Pope John Paul II declared him nothing more than a legend). If you could lift the minuscule visor, you'd see that the carved ivory face of St. George is actually the Wittelsbach duke (the dragon represents the "evil" forces of Protestantism).

In the next room (#4), notice the vividly carved ivory crucifixes from 1630 (#157 and #158, on the right). These incredibly realistic

sculptures were done by local artist Georg Petel, a friend of Peter Paul Rubens (whose painting of Christ on the cross—which you'll see across town in the Alte Pinakothek—is Petel's obvious inspiration). Look at the flesh of Jesus' wrist pulling around the nails.

Continue into Room 5. The free-standing glass case (#245) holds the never-used royal crowns of Bavaria. Napoleon ended the Holy Roman

Empire and let the Wittelsbach family rule as kings of Bavaria. As a sign of friendship, this royal coronation gear was made in Paris by the same shop that crafted Napoleon's crown. But before the actual coronation, Bavaria joined in an all-Europe anti-Napoleon alliance, and suddenly these were too French to be used.

Cuvilliés Theater

The exquisite Cuvilliés Theater is in a northern wing of the Residenz complex, best entered from Residenzstrasse. Your visit consists of

just one small but plush theater hall. It's so heavily restored, you can almost smell the paint. In 1751, this was Germany's ultimate Rococo theater. Mozart conducted here several times. Designed by the same brilliant dwarf architect who did the Amalienburg Palace, this theater is dazzling enough to send you back to the days of divine monarchs.

Cost and Hours: €3.50, €13 combo-ticket with museum and treasury, covered by Bavaria's 14-day ticket (Mehrtages-ticket); April-mid-Sept Mon-Sat 14:00-18:00, Sun 9:00-18:00; mid-Sept-March Mon-Sat 14:00-17:00, Sun 10:00-17:00; last entry one hour before closing, no English information provided.

Munich's Cluster of Art Museums

This cluster of blockbuster museums (the Alte, Neue, and Moderne Pinakotheks, the Museum Brandhorst, the Lenbachhaus, and the Glyptothek) displays art spanning from the 14th century to the 21st. The Glyptothek and Lenbachhaus are right by the König-splatz stop on the U-2 subway line. The three Pinakothek museums and the Brandhorst are just to the northeast. Handy tram #27 whisks you right to the Pinakothek stop from Karlsplatz (between the train station and Marienplatz). You can also take bus #100 from the train station, or walk 10 minutes from the Theresienstrasse or Königsplatz stops on the U-2 line.

A €12 combo-ticket covers any two of the three Pinakotheks, plus the Brandhorst. On Sundays, these museums and the Glyp-tothek let you in for just a token €1, but charge for the useful au-dioguides (normally included).

▲▲Alte Pinakothek

Bavaria's best painting gallery (the "Old Art Gallery," pronounced ALL-tuh pee-nah-koh-TEHK) shows off a world-class collection of European masterpieces from the 14th to 19th century, starring the two tumultuous centuries (1450-1650) when Europe went from

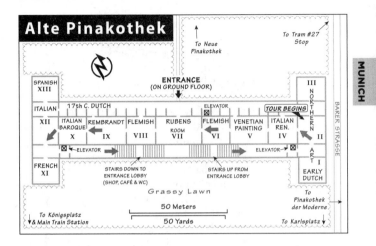

Alte Pinakothek

To Tram #27 Stop

To Neue Pinakothek

↑ **ENTRANCE** (ON GROUND FLOOR)

SPANISH XIII

ITALIAN XII

17th C. DUTCH

ITALIAN BAROQUE X

REMBRANDT IX

FLEMISH VIII

RUBENS ROOM VII

FLEMISH VI

VENETIAN PAINTING V

ITALIAN REN. IV

III NORTHERN

ELEVATOR

TOUR BEGINS

⊠ ELEVATOR

II

⊠ ←ELEVATOR

ELEVATOR→ ⊠

FRENCH XI

STAIRS DOWN TO ENTRANCE LOBBY (SHOP, CAFÉ & WC)

STAIRS UP FROM ENTRANCE LOBBY

A R T I

EARLY DUTCH

BARER STRASSE

Grassy Lawn

50 Meters

50 Yards

To Königsplatz & Main Train Station

To Karlsplatz

To Pinakothek der Moderne

MUNICH

medieval to modern. See paintings from the Italian Renaissance (Raphael, Leonardo, Botticelli, Titian) and the German Renaissance it inspired (Albrecht Dürer). The Reformation of Martin Luther eventually split Europe into two subcultures—Protestants and Catholics—with their two distinct art styles (exemplified by Rembrandt and Rubens, respectively).

Cost and Hours: €7, €1 on Sun, covered by €12 combo-ticket, open Wed-Sun 10:00-18:00, Tue 10:00-20:00, closed Mon, last entry 30 minutes before closing, free and excellent audioguide (€4.50 on Sun), obligatory lockers with refundable €2 deposit, no flash photos; U-2: Theresienstrasse, tram #27, or bus #100; Barer Strasse 27, tel. 089/2380-5216, www.pinakothek.de/alte-pinakothek.

❂ **Self-Guided Tour:** All the paintings we'll see are on the upper floor, which is laid out like a barbell. This tour starts at one fat end and works its way through the "handle" to the other end. From the ticket counter, head toward the back wall and walk up the stairway to the left. Go through two sets of doors into Room IIa, then make a left into Room II.

German Renaissance—Room II: Albrecht Altdorfer's *The Battle of Issus (Schlacht bei Issus)* shows a world at war. Masses of soldiers are swept along in the currents and tides of a battle completely beyond their control, their confused motion reflected in the swirling sky. We see the battle from a great height, giving us a godlike perspective. Though the painting depicts Alexander the Great's victory over the Persians (find the Persian king Darius turning and fleeing), it could as easily have been Germany in the 1520s. Christians were fighting Muslims, peasants battled masters, and Catholics and Protestants were squaring off for a century of conflict. The armies melt into a huge landscape, leaving the impression that the battle goes on forever.

Albrecht Dürer's larger-than-life *Four Apostles* (*Johannes und Petrus* and *Paulus und Marcus*) are saints of a radical new religion: Martin Luther's Protestantism. Just as Luther challenged Church authority, Dürer—a friend of Luther's—strips these saints of any rich clothes, halos, or trappings of power and gives them down-to-earth human features: receding hairlines, wrinkles, and suspicious eyes. The inscription warns German rulers to follow the Bible rather than Catholic Church leaders. The figure of

Mark—a Bible in one hand and a sword in the other—is a fitting symbol of the dangerous times.

Dürer's *Self-Portrait in Fur Coat* (*Selbstbildnis im Pelzrock*) looks like Jesus Christ but is actually 28-year-old Dürer himself, gazing out, with his right hand solemnly giving a blessing. This is the ultimate image of humanism: the artist as an instrument of God's continued creation. Get close and enjoy the intricately braided hair, the skin texture, and the fur collar. To the left of the head is Dürer's famous monogram—"A.D." in the form of a pyramid.

Italian Renaissance—Room IV: With the Italian Renaissance—the "rebirth" of interest in the art and learning of ancient Greece and Rome—artists captured the realism, three-dimensionality, and symmetry found in classical statues. Leonardo da Vinci's *Virgin and Child (Maria mit dem Kinde)* need no halos—they radiate purity. Mary is a solid pyramid of maternal love, flanked by Renaissance-arch windows that look out on the hazy

distance. Baby Jesus reaches out to play innocently with a carnation, the blood-colored symbol of his eventual death.

Raphael's *Holy Family at the Canigiani House (Die hl. Familie aus dem Hause Canigiani)* takes Leonardo's pyramid form and runs with it. Father Joseph forms the peak, with his staff as the strong central axis. Mary and Jesus (on the right) form a pyramid-within-the-pyramid, as do Elizabeth and baby John the Baptist on the left. They all exchange meaningful contact, safe within the bounds of the stable family structure.

In Botticelli's *Lamentation over Christ (Die Beweinung Christi)*, the Renaissance "pyramid" implodes, as the weight of the dead Christ drags everyone down, and the tomb grins darkly behind them.

Venetian Painting—Room V: In Titian's *Christ Crowned with Thorns (Die Dornenkrönung)*, a powerfully built Christ sits silently enduring torture by prison guards. The painting is by Venice's greatest Renaissance painter, but there's no symmetry, no pyramid form, and the brushwork is intentionally messy and Impressionistic. By the way, this is the first painting we've seen done on canvas rather than wood, as artists experimented with vegetable oil-based paints.

Rubens and Baroque—Room VII: Europe's religious wars split the Continent in two—Protestants in the northern countries, Catholics in the south. (Germany itself was divided, with Bavaria remaining Catholic.) The Baroque style, popular in Catholic countries, featured large canvases, bright colors, lots of flesh, rippling motion, wild emotions, grand themes...and pudgy winged babies, the sure sign of Baroque. This room holds several canvases by the great Flemish painter Peter Paul Rubens.

In Rubens' 300-square-foot *Great Last Judgment (Das Grosse Jüngste Gericht)*, Christ raises the righteous up to heaven (left side) and damns the sinners to hell (on the right). This swirling cycle of nudes was considered risqué and kept under wraps by the very monks who'd commissioned it.

Rubens and Isabella Brant shows the artist with his first wife, both of them the very picture of health, wealth, and success. They lean together unconsciously, as people in love will do, with their hands clasped in mutual affection. When his first

MUNICH

wife died, 53-year-old Rubens found a replacement—16-year-old Hélène Fourment, shown in an adjacent painting (just to the left) in her wedding dress. You may recognize Hélène's face in other Rubens paintings.

The Rape of the Daughters of Leucippus (Der Raub der Töchter des Leukippos) has many of Rubens' most typical elements—fleshy, emotional, rippling motion; bright colors; and a classical subject. The legendary twins Castor and Pollux crash a wedding and steal the brides as their own. The chaos of flailing limbs and rearing horses is all held together in a subtle X-shaped composition. Like the weaving counterpoint in a Baroque fugue, Rubens balances opposites.

Notice that Rubens' canvases were—to a great extent—cranked out by his students and assistants from small "cartoons" the master himself made (displayed in the side room).

Rembrandt and Dutch—Room IX: From Holland, Rembrandt van Rijn's *Six Paintings from the Life of Christ* are a down-

to-earth look at supernatural events. The *Adoration (Die Anbetung der Hirten)* of Baby Jesus takes place in a 17th-century Dutch barn with ordinary folk as models. The canvases are dark brown, lit by strong light. The *Adoration*'s light source is the Baby Jesus himself—literally the "light of the world." In the *Deposition (Kreuzabnahme)*, the light bounces off Christ's pale body onto his mother Mary, who has fainted in the shadows, showing how his death also hurts her. The drama is underplayed, with subdued emotions. In the *Raising of the Cross (Kreuzaufrichtung)*, a man dressed in blue is looking on—a self-portrait of Rembrandt.

▲Neue Pinakothek

The Alte Pinakothek's sister is a twin building across the street, showing off paintings from 1800 to 1920: Romanticism, Realism, Impressionism, *Jugendstil*, Claude Monet, Pierre-Auguste Renoir, Vincent van Gogh, Francisco Goya, and Franz von Stuck—Munich's answer to Gustav Klimt.

Cost and Hours: €7, €1 on Sun, covered by €12 combo-ticket, open Thu-Mon 10:00-18:00, Wed 10:00-20:00, closed Tue, well-done audioguide is usually free but €4.50 on Sun, classy Café Hunsinger in basement spills into park; U-2: Theresienstrasse, tram

#27, or bus #100; Barer Strasse 29 but enter on Theresienstrasse, tel. 089/2380-5195, www.pinakothek.de/neue-pinakothek.

▲Pinakothek der Moderne

This museum picks up where the other two leave off, covering the 20th century. Four permanent displays (graphics, design, archi-

tecture, and paintings) are layered within the striking minimalist architecture. You'll find works by Pablo Picasso, Salvador Dalí, Joan Miró, René Magritte, Max Beckmann, Max Ernst, and abstract artists. The big, white, high-ceilinged building itself is worth a look. Even if you don't pay to visit the exhibits, step into the free entrance hall to see the sky-high atrium and the color-ful blob-column descending the staircase.

Cost and Hours: €10, €1 on Sun, covered by €12 combo-ticket, open Tue-Sun 10:00-18:00, Thu until 20:00, closed Mon, audioguide is usually free but €4.50 on Sun; U-2: Theresienstrasse, tram #27, or bus #100; Barer Strasse 40, tel. 089/2380-5360, www.pinakothek.de/pinakothek-der-moderne.

Other Nearby Art Museums

The museum quarter has three more highly regarded muse-ums, but for the typical tourist on a quick visit they probably don't merit a visit. However, if you have a special interest in art, you'll want to know about them. The **Museum Brand-horst** covers the end of the 20th century and the begin-

ning of the 21st. Its collection is contained in a striking building with thousands of colored cylinders lining the outside (closed Mon, www.museum-brandhorst.de). The **Lenbachhaus** features the best

collection of the early Modern-ist movement known as Blaue Reiter (Blue Rider), a branch of Expressionism that flourished from 1911 to 1914. When Was-sily Kandinsky, Paul Klee, Franz Marc, Gabriele Münter, and some of their art-school cronies got fed up with being told how and what to paint, they formed the Blaue Reiter around a common ideology: to strive for new forms that expressed spiritual truth (closed Mon, www.lenbachhaus.de). And the **Glyptothek** is an impressive collection of Greek and Roman sculpture started by King Ludwig I (closed Mon, www.antike-am-koenigsplatz.mwn. de/glyptothek).

The English Garden and Nearby

▲English Garden (Englischer Garten)

Munich's "Central Park," the largest one on the Continent, was laid out in 1789 by an American. More than 100,000 locals commune with nature here on sunny summer days. The park stretches three miles from the center, past the university and the trendy, bohemian Schwabing quarter. For the best quick visit, take bus #100 or tram #18 to the Nationalmuseum/Haus der Kunst stop. Under the bridge, you may see surfers. Follow the path downstream into  the garden. Just beyond the hilltop temple (walk up for a postcard view of the city), you'll find the big Chinese Tower beer garden and other places to enjoy a drink or a meal (described later, under "Eating in Munich"). Afterward, instead of retracing your steps, you can walk (or take bus #54 a couple stops) to the Giselastrasse U-Bahn station and return to town on the U-3 or U-6.

A rewarding respite from the city, the park is especially fun—and worth ▲▲—on a bike under the summer sun and on warm evenings (unfortunately, there are no bike-rental agencies in or near the park). Caution: While local law requires sun-worshippers to wear clothes on the tram, the park is sprinkled with buck-naked sunbathers—quite a shock to prudish Americans (they're the ones riding their bikes into the river and trees).

Haus der Kunst

Built by Hitler as a temple of Nazi art, this bold and fascist building—a rare surviving example of a purpose-built Nazi structure—is now an impressive shell for various temporary art exhibits. Ironically, the art now displayed in Hitler's "house of art" is the kind that annoyed the Führer most—modern. Its cellar, which served as a nightclub for GIs in 1945, is now the extremely exclusive P-1 nightclub.

Cost and Hours: €5-10 per exhibit, combo-tickets save money if seeing at least two exhibits, daily 10:00-20:00, Thu until 22:00, little information in English but some exhibits may have English handouts, at south end of English Garden, tram #18 or bus #100

Green Munich

Although the capital of a very conservative part of Germany, Munich has long been a liberal stronghold. For nearly two decades, the city council has been controlled by a Social Democrat/Green Party coalition. The city policies are pedestrian-friendly—you'll find much of the town center closed to normal traffic, with plenty of bike lanes and green spaces. As you talk softly and hear birds rather than motors, it's easy to forget you're in the center of a big city. On summer Mondays, the peace and quiet make way for "blade Monday"—when streets in the center are closed to cars and as many as 30,000 inline skaters swarm around town in a giant rolling party.

---

from station to Nationalmuseum/Haus der Kunst, Prinzregentenstrasse 1, tel. 089/211-270, www.hausderkunst.de.

Nearby: Just beyond the Haus der Kunst, where Prinzregentenstrasse crosses the Eisbach canal, you can watch adventure-seekers surfing in the rapids created as the small river tumbles underground.

Bavarian National Museum (Bayerisches Nationalmuseum)
This tired but interesting collection features Tilman Riemenschneider woodcarvings, manger scenes, traditional living rooms, and old Bavarian houses.

Cost and Hours: €5, €1 on Sun, open Tue-Sun 10:00-17:00, Thu until 20:00, closed Mon, tram #18 or bus #100 from station to Nationalmuseum/Haus der Kunst, Prinzregentenstrasse 3, tel. 089/211-2401, www.bayerisches-nationalmuseum.de.

Deutsches Museum

Germany's answer to our Smithsonian National Air and Space Museum, the Deutsches Museum traces the evolution of science and technology. The main branch of the Deutsches Museum is centrally located. The two other branches—the Museum of Transportation and the Flight Museum—are situated outside the city center, but are worth the effort for enthusiasts. You can pay separately for each museum, or buy one €15 combo-ticket, which covers all three. Since this ticket has no time limit, you can spread out your visits to the various branches over your entire stay.

▲Deutsches Museum (Main Branch)

Enjoy wandering through well-described rooms of historic airplanes, spaceships, mining, the harnessing of wind and water power, hydraulics, musical instruments, printing, chemistry, computers, astronomy, and nanotechnology...it's the Louvre of technical know-how. The museum is designed to be hands-on; if you see a button, push it. But with 11 acres of floor space and 10 miles of exhibits, from astronomy to zymurgy, even those on roller skates will need to be selective. While the museum was a big deal a generation ago, today it feels to many a bit dated, dusty, and overrated. It's far too vast and varied to cover completely. The key is to study the floor plan that shows all the departments and simply visit the ones that interest you. Many sections of the museum are well-described in English. The much-vaunted high-voltage demonstrations (3/day, 15 minutes, all in German) show the noisy creation of a five-foot bolt of lightning.

Cost and Hours: €8.50, €15 combo-ticket includes Museum of Transportation and Flight Museum, daily 9:00-17:00, worthwhile €4 English guidebook, self-service cafeteria, tel. 089/21791, www.deutsches-museum.de.

Getting There: Take tram #16 to the Deutsches Museum stop. Alternatively, take the S-Bahn or tram #18 to Isartor, then walk 300 yards over the river, following signs.

Visiting the Museum: If you don't mind a very long, winding, one-way route that feels like a subterranean hike, start off in the **mines** (mines closed during daily German-language tours at 9:45 and 13:45). This exhibit traces the history of mining since prehistoric times. Enter just past the coat-check desk (just keep on going—there's only one way) through a vacant mine shaft with lots of old mining gear. While descriptions are only in German, the reconstructions of coal, potash, and salt mines are still impressive. When you emerge from the mines, skip the mineral oil and natural gas section *(Erdöl und Erdgas)* and follow the signs for *Ausgang* (exit).

The fascinating, compact exhibit on **marine navigation** (on the ground floor) has models of sail, steam, and diesel vessels, from early canoes to grand sailing ships. Take the staircase down into the galley, below the main floor, to check out how life on passenger ships has changed—and don't miss the bisected U1 submarine. This first German submarine, dating from 1906, has been in the museum since 1921.

Flying high above the masts of the marine navigation exhibit is the section on **aeronautics** (first floor). Displays cover the most basic airborne flights (flying insects and seed pods), Otto Lilienthal's successful efforts in 1891 to imitate bird flight, and the development of hot-air balloons and gas-powered zeppelins. Many of the planes here are original, including the Wright brothers' Type A (1909), fighters and cargo ships from the two World Wars, and the first functioning helicopter, made in 1936. Climb into the planes whenever permitted, and try out the flight simulator.

The **astronautics** exhibit is located on the second floor. Back in the 1920s, Germany was working on rocket-propelled cars and sleds. Germany's research provided the US and Soviet space teams with much of their technical know-how. Here, you can peer at models of the V-2 (one of the first remote-controlled rockets/weapons, from World War II), motors from the American Saturn rockets, and various space capsules, including Spacelab. The main focus is the walk on the moon, the Apollo missions, and the dogs-in-space program (monkeys, too)...but if you've ever been curious about how space underwear works, you'll find your answer here.

The third floor traces the **history of measurement,** including time (from a 16th-century sundial and an 18th-century clock to a scary Black Forest wall clock complete with grim reaper), weights, geodesy (surveying and mapping), and computing (from 18th-century calculators to antiquated computers from the 1940s and 1950s).

On your way to the state-of-the-art **planetarium** (worth a visit if open, requires €2 extra ticket, lecture in German), poke your head out into the **sundial garden** located above the third floor. Even if you're not interested in sundials, this is a great place for a view of the surrounding landscape. On a clear day, you can see the Alps.

▲Museum of Transportation (Verkehrszentrum)

You don't need to be an engineer or race-car driver to get a kick out of this fun museum. In 2003, the Deutsches Museum celebrated its centennial by opening this annex across town that shows off all aspects of transport, from old big-wheeled bikes to Benz's first car (a three-wheeler from the 1880s) to sleek ICE super-trains. It's housed in three giant hangar-like exhibition halls near the Oktoberfest grounds, a.k.a. Theresienwiese. All the exhibits are in both English and German.

Cost and Hours: €6, €15 combo-ticket includes Deutsches Museum and Flight Museum, daily 9:00-17:00, Theresienhöhe 14a, tel. 089/5008-06762, www.deutsches-museum.de.

Getting There: Take the U-4 or U-5 to Schwanthalerhöhe and follow signs for *Deutsches Museum* from the platform. The museum is just a few steps from the station exit.

Tours: The free tours daily at 11:00, 13:30, and 14:30 (each focusing on one of the museum's three halls) are primarily in German, but worth tagging along on for a chance to climb into the old carriage in Hall 2 (only allowed as part of the tour). The metal track simulates what it would have felt like to travel in the 18th century over different terrain (grass and cobblestones—pretty uncomfortable).

Visiting the Museum: True to the Deutsches Museum's interactive spirit, the Museum of Transportation is totally hands-on, and comes with plentiful English explanations. The museum asks what our lives would be like without transportation, and the exhibits show how modes of transportation developed from Neolithic "bone" skates (predecessors to today's inline skates) to 19th-century Lapland skis, to today's snowboards and fast cars.

Hall 1 focuses on urban transport, with special attention to Munich. Climb into the original 1967 U-Bahn car, marvel at a cross-section of the intricate and multilayered subway system, learn about the history of the bicycle, and admire the vintage cars arrayed into mock traffic jams. Twice a day (10:00-10:30 and 15:30-16:00; confirm times) they fire up an S-Bahn simulator and let visitors pretend to drive the train.

Hall 2 gives you a look at the development of long-distance overland travel. The focus here is on trains and coach travel (serious train buffs, however, will be more excited by the Deutsche Bahn Museum in Nürnberg). Don't miss the Maffei S3/6, a.k.a. "The Pride of Bavaria" (in its heyday the fastest steam engine, at nearly 80 miles per hour); climb aboard the clever old postal train car (complete with a mail slot on the side); and check out the 1950s panorama bus that shuttled eager tourists to fashionable destinations such as Italy.

Hall 3 is all about fun: motorcycles, bicycles, skis, and race cars. Famous prewar models include the deluxe Mercedes-Benz 370 (1930s) and the Auto Union Type C "Grand Prix" race car. Other tiny racers—which resemble metal pickles to the uninitiated—include the 1950s Mercedes-Benz 300 SLR and the famous Messerschmitt 200. You'll also find early 18th-century bicycles based on Leonardo da Vinci's drawings. Before the invention of the pedal crank, bikes were just silly-looking scooters for adults.

Flight Museum (Flugwerft Schleissheim)

Fans of all things winged will enjoy the Deutsches Museum's Flight Museum, with more than 50 planes, helicopters, gliders, and an original Europa rocket housed in a historical aerodrome on a former military airfield. Inside the museum, try a helicopter simulator (for an extra charge) and watch antique planes being restored in the glass-walled workshop. The museum is well-done and has English explanations, but probably only those interested in the history of flight will find the trek worthwhile.

Cost and Hours: €6, €15 combo-ticket includes Deutsches Museum and Museum of Transportation, daily 9:00-17:00; tiny café, indoor benches provided for picnicking, other eating options in neighborhood; 20-minute S-Bahn trip from Marienplatz, take S-1 (direction: Freising Flughafen) and get off at Oberschleissheim (trip covered by Munich XXL day pass), then walk 15 minutes

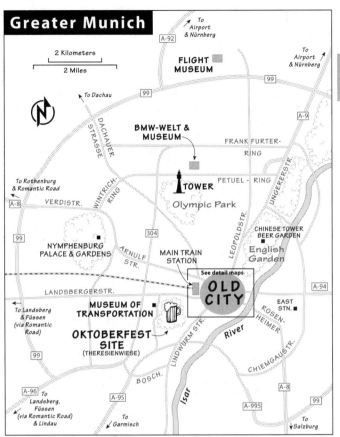

Greater Munich

following "Museen" signs to Effnerstrasse 18, tel. 089/3157-1410, www.deutsches-museum.de.

Sights Outside the City Center

Greater Munich
The following destinations are in Munich, but on the outskirts of town.

▲▲Nymphenburg Palace Complex
Nymphenburg Palace and the surrounding one-square-mile park are a great place for a royal stroll or discreet picnic. Indoors, you can tour the Bavarian royal family's summer quarters, and visit the Royal Stables Museum plus playful extras such as a hunting lodge (Amalienburg), bathhouse (Badenburg), pagoda (Pagodenburg),

and artificial ruins (Magdalenenklause). There is also a humble natural history museum in this complex.

Cost and Hours: The park is open daily 6:30-dusk and free to enter. You pay only to enter the buildings: €6 for just the palace; €11.50 combo-ticket for the palace, Royal Stables Museum, and outlying sights open in summer; covered by Bavaria's 14-day ticket (Mehrtagesticket). All of these sights are open daily April-mid-Oct 9:00-18:00, mid-Oct-March 10:00-16:00—except for Amalienburg and the other small palaces in the park, which are closed mid-Oct-March. Tel. 089/179-080, www.schloss-nymphenburg.de.

Getting There: The palace is three miles northwest of central Munich. From the center, take tram #17 from the Karlstor or the train station (15 minutes to palace), getting off at the Schloss Nymphenburg stop. From the bridge by the tram stop, you'll see the palace—a 10-minute walk away. A pleasant bike path follows Arnulfstrasse from the train station all the way to Nymphenburg (a 30-minute pedal).

Eating: A café serves lunches in the former palm-tree house, behind and to the right of the palace (open year-round). More eating options are near the tram stop, including a bakery with sandwiches.

Nymphenburg Palace

In 1662, after 10 years of trying, the Bavarian ruler Ferdinand Maria and his wife, Henriette Adelaide of Savoy, finally had a son, Max Emanuel. In gratitude for a male heir, Ferdinand gave this land to his Italian wife, who proceeded to build an Italian-style Baroque palace. Their son expanded the palace to today's size. For 200 years, this was the Wittelsbach family's summer escape from Munich. (They still refer to  themselves as princes and live in one wing of the palace.)

The palace interior, while interesting, is much less extensive than the Residenz. Your visit is limited to 16 main rooms on one floor: the Great Hall (where you start), the King's Wing (to the right as you approach the palace), and the Queen's Wing (to the left). The place is stingy on information—not even providing a map without charging—and the rooms only have meaning if you invest in the €3.50 audioguide. I've described most of what you'll see, next.

Visiting the Palace: The **Great Hall** in the middle was the dining hall, site of big Wittelsbach family festivals. One of the grandest Rococo rooms in Bavaria, it was decorated by Johann Baptist Zimmermann (of Wieskirche fame) and François de Cuvil-

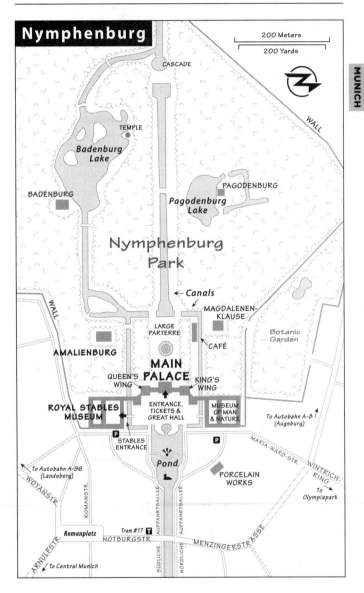

Nymphenburg

200 Meters
200 Yards

CASCADE

TEMPLE

Badenburg Lake

BADENBURG

PAGODENBURG

Pagodenburg Lake

Nymphenburg Park

← *Canals*

MAGDALENEN-KLAUSE

Botanic Garden

LARGE PARTERRE

AMALIENBURG

CAFÉ

MAIN PALACE

QUEEN'S WING

KING'S WING

ROYAL STABLES MUSEUM

ENTRANCE, TICKETS & GREAT HALL

MUSEUM OF MAN & NATURE

To Autobahn A-8 (Augsburg)

STABLES ENTRANCE

MARIA-WARD-STR.

To Autobahn A-96 (Landsberg)

Pond

PORCELAIN WORKS

WINTRICH-RING

To Olympiapark

WOTANSTR.

ROMANSTR.

Romanplatz

Tram #17

NÖTBURGSTR.

SÜDLICHE AUFFAHRTSALLEE

NÖRDLICHE AUFFAHRTSALLEE

MENZINGERSTRASSE

ARNULFSTR.

To Central Munich

WALL

WALL

MUNICH

liés in about 1760. The painting on the ceiling shows a pagan heavenly host of Olympian gods, a scene designed to help legitimize the supposedly divine rule of the Wittelsbachs. The windows connect you with the lavish gardens.

From here, the two wings (the King's and the Queen's) are mirror images of one another: antechamber, audience chamber, bedchamber, and private living quarters.

The **King's Wing** (Rooms 2-9) has walls filled with Wittelsbach portraits and stories. In the second room straight ahead, old paintings of Nymphenburg show how there was nothing but countryside between it and downtown when it was built. Find the painting of Fürstenried Palace (in another Munich suburb), and look for the twin onion domes of the Frauenkirche in the distance. Imagine the logistics when the royal family—with their entourage of 200—decided to move out to the summer palace. The Wittelsbachs were high rollers; from 1624 until 1806, one of the seven electors of the Holy Roman Emperor was always a Wittelsbach. In 1806, when Napoleon put an end to the Empire, he permitted the Wittelsbachs to call themselves kings instead of just dukes, duchesses, and electors.

In the **Queen's Wing** (Rooms 10-20), head down the long hall. Near the end, you'll come to **King Ludwig I's Gallery of Beauties.** The gallery is decorated with portraits of 36 beautiful women—all of them painted by Joseph Stieler from 1827 to 1850. King Ludwig I was a consummate girl-watcher who prided himself on the ability to appreciate beauty regardless of social rank. He would pick the prettiest women from the general public and, with one of the most effective pickup lines of all time, invite them to the palace for a portrait. Who could refuse? The portraits were on public display in the Residenz and catapulted their subjects into stardom. Ludwig may not have been picky about status—the women range from royal princesses to a humble cobbler's daughter—but he sure seemed to prefer brunettes. Find Helene Sedlmayr, the cobbler's daughter, in a dress way beyond her budget. She married the king's valet, had 10 kids, and lived until 1898. Also look for Lola Montez, a dancer who became the king's mistress (see "The History of Munich, Part 1" sidebar). The portraits reflect the modest Biedermeier style, as opposed to the more flamboyant Romanticism of the same period. The dimly lit room is erotically charged, in a Prince Charles kind of way. If only these creaking floors could talk.

The next rooms are decorated in the Neoclassical style of the Napoleonic era. Furthest in, find the room where Ludwig II was born on August 25, 1845. Royal births were carefully witnessed, and the mirror allowed for a better view. While Ludwig's death was shrouded in mystery, his birth was well-documented.

Palace Grounds

The wooded grounds extend far back beyond the formal gardens and are popular with joggers and walkers (biking is not allowed). Find a bench for a low-profile picnic. The park is laced with canals and small lakes, where court guests once rode on Venetian-style gondolas.

Amalienburg

Three hundred yards from Nymphenburg Palace, hiding in the park (head into the sculpted garden and veer to the left, following signs), you'll find a fine little Rococo hunting lodge which takes just a few minutes to tour. In 1734, Elector Karl Albrecht had it built for his wife, Maria Amalia. Amalienburg was designed by François de Cuvilliés and decorated by Johann Baptist Zimmermann. It's the most worthwhile of the four small

"extra" palaces buried in the park that are included on the combo-ticket. The others are the Pagodenburg, a Chinese-inspired pavilion; Badenburg, an opulent bathing house and banquet hall; and the Magdalenenklause, a mini-palace that looks like a ruin from the outside but has an elaborate altar and woody apartments inside.

Visiting Amalienburg: As you approach, circle to the front and notice the facade. Above the pink-and-white grand entryway, Diana, goddess of the chase, is surrounded by themes of the hunt and flanked by busts of satyrs. The queen would shoot from the perch atop the roof. Behind a wall in the garden, dogs would scare non-flying pheasants. When they jumped up in the air above the wall, the sporting queen—as if shooting skeet—would pick the birds off.

Tourists now enter this tiny getaway through the back door. Doghouses under gun cupboards fill the first room. In the fine yellow-and-silver bedroom, the bed is flanked by portraits of Karl Albrecht and Maria Amalia—decked out in hunting attire. She liked her dogs. The door under the portrait leads to stairs to the rooftop pheasant-shooting perch. The relief on the door's lower panel shows Vulcan forging arrows for amorous cupids.

The mini-Hall of Mirrors is a blue-and-silver commotion of Rococo nymphs designed by Cuvilliés. In the next room, paintings depict court festivities, formal hunting parties, and no-contest kills (where the animal is put at an impossible disadvantage—like shooting fish in a barrel). Finally, the unfinished-feeling kitchen is decorated with Chinese-style drawings on Dutch tile.

Royal Stables Museum (Marstallmuseum)

This huge garage (to the left of the main palace as you approach the complex) is full of gilded coaches that will make you think of Cinderella's journey to the king's ball. Upstairs, there's also a porcelain exhibit. If you don't want to visit the main palace, you can buy a €4.50 ticket just for this museum. There is no audioguide.

Visiting the Museum: Wandering through the collection,

MUNICH

you can trace the evolution of 300 years of coaches—getting lighter and with better suspension as they were harnessed to faster horses. A highlight is just inside the entrance: the 1742 Karl Albrecht coronation coach. When the Elector Karl Albrecht was chosen as Holy Roman Emperor, he rode in this coach, drawn by eight horses. Kings got only six. The carousel for the royal kids made development of dexterity fun—lopping off noses and heads and tossing balls through the snake. The glass case is filled with accessories.

In the room after the carousel, find the painting on the right of "Mad" King Ludwig II on his sleigh at night. In his later years, Ludwig was a Howard Hughes-type recluse who stayed away from the public eye and only went out at night. (At his nearby Linderhof Palace, he actually had a hydraulic-powered dining table that would rise from the kitchen below, completely set for the meal—so he wouldn't be seen by his servants.) In the next room, you'll find Ludwig's sleighs. Ludwig's over-the-top coaches were Baroque. But this was 1870. The coaches, like the king, were in the wrong century. Notice the photos (c. 1865, in the glass case) of Ludwig and the Romantic composer Richard Wagner. Ludwig cried on the day Wagner was married. Hmmm.

Across the passage from the museum entrance, the second hall is filled with more practical coaches for everyday use. At the end of that hall, head upstairs to see a collection of **Nymphenburg porcelain** (described by an English loaner booklet at the entrance). Historically, royal families such as the Wittelsbachs liked to have their own porcelain plants to make fit-for-a-king plates, vases, and so on. The Nymphenburg Palace porcelain works is still in operation (not open to the public). Find the large room with copies of old masters from the Wittelsbach art collection (now at the Alte Pinakothek). King Ludwig I had these paintings copied onto porcelain for safekeeping into the distant future. Take a close look—they're exquisite.

▲▲BMW-Welt and Museum

A brand with a rich heritage, an impressive display of futuristic architecture, and an enthusiastic welcome to the public combine to make the headquarters of BMW ("bay-em-VAY" to Germans) one of the top sights in Munich. This vast complex—built on the site of Munich's first airstrip and home to the BMW factory since 1920—has four components: the headquarters (in the building nicknamed "the Four Cylinders"—not open to the public), the factory (tourable with advance reservations), the showroom (called BMW-Welt—"BMW World"), and the BMW Museum.

The **BMW-Welt** building itself—a cloud-shaped, glass-and-steel architectural masterpiece—is reason enough to visit. It's free and filled with exhibits designed to enthuse car lovers so they'll find a way to afford a Beamer. While the adjacent museum reviews the BMW past, BMW-Welt shows you the present and gives you a breathtaking look at the future. With interactive stations, high-powered videos, an inviting cafeteria, and lots of horsepower, this is where customers come to pick up their new Beamers, and where hopeful customers-to-be come to nurture their automotive dreams.

In the futuristic **BMW Museum,** a bowl-shaped building encloses a world of floating walkways linking exhibits highlighting BMW motorcycle and car design and technology through the years. Employing seven themes and great English descriptions, the museum traces the Bavarian Motor Works' history since 1917, when the company began making airplane engines. Motorcycles came next, followed by the first BMW sedan in 1929. You'll see how design was celebrated here from the start. Exhibits showcase motorsports, roadsters, and luxury cars. Stand on an *E* for English to hear the chief designer talk about his favorite cars in the "treasure trove." The Info Bar lets you review 90 years of history with the touch of a finger. And the 1956 BMW 507 is enough to rev almost anyone's engine.

Cost and Hours: BMW-Welt is free and open daily (building open 7:30-24:00, exhibits open 9:00-18:00). The museum costs €9 (Tue-Sun 10:00-18:00, closed Mon, tel. 089/125-016-001, www.bmw-welt.com). English tours are offered of both the Welt (€7, daily at 14:00, 80 minutes) and the museum (€3, 1.5 hours, call ahead for times). Factory tours must be booked long in advance (€8, 2.5 hours, Mon-Fri only, ages 7 and up, book by calling 089/125-016-001, more info at www.bmw-werk-muenchen.de; ask at the BMW-Welt building about cancellations—open spots are released to the public a half-hour before each tour).

Getting There: It's very easy: Ride the U-3 to Olympia-Zentrum; the stop faces the BMW-Welt entry. To reach the museum, walk through BMW-Welt and over the swoopy bridge.

Olympic Park (Olympiapark München)

Munich's great 1972 Olympic stadium and sports complex is now a lush park. You can get a good look at the center's striking "cob-web" style of architecture while enjoying the park's picnic potential. In addition, there are several activities on offer at the park, including a tower (Olympiaturm) with a commanding but so-high-it's-boring view from 820 feet and an excellent swimming pool, the Olympia-Schwimmhalle. With the construction of Munich's Allianz Arena for the 2006 World Cup, Olympic Park has been left in the past, and has melted into the neighborhood as simply a fine park and swimming pool.

Cost and Hours: Tower—€5.50, daily 9:00-24:00, tel. 089/30670, www.olympiapark.de. Pool—€4.30, daily 7:00-23:00, tel. 01801-796-223, www.swm.de. The U-3 runs from Marienplatz directly to the Olympia-Zentrum stop.

▲Isar River Bike Ride

Munich's river, lined by a gorgeous park, leads bikers into the pristine countryside in just a few minutes. From downtown (easy access from the English Garden or Deutsches Museum), follow the riverside bike path south (upstream) along the east (left) bank. You can't get lost. Just stay on the lovely bike path. It crosses the river after a while, passing tempting little *Biergartens* and lots of Bavarians having their brand of fun—including gangs enjoying Munich's famous river party rafts. Go as far as you like, then retrace your route to get home. The closest bike rental is at Munich Walk, by the Isartor.

Near Munich

The following sights are a short train or bus ride away from Munich.

▲▲Dachau Concentration Camp Memorial (KZ-Gedenkstätte Dachau)

Dachau was the first Nazi concentration camp (1933). Today, it's an easily accessible camp for travelers and an effective voice from our recent but grisly past, pleading "Never again." A visit here is a valuable experience and, when

approached thoughtfully, well worth the trouble. After this powerful sightseeing experience, many people gain more respect for history and the dangers of mixing fear, the promise of jobs, blind patriotism, and an evil government. You'll likely see lots of students here, as all Bavarian schoolchildren are required to visit a concentration camp. It's interesting to think that little more than a couple of generations ago, people greeted each other with a robust *"Sieg Heil!"* Today, almost no Germans know the lyrics of their national anthem, and German flags are a rarity outside of major soccer matches.

Cost and Hours: Free, daily 9:00-17:00, last entry 30 minutes before closing. Though the museum shuts down at 17:00, the grounds are unofficially open until about 17:30 or 18:00 (as it takes a while for people to walk back to the entrance). The museum discourages parents from bringing children under age 12.

Planning Your Time: Allow yourself about five hours here (four at a minimum), including your round-trip from central Munich. Giving yourself at least two and a half hours at the camp itself lets you see it at a comfortable pace (with just two hours, it's doable but rushed, and you'll have to skip the movie).

Getting There: The camp is a 45-minute trip from downtown Munich. Take the S-2 subway (direction: Petershausen) from any of the central S-Bahn stops in Munich to Dachau (3/hour, 20-minute trip from Hauptbahnhof). Then, at Dachau station, go down the stairs and follow the crowds out to the bus platforms; find the one marked *KZ-Gedenkstätte-Concentration Camp Memorial Sight.*

Here, catch bus #726 and ride it seven minutes to the KZ-Gedenk-stätte stop (3/hour). Before you leave this bus stop, be sure to note the return times back to the station. To return to Munich, you'll catch the S-2 again at Dachau station (direction: Erding or Markt Schwaben).

The Munich XXL day pass covers the entire trip, both ways (€7.80/person, €13.60/partner ticket for up to 5 adults). If you've already invested in a three-day Munich transport pass (which covers only the white/inner zone), you can save a couple euros by buying and stamping single tickets (€2.60/person each way) to cover the part of the trip that's in the green zone. You can also take a guided tour from Munich.

Drivers follow Dachauer Strasse from downtown Munich to Dachau-Ost, then follow *KZ-Gedenkstätte* signs.

The Town: The town of Dachau is more pleasant than its unfortunate association with the camp on its outskirts, and tries hard to encourage you to visit its old town and castle (www.dachau.de). With 40,000 residents and quick access to downtown Munich, Dachau is now a high-priced and in-demand place to live.

Visitors Center: Coming from the bus stop or parking lot, you'll first see the visitors center, outside the camp wall. It doesn't have any exhibits, but does have some useful services: a café serving simple lunches (sandwiches and €5-6 pasta dishes), a bookstore with a modest selection of English-language books on Holocaust themes, and a small WC (more WCs in the museum inside the camp). At the information desk, you can rent an audioguide or sign up for a tour.

Tours: The €3.50 **audioguide** covers the grounds and museum; its basic itinerary includes 1.5 hours of information. It gives you a few extras (mainly short reminiscences by two camp survivors and three members of the Allied forces who liberated the camp), but isn't essential, since the camp is fully labeled in English (must leave ID, rental desk closes right at 17:00). Two different **guided walks** in English are offered, starting from the visitors center (€3, daily at 11:00 and 13:00, 2.5 hours; limited to 30 people, so show up early—especially in summer, 13:00 walk fills up first; call or visit website to confirm times, tel. 08131/669-970, www.kz-gedenkstaette-dachau.de).

Background: While a relatively few 32,000 inmates died in Dachau between 1933 and 1945 (in comparison, more than a million were killed at Auschwitz in Poland), the camp is notorious because it was the Nazis' first. It was originally established to house political prisoners and opponents of the Nazi regime, and only later played a role in World War II. In the 1930s, the camp was located outside built-up areas, and was surrounded by a mile-wide restricted area. It was a work camp, where inmates were used for slave labor, including constructing the buildings that you see. A huge training center stood next to the camp. The people who ran the entire concentration-camp system during the war were trained here, and it was former Dachau officials who went on to manage the death camps farther east, mostly in Nazi-occupied Poland. For example, the first commandant at Auschwitz, Rudolf Höss, worked at Dachau from 1934 to 1938.

After war broke out, the regime found more purposes for Dachau: a departure point for people shipped east to the gas chambers, a special prison for priests, a center for barbaric medical experimentation on inmates, and finally—as the Nazis retreated—a transfer destination for prisoners from other camps. Oddly, Dachau actually housed people longer *after* the war than during the war. From 1945 to 1948, Nazi officials arrested by the Allies were interned here. After that (from 1948 to 1964), ethnic Germans expelled from Eastern Europe lived in the barracks, which were like a small town, with a cinema, shops, and so on. The last of the barracks was torn down in 1964, and the museum opened the following year.

❍ Self-Guided Tour: Walking past the visitors center, turn right into the main compound. You enter, like the inmates did, through the infamous **iron gate** with the taunting slogan *Arbeit macht frei* ("Work makes you free"). Inside are the four key experiences of the memorial: the museum, the bunker behind the museum, the restored barracks, and a pensive walk across the huge but now-empty camp

to the memorials and crematorium at the far end.

Museum: The large camp maintenance building to your right has been converted into a gripping museum. Walk toward the forecourt of the building and you'll

see the museum entrance. Just inside is a small bookshop that funds a nonprofit organization (founded by former prisoners) that researches and preserves the camp's history. Here you can pick up a €0.50 information sheet, or buy the excellent 200-page book with a CD (€15) that contains the same text and images that you'll see in the museum.

In the middle of the museum building is a **theater,** which

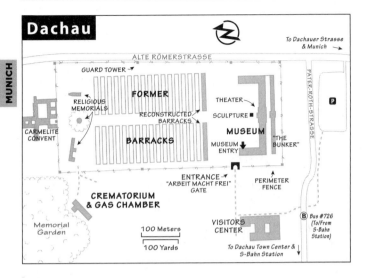

shows a powerful 22-minute documentary movie dating from the 1960s (English showings generally at 10:00, 11:30, 12:30, 14:00, and 15:00; confirm times at visitors center, ages 12 and up only).

The museum is organized chronologically, focusing on three stages in the history of the camp: before the war (1933-1938), early in the war (1939-1942), and late in the war (1942-1945). Exhibits are thoughtfully and completely described in English, and computer touch-screens let you watch early newsreels.

In its first years, the camp was basically a political prison designed for opponents of the Nazi regime, and it could hold just under 3,000 inmates. Aside from political activists, these prisoners included homosexuals, Jehovah's Witnesses, Gypsies, so-called career criminals, and Germans who had been deported back home after trying to emigrate. As Nazi extremism increased, the camp operated with less and less regard for the rule of law, and after the Nazis whipped up domestic anti-Semitism, a number of German Jews were also sent to Dachau.

Prisoners had a regimented life, with lights out at 21:00, a wake-up call at 4:00 in the morning, and an 11-hour workday, plus standing for roll call at 5:15 and 19:00. In 1937 and 1938, the camp was expanded and the building that now houses the museum was built, as well as barracks intended to hold 6,000 prisoners.

Once Germany invaded Poland in 1939, fewer local detainees arrived at the camp, replaced by more and more prisoners from Poland and Czechoslovakia. Dachau was also the place of detention for almost 2,000 Polish Catholic clergymen and for former fighters in the Spanish Civil War. During these years, Dachau prisoners were used as convenient guinea pigs for war-related medical experiments of human tolerance for air pressure, hypothermia, and biological agents like malaria; the photos of these victims may be the most painful in the museum. After the Nazis put their plans for exterminating Europe's Jews in motion, Jewish prisoners at Dachau were typically sent east to the extermination camps in Poland and killed.

Once the tide of war started to turn in 1942 and 1943, both Nazi measures and camp conditions became more and more desperate. Inmates were now seen as a source of slave labor for the German war machine. Many were put to work in sub-camps (in nearby towns) making armaments. As the Allies closed in on both fronts, prisoners from concentration camps in France, the Low Countries, and Eastern Europe were transferred to Dachau, and the number of Jewish internees rose again. Disease broke out, and food ran short in the winter of 1944-1945. With coal for the crematorium running low, the corpses of those who died were buried in mass graves outside the camp site. Though the Nazis moved some camp inmates to the mountains of the Tirol in the spring of 1945, more than 30,000 people were jammed into Dachau's 34 barracks when the Allies arrived on April 29. Two thousand of them were so weak or sick that they died in the weeks after liberation.

• *Consider using the WC before leaving the museum building (there aren't any bathrooms elsewhere within the camp walls). Find the side door, at the end of the exhibition, which leads out to the long, low bunker behind the museum building.*

Bunker: This was a cellblock for prominent "special prisoners," such as failed Hitler assassins, German religious leaders, and politicians who challenged Na-zism. Most of the 136 cells are empty, but exhibits in a few of them (near the entrance) profile the inmates and the SS guards who worked at Dachau, and allow you to listen to some in-mates' testimonies. Look into cell #65, which was divided by partitions (now gone) into

"standing cells," with less than three square feet of floor space. In-mates were tortured here by being forced to stay on their feet for days at a time.

• *Exit the bunker, and walk around past the* Arbeit macht frei *gate to the big square between the museum and the reconstructed barracks, which was used for roll call. In front of the museum, notice the power-ful* **memorial** *to the victims created in 1968 by Nandor Glid, a Jewish Holocaust survivor and artist, which includes humanity's vow:* Never Again. *Cross the square to the farther of the two reconstructed...*

Barracks: Take a quick look inside to get an idea of what sleeping and living conditions were like in the camp. There were 34 barracks, each measuring about 10 yards by 100 yards. When the camp was at its fullest, there was only about one square yard of living space per inmate.

• *Now walk between the two reconstructed barracks and down the tree-lined path past the foundations of the other barracks. At the end of the camp, in space that once housed the camp vegetable garden, rabbit farm, and brothel, there are now three places of meditation and worship (Jewish to your right, Catholic straight ahead, and Protestant to your left). Beyond them, just outside the camp, is a Carmelite convent. Turn left toward the corner of the camp and find the small bridge leading to the...*

Camp Crematorium: A memorial garden surrounds the two camp crematorium buildings, which were used to burn the bodies

of prisoners who had died or been killed. The newer, larger concrete crematorium was built to replace the smaller wooden one. One of its rooms is a **gas chamber,** which worked on the same principles as the much larger one at Auschwitz, and was originally disguised as a shower room (the fittings are gone now). It was never put to use at Dachau for mass murder, but some historians suspect that a few people were killed in it experimentally. In the garden near the buildings is a Russian Orthodox shrine.

To end your visit, retrace your steps back to the visitors center and bus stop.

▲Andechs Monastery

This monastery crouches quietly with a big smile between two lakes just south of Munich. For a fine Baroque church in a rural Bavarian setting at a monastery that serves hearty cafeteria-quality food and perhaps the best beer in Germany, consider a short side-trip here. The cafeteria terrace offers first-class views and second-class prices. Don't miss the stroll up to the church, where you can sit peacefully and ponder the striking contrasts a trip through Germany offers.

Cost and Hours: Free, *Biergarten* open daily 10:00-20:00, church open until 18:00, tel. 08152/3760, www.andechs.de.

Getting There: Reaching Andechs from Munich without a car is doable with a little planning. Bus #951 stops at the monastery on its run between Herrsching (at the end of the S-8 subway line) and Starnberg Nord (on the S-6 line). Bus #958 runs to Andechs from Tutzing (also on the S-6 line). Use the online schedules at www.bahn.com or www.mvv-muenchen.de to find a convenient connection (use Kloster Andechs as your destination; trip takes 1-1.5 hours, buy Munich *Gesamtnetz* day pass for €11.20 or pay €20.40 for the partner pass good for up to 5 people). You can also take the S-8 train to Herrsching, then hike, bike, or catch a taxi for the three miles to the monastery.

More Day Trips from Munich

For day trips to many Bavarian destinations, including the first four listed here, consider traveling by train with the **Bayern-Ticket.** It covers up to five people from Munich to anywhere in Bavaria (plus Salzburg) and back for a very low price (€22 for the first person plus €4 for each additional person, €2 more if bought at counter instead of machine, not valid before 9:00 Mon-Fri, valid only on slower "regional" trains—most of them labeled on schedules as either "RB," "RE," or "IRE," also valid on city transport). The ticket is explained in *The Inside Track* newsletter and sold at EurAide.

▲▲▲"Mad" King Ludwig's Castles

The spectacular Neuschwanstein and Linderhof castles make a great day trip. Your easiest option is to take a tour. Without a tour, only Neuschwanstein is easy (2 hours by train to Füssen, then 10-minute bus ride to the castle). Or spend the night in Füssen. For all the details, see the next chapter.

▲▲Nürnberg

A handy but expensive ICE express train zips you to Nürnberg in about an hour (departures several times an hour), making this very historic city a viable day trip from Munich. Cheaper RE trains, covered by the Bayern-Ticket, take a little longer.

▲▲▲Salzburg

This Austrian city is an easy day trip and offers some exciting sightseeing (hourly trains from Munich get you there in less than 2 hours). For details, see the Salzburg chapter.

▲▲▲Berchtesgaden

This resort, near Hitler's Eagle's Nest getaway, is easier as a side-trip from Salzburg (just 12 miles from there).

MUNICH

Shopping in Munich

While the whole city is great for shopping, the most glamorous area is around Marienplatz. It's fun to window-shop, even if you have no plans to buy. Here are a few stores and streets to consider.

Department Stores: You'll see lots of modern department stores. Locals rate them this way: **C&A** (which sells only clothing) is considered cheap yet respected, **Kaufhof** (which sells everything) is mid-range, and **Karstadt** is upmarket. **Beck's,** an even more upscale department store at Marienplatz, has been a local institution since 1861. With six floors of expensive designer clothing (plus some music, stationery, and cosmetics), this is the place to go for a €200 pair of jeans. Beck's has long been to fabrics what Dallmayr is to fine food—too expensive to actually buy anything in, but fun to browse (Mon-Sat 10:00-20:00, closed Sun). Also on Marienplatz is the big **Hugendubel bookstore,** though their English selection is modest.

Weinstrasse/Theatinerstrasse: Shoppers will want to stroll from Marienplatz down the pedestrianized Weinstrasse (it begins to the left as you face New Town Hall). After a few short blocks, the street name changes to Theatinerstrasse; look for **Fünf Höfe** on your left, a delightful mall filled with Germany's top shops (open Mon-Sat until 20:00, closed Sun). Named for its five courtyards, this is where tradition meets modern. Note how its Swiss architects (who also designed Munich's grand Allianz soccer stadium for the 2006 World Cup) play with light and color. Even if you're not a shopper, wander through the **Kunsthalle** to appreciate the architecture, the elegant window displays, and the sight of Bavarians living very well.

For fine-quality (and very expensive) traditional clothing, detour a block west along Maffeistrasse to **Loden-Frey Verkaufshaus.** The third floor of this fine department store is dedicated to classic Bavarian wear for men and women (Mon-Sat 10:00-20:00, closed Sun, Maffeistrasse 7, tel. 089/210-390, www.loden-frey.com).

Theatinerstrasse spills out onto Odeonsplatz, where you'll find the **Nymphenburg Porcelain Store** (Mon-Fri 10:00-18:30, Sat 10:00-18:00, closed Sun, Odeonsplatz 1, tel. 089/282-428, www.nymphenburg.com).

Maximilianstrasse: Built by Maximilian II in the 1850s, this street was designed for shoppers. Today it's home to Munich's most exclusive shops.

Lowbrow Tips: For that beer stein you promised to take home to your uncle, try the shops on the pedestrian zone by St. Michael's Church and the gift shops that surround the Hofbräuhaus. Or look for Servus Heimat, an amusing souvenir and antique shop with locations in the courtyard of the Munich City Museum (Mon-Sat 10:00-22:00, Sun 10:00-18:00, St.-Jakobs-Platz 1, tel. 089/2370-2380, www.servusheimat.com) and elsewhere. If you're looking for a used cell phone or exotic groceries, the area south of the train station is a lot of fun.

Sleeping in Munich

Unless you hit Munich during a fair, convention, or big holiday, you can sleep reasonably here. Lots of student hotels around the station house anyone who's young at heart for €25, and it's possible to find a fine double with breakfast in a good basic hotel for €90. I've listed accommodations in two neighborhoods: within a few blocks of the central train station (Hauptbahnhof), and in the old center, between Marienplatz and Sendlinger Tor. Many of these places have complicated, slippery pricing schemes. I've listed the normal non-convention, non-festival prices. There are major conventions about 30 nights a year—prices increase from 20 percent to as much as 300 percent during Oktoberfest (Sept 20-Oct 5 in 2014; reserve well in advance). On the other hand, during slow times, you may be able to do better than the rates listed here—always ask. Sunday is very slow and usually comes with a huge discount if you ask.

Near the Train Station

Good-value hotels cluster in the multicultural area immediately south of the station. It feels seedy after dark (erotic cinemas and men with moustaches loitering in the shadows), but it's dangerous only for those in search of trouble. Still, hotels in the old center (listed later) might feel more comfortable to some.

$$$ Marc München—polished, modern, and with 80 newly renovated rooms—is a good option if you need a little more luxury than the other listings here. It's just half-block from the station on a relatively tame street, and has four-star comforts like a nice lobby and classy breakfast spread. The cheaper "superior king" rooms are fine (around Sb-€127, Db-€147); the more expensive rooms (Sb-€137-197, Db-€167-217) add more cost than value (no triples, 10 percent discount with this book and direct reservation except during events, parking-€10-16/day, air-con, non-smoking, guest computer, free cable Internet and Wi-Fi, Senefelderstrasse 12, tel. 089/559-820, www.hotel-marc.de, info@hotel-marc.de).

$$ Hotel Monaco is a delightful and welcoming little hideaway, tucked inside the fifth floor of a giant nondescript building two blocks from the station. Emerging from the elevator, you're warmly welcomed by Christine and her staff into a flowery, cherub-filled oasis. It's homey, with 24 clean and fresh rooms, and lots of special touches (S-€57, Sb-€77, D-€75, Db-€91-96, Tb-€133,

MUNICH

Sleep Code

(€1 = about $1.30, country code: 49, area code: 089)
S = Single, **D** = Double/Twin, **T** = Triple, **Q** = Quad, **b** = bathroom, **s** = shower only. Unless otherwise noted, credit cards are accepted, a buffet breakfast is included, there is an elevator but no air-conditioning, and English is spoken.

To help you sort easily through these listings, I've divided the accommodations into three categories based on the price for a standard double room with bath:

$$$ Higher Priced—Most rooms €130 or more.
 $$ Moderately Priced—Most rooms between €90-130.
  $ Lower Priced—Most rooms €90 or less.

Prices can change without notice; verify the hotel's current rates online or by email. For the best prices, always book direct.

€8/person less without breakfast—but I wouldn't skip it, cash preferred with one-night stay, non-smoking, guest computer, free Wi-Fi, Schillerstrasse 9, entrance on Adolf-Kolping-Strasse, tel. 089/545-9940, www.hotel-monaco.de, info@hotel-monaco.de).

$$ Hotel Uhland is a stately mansion that rents 29 delightful rooms in a safe-feeling, less-seedy residential neighborhood a slightly longer walk from the station than the others in this section (toward the Theresienwiese Oktoberfest grounds). It's been in the Hauzenberger family for 50 years (Sb-€75-80, small Db-€95, big Db-€105-118, Tb-€130-143, price depends on room size, great family rooms, online deals, non-smoking, free Wi-Fi, limited free parking; from station, take bus #58 to Georg-Hirth-Platz, or walk 15 minutes: go up Goethestrasse and turn right on Pettenkoferstrasse, cross Georg-Hirth-Platz to Uhlandstrasse and find #1; tel. 089/543-350, www.hotel-uhland.de, info@hotel-uhland.de).

$$ Hotel Belle Blue, three blocks from the station, has 30 fresh, modern rooms with air-conditioning. And yes, the decor is in shades of blue (Sb-€79, Db-€95, non-smoking rooms, free cable Internet and Wi-Fi, Schillerstrasse 21, tel. 089/550-6260, www.hotel-belleblue.de, info@hotel-belleblue.com, Irmgard).

$$ Hotel Bristol is bright and efficient, with 56 comfortable, business-like rooms. While walkable from the station, it's actually just across the street from the Sendlinger Tor U-Bahn station, one stop from the train station on the U-1 or U-2 (Sb-€89, Db-€99, non-smoking rooms, guest computer, free Wi-Fi, air-con in lobby, Pettenkoferstrasse 2, tel. 089/5434-8880, www.bristol-munich.de, info@bristol-munich.de).

$$ Hotel Deutsches Theater is a brass-and-marble-filled place with 27 tight, modern three-star rooms. The back rooms face the courtyard of a neighboring theater—when there's a show, there can be some noise (Sb-€68, Db-€97, Tb-€136, pricier suites, €9/ person less without breakfast, non-smoking floors, free Wi-Fi, Landwehrstrasse 18, tel. 089/545-8525, www.hoteldeutschestheater.de, info@hoteldeutschestheater.de).

$$ Hotel Europäischer Hof, across the street from the station, is a huge, impersonal hotel with 150 decent rooms. During cool weather when you can keep the windows shut, the street-facing rooms are an acceptable option. The quieter, courtyard-facing rooms are more expensive and a lesser value, except for a few cheap rooms with shared bath—you'll have to email about these, as they're not listed on the website (streetside Sb-€82, Db-€97; courtyard S-€50, D with head-to-toe twin beds-€57; 10 percent discount on prevailing rates with this book and direct advance reservation, *or* if you pay cash—no double discounts; no discounts during conventions, major events, and Oktoberfest weekends; check website for current rates, non-smoking rooms, family rooms, guest computer, free Wi-Fi by reception, free cable Internet in rooms with bath, parking-€13.50/day, Bayerstrasse 31, tel. 089/551-510, www. heh.de, info@heh.de).

$ Hotel Royal is one of the best values in the neighborhood (as long as you can look past the strip joints flanking the entry). While a bit institutional, it's clean, entirely non-smoking, and plenty comfortable. Most importantly, it's energetically run by Pasha and Christiane. Each of its 40 rooms is fresh and bright (Sb-€54-69, Db-€74-89, Tb-€94-109, Qb-€99-129, lower prices generally Nov-March, book direct for a 10 percent discount off the prevailing price with this book, ask for a room on the quiet side— especially in summer when you'll want the window open, guest computer, free Wi-Fi, Schillerstrasse 11a, tel. 089/5998-8160, www.hotel-royal.de, info@hotel-royal.de).

$ Litty's Hotel is a basic hotel with 37 small rooms run by Verena and Bernd Litty (S-€48, Sb-€56, D-€68, Ds-€76, Db-€84, T-€87, free Wi-Fi at reception reaches lower floors, near Schillerstrasse at Landwehrstrasse 32c, tel. 089/5434-4211, www.littyshotel.de, info@littyshotel.de).

$ The CVJM (YMCA), open to all ages, rents 85 beds in clean, slightly worn rooms with sinks in the rooms and showers and toilets down the hall. Doubles are head-to-head; triples are like doubles with a bunk over one of the beds (S-€36, D-€61, T-€83, €28/bed in a shared triple, guests over 26 pay €3/person more, cheaper for 3 nights or more and in winter; only €10/night per person more during Oktoberfest—reserve at least 6 months ahead for Oktoberfest weekdays, a year ahead for Oktoberfest weekends; includes

MUNICH

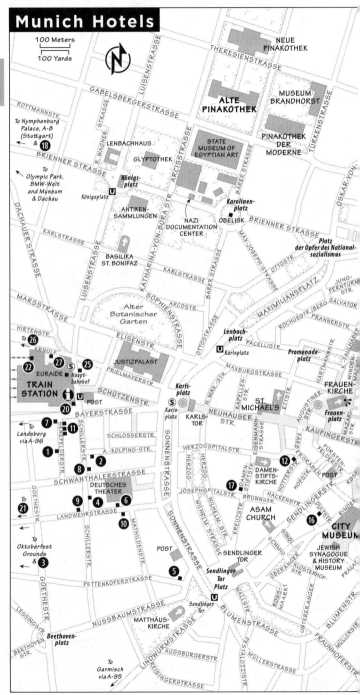

Munich Hotels

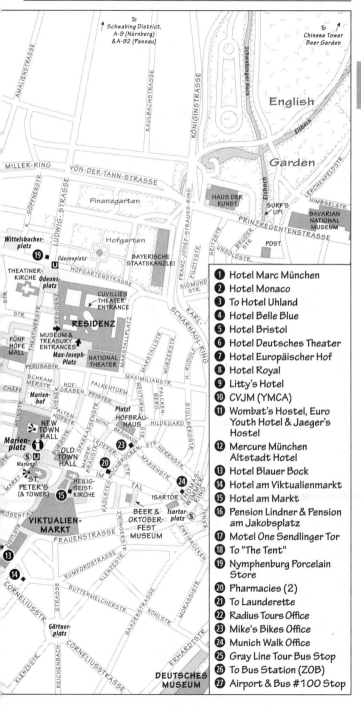

MUNICH

1. Hotel Marc München
2. Hotel Monaco
3. To Hotel Uhland
4. Hotel Belle Blue
5. Hotel Bristol
6. Hotel Deutsches Theater
7. Hotel Europäischer Hof
8. Hotel Royal
9. Litty's Hotel
10. CVJM (YMCA)
11. Wombat's Hostel, Euro Youth Hotel & Jaeger's Hostel
12. Mercure München Altstadt Hotel
13. Hotel Blauer Bock
14. Hotel am Viktualienmarkt
15. Hotel am Markt
16. Pension Lindner & Pension am Jakobsplatz
17. Motel One Sendlinger Tor
18. To "The Tent"
19. Nymphenburg Porcelain Store
20. Pharmacies (2)
21. To Launderette
22. Radius Tours Office
23. Mike's Bikes Office
24. Munich Walk Office
25. Gray Line Tour Bus Stop
26. To Bus Station (ZOB)
27. Airport & Bus #100 Stop

sheets, breakfast, and guest computer, but no lockers; cheap Wi-Fi by reception, Landwehrstrasse 13, tel. 089/552-1410, www.cvjm-muenchen.org/hotel, hotel@cvjm-muenchen.org).

"Hostel Row" on Senefelderstrasse, a Block from the Station

All three of the following hostels are casual and well-run, with friendly and creative management, and all cater expertly to the needs of young beer-drinking backpackers enjoying Munich on a shoestring. With 900 cheap dorm beds, this is a spirited street. There's no curfew, and each has a lively bar that rages until the wee hours (Euro Youth's is open the latest—until 4:00 in the morning), along with staff who speak English as the primary language. All have 24-hour receptions, pay guest computer, free Wi-Fi, laundry facilities, lockers, and included linens; none has a kitchen, but each offers a buffet breakfast for €4-5. Sleep cheap in big dorms, or spend a little more for a two-, three-, or four-bed room. Prices vary with demand, and can range a little higher than the rates listed here in summer, quite a bit higher for Oktoberfest, and quite a bit lower in the off-season, when you might find a dorm bed for €12.

$ Wombat's Hostel, perhaps the most hip and colorful, rents cheap doubles and six- to eight-bed dorms with lockers. Each bedroom is fresh and modern, with its own bathroom, and there's a relaxing and peaceful winter garden (300 beds, 8-bed dorms-€26/bed, 6-bed dorms-€29/bed, Db-€80, Senefelderstrasse 1, tel. 089/5998-9180, www.wombats-hostels.eu, office@wombats-munich.de).

$ Euro Youth Hotel fills a rare pre-WWII building (200 beds, 10- to 12-bed dorms-€23.50/bed, 3- to 5-bed dorms-€27/bed; D-€73, Db-€89, breakfast included for private rooms; Senefelderstrasse 5, tel. 089/5990-8811, www.euro-youth-hotel.de, info@euro-youth-hotel.de, run by Alfio and Andy).

$ Jaeger's Hostel rounds out this trio, with 300 cheap beds and all the fun and efficiency you'd hope for in a hostel—plus the only air-conditioning on the street. If you're not looking to party, this is your hostel—it seems to be the quietest (40-bed dorm-€19/bed, 8-bed dorm-€27/bed, 4- to 6-bed rooms-€29/bed, hotel-quality Sb-€59, Db-€78, towel-€1/day if staying in dorm, Senefelderstrasse 3, tel. 089/555-281, www.jaegershostel.de, office@jaegershostel.de).

In the Old Center

A few good deals remain in the area south of Marienplatz, going toward the Sendlinger Tor. This neighborhood feels more genteel than the streets around the train station, and is convenient for sightseeing.

$$$ Mercure München Altstadt Hotel is reliable, with all the modern comforts in its 75 business-class rooms, and is well-located on a boring, quiet street very close to the Marienplatz action. It's a chain, and a bit bland, but has fine services and decent prices (Sb-€124, Db-€166, parking-€20/day, non-smoking, air-con, guest computer, free Wi-Fi, a block south of the pedestrian zone at Hotterstrasse 4, tel. 089/232-590, www.mercure-muenchen-altstadt.de, h3709@accor.com).

$$$ Hotel Blauer Bock, formerly a dormitory for Benedictine monks, has been on the same corner near the Munich City Museum since 1841. Its 69 recently remodeled rooms are a little spartan for the price, but the location is nice. Various online discounts (senior, Sunday, nonrefundable) can save you €10-20/room (S-€67, Sb-€99-135, D-€90, Db-€155, fancy premium Db-€210, extra bed-€40, guest computer, free Wi-Fi, parking-€22/day, Sebastiansplatz 9, tel. 089/231-780, www.hotelblauerbock.de, info@hotelblauerbock.de).

$$ At Hotel am Viktualienmarkt, everything about this 26-room hotel is small but well-designed, including the elevator and three good-value, tiny singles. It's on a small side street a couple of blocks from the Viktualienmarkt. Coming from the train station, you can take tram #16 to Reichenbachplatz nearly to the door (tiny Sb-€59, larger Sb-€89, Db-€129, Tb-€169, Qb-€179, Quint/b-€229; guest computer, free Wi-Fi in common areas, free cable Internet in rooms; Utzschneiderstrasse 14, tel. 089/231-1090, www.hotel-am-viktualienmarkt.de, reservierung@hotel-am-viktualienmarkt.de)

$$ Hotel am Markt, not to be confused with the listing above, is a lesser value right next to the Viktualienmarkt. It has old-feeling hallways but 32 decent rooms, and is a better deal if you skip the expensive breakfast (Sb-€86, Db-€123-133, Tb-€166-176, prices depend on room size, €12/person less without breakfast, free Wi-Fi, Heiliggeiststrasse 6, tel. 089/225-014, www.hotel-am-markt.eu, service@hotel-am-markt.eu).

$$ Pension Lindner is clean and quiet, with nine pleasant pastel-bouquet rooms off a bare stairway (S-€45, D-€75, Db-€100, T-€105, Tb-€130, €5 discount on doubles and triples if you pay cash, tiny elevator, free Wi-Fi, Dultstrasse 1, tel. 089/263-413, www.pension-lindner.com, info@pension-lindner.com, Marion Sinzinger).

$$ Pension am Jakobsplatz, downstairs from Pension Lindner, has four basic but pleasant rooms. Two have fully private facilities, and the other two have a sink and shower but share a toilet. Showers here are in-room (Ss-€70-80, Sb-€80-90, Ds-€80-90, Db-€90-100, non-smoking, guest computer, free Wi-Fi, Dultstrasse 1, tel. 089/2323-1556, mobile 0173-973-4598, www.

pension-jakobsplatz.de, info@pension-jakobsplatz.de, Christoph Zenker and son Marco).

$$ Motel One Sendlinger Tor, across from the Sendlinger Tor tram and U-Bahn stop, is a huge 241-room, busy, inexpensive chain hotel with rushed staff in a fine location. The rooms are a good value and tend to sell out a few weeks in advance. When booking on their website, make sure to choose the Sendlinger Tor location—they have six other hotels in Munich (Sb-€77, Db-€99, €7.50/person less without breakfast, non-smoking, free Wi-Fi, parking-€15/day, Herzog-Wilhelm-Strasse 28, tel. 089/5177-7250, www.motel-one.com, muenchen-sendlingertor@motel-one.com).

Away from the Center

$ The Tent—a venerable Munich institution officially known as the International Youth Camp Kapuzinerhölzl—offers 400 spots in three huge circus tents near Nymphenburg Palace. It never fills up, though you are encouraged to reserve online. Choose a mattress on a wooden floor (€7.50) or a bunk bed (€10.50), or pitch your own tent (€5.50/tent plus €5.50/person). Blankets, hot showers, lockers (bring or buy a lock), a kitchen, and Wi-Fi are all included; breakfast is a few euros extra. It can be a fun but noisy experience—kind of a cross between a slumber party and Woodstock. It feels quite

wholesome, but I wouldn't bring kids—it's really for young adults. There's a cool table-tennis-and-Frisbee atmosphere throughout the day, nightly campfires, and no curfew, though silence is requested after 1:00 (open early June-early Oct only, prices a little higher during Oktoberfest, cash only, pay guest computer, self-service laundry, bikes-€9/day, catch tram #17 from train station for 18 minutes to Botanischer Garten, direction Amalienburgstrasse, then go right down Franz-Schrank-Strasse—it's behind the trees at the end of the street, tel. 089/141-4300, www.the-tent.com, cu@the-tent.com).

More Hotels in Munich

If my listings above are full, here are some others to consider.

Within walking distance of the Viktualienmarkt, consider artsy **$$$ Hotel Olympic,** with 38 fresh, relaxing rooms (Db-€160-250, Hans-Sachs-Strasse 4, tel. 089-231-890, www.hotel-olympic.de, info@hotel-olympic.de); classy yet homey **$$$ Hotel Admiral** (Db-€160-300, Kohlstrasse 9, tel. 089-216-350, www.hotel-admiral.de); and **$$ Hotel Isartor,** with 68 comfortable but plain rooms (Db-€119-214, Baaderstrasse 2-4, tel. 089-216-3340, www.hotel-isartor.de).

Near Sendlinger Tor, alpine-bright and sunny **$$ Hotel Mueller**, offers 44 cozy rooms (Db-€109-369, Fliegenstrasse 4, tel. 089-232-3860, www.hotel-mueller-muenchen.de), while **$$ Carat Hotel** is a glossy slumber-mill popular with groups. Its streetside rooms have rare air-conditioning and its 48 apartments have kitchenettes (Db-€89-389, Lindwurmstrasse 13, tel. 089-230-380, www.carat-hotel-muenchen.de).

An easy tram or U-bahn ride from Marienplatz, **$$$ Hotel Europa Muenchen** has four-star American-style comfort and amenities in an impersonal, blocky structure (Db-€132-156, Dachauerstrasse 115, tel. 089-542-420, www.hotel-europa.de).

Eating in Munich

Munich cuisine is traditionally seasoned with beer. In beer halls, beer gardens, or at the Viktualienmarkt, try the most typical meal in town: *Weisswurst* (white-colored veal sausage—peel off the skin before eating, often available only until noon) with *süsser Senf* (sweet mustard), a salty *Brezel* (pretzel), and *Weissbier* ("white" wheat beer). Another traditional favorite is *Obatzda* (a.k.a. *Obatzter*), a mix of soft cheeses, butter, paprika, and often garlic or onions that's spread on bread. *Brotzeit*, literally "bread time," gets you a wooden platter of cold cuts, cheese, and pickles and is a good option for a light dinner.

I'm here for the beer-hall and beer-garden fun (my first several listings). But when the *Wurst und Kraut* get to be too much for you, Munich has plenty of good alternatives; I've listed my favorites later in this section.

Bavarian restaurants are now smoke-free. The only ashtrays you'll see throughout Bavaria are outside.

Beer Halls, Beer Gardens, and Bavarian Food

Nothing beats the Hofbräuhaus (the only place in town where you'll find oompah music) for those in search of the boisterous, clichéd image of the beer hall. Locals prefer the innumerable beer gardens. On a warm day, when you're looking for the authentic outdoor beer-garden experience, your best options are the Augustiner (near the train station), the small beer garden at the Viktualienmarkt (near Marienplatz), or the sea of tables in the English Garden.

Near Marienplatz

The **Hofbräuhaus** (HOAF-broy-house) is the world's most famous beer hall. While it's grotesquely touristy and filled with sloppy

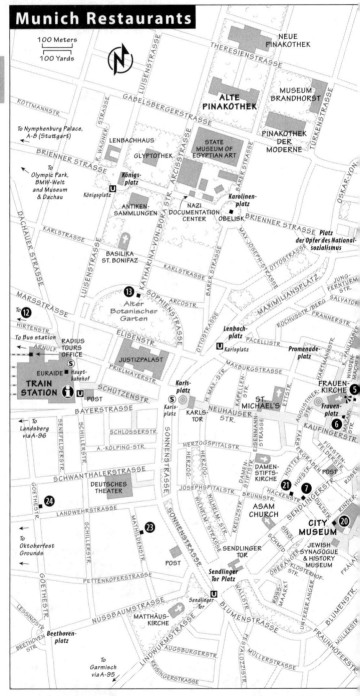

Munich Restaurants

100 Meters
100 Yards

NEUE PINAKOTHEK

THERESIENSTRASSE

ALTE PINAKOTHEK

MUSEUM BRANDHORST

GABELSBERGERSTRASSE

ROTTMANNSTR.

To Nymphenburg Palace,
A-8 (Stuttgart)

LENBACHHAUS

GLYPTOTHEK

STATE MUSEUM OF EGYPTIAN ART

PINAKOTHEK DER MODERNE

BRIENNER STRASSE

To Olympic Park,
BMW-Welt
and Museum
& Dachau

Königsplatz

Königsplatz

ANTIKEN-SAMMLUNGEN

NAZI DOCUMENTATION CENTER

Karolinenplatz

OBELISK

BRIENNER STRASSE

Platz der Opfer des National-sozialismus

KARLSTRASSE

BASILIKA ST. BONIFAZ

KARLSTRASSE

MAXIMILIANSPLATZ

JUNG-FERNTURM STR.

DACHAUER STRASSE

MARSSTRASSE

13

Alter Botanischer Garten

SOPHIENSTRASSE

ARCOSTR.

Lenbach-platz

PACELLISTR.

Promenade-platz

SALVATOR

KOCHUSTR.

PERG.

PRANNERSTR.

To **12**

HIRTENSTR.

To Bus station

RADIUS TOURS OFFICE

ARNULF.

ELISENSTR.

JUSTIZPALAST

PRIELMAYERSTR.

Karlsplatz

Karls-platz

MAXBURGSTRASSE

ST. MICHAEL'S

FRAUEN-KIRCHE **5**

EURAIDE

Haupt-bahnhof

TRAIN STATION

POST

SCHÜTZENSTR.

KARLS-TOR

NEUHAUSER STR.

Frauen-platz **6**

KAUFINGERSTR.

To Landsberg
via A-96

BAYERSTRASSE

SCHLOSSERSTR.

A.-KOLPING-STR.

HERZOGSPITALSTR.

HERZOG.

DAMEN-STIFTS-KIRCHE

HOTTER.

BURGGARTEN.

POST

SCHWANTHALERSTRASSE

DEUTSCHES THEATER

JOSEPHSPITALSTR.

21

HACKEN.

7

SENDLINGERSTR.

24

LANDWEHRSTRASSE

ASAM CHURCH

CITY MUSEUM **20**

To Oktoberfest
Grounds

23

MATHILDENSTR.

SENDLINGER TOR

JEWISH SYNAGOGUE & HISTORY MUSEUM

POST

PETTENKOFERSTRASSE

Sendlinger Tor Platz

Beethoven-platz

NUSSBAUMSTRASSE

MATTHÄUS-KIRCHE

Sendlinger Tor

BLUMENSTRASSE

To Garmisch
via A-95

LINDWURMSTRASSE

AUGSBURGERSTR.

FRAUNHOFERSTR.

MUNICH

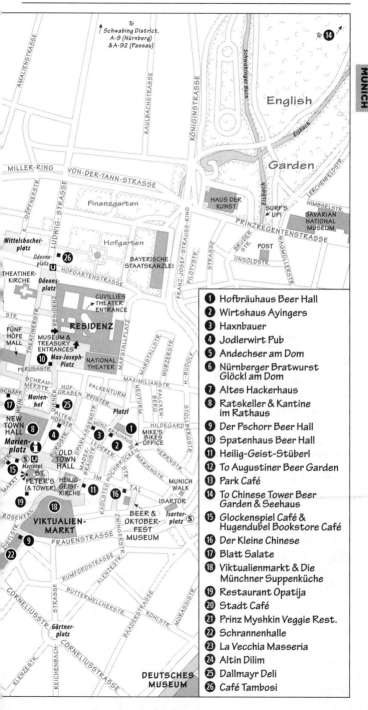

1. Hofbräuhaus Beer Hall
2. Wirtshaus Ayingers
3. Haxnbauer
4. Jodlerwirt Pub
5. Andechser am Dom
6. Nürnberger Bratwurst Glöckl am Dom
7. Altes Hackerhaus
8. Ratskeller & Kantine im Rathaus
9. Der Pschorr Beer Hall
10. Spatenhaus Beer Hall
11. Heilig-Geist-Stüberl
12. To Augustiner Beer Garden
13. Park Café
14. To Chinese Tower Beer Garden & Seehaus
15. Glockenspiel Café & Hugendubel Bookstore Café
16. Der Kleine Chinese
17. Blatt Salate
18. Viktualienmarkt & Die Münchner Suppenküche
19. Restaurant Opatija
20. Stadt Café
21. Prinz Myshkin Veggie Rest.
22. Schrannenhalle
23. La Vecchia Masseria
24. Altin Dilim
25. Dallmayr Deli
26. Café Tambosi

backpackers and tour groups, it's still a lot of fun—a Munich must. Even if you don't eat here, check it out to see 200 Japanese people drinking beer in a German beer hall...across from a Hard Rock Café. Germans go for the entertainment—to sing "Country Roads," see how Texas girls party, and watch tourists try to chug beer.

You can drop by anytime for a large or light meal (my favorite: €7 for *Schweinswurst mit Kraut*—pork sausages with sauerkraut), or for just a drink. Even though the visitors outnumber the locals, the food here is good. Choose from four zones: the rowdy main hall on the ground floor, a quieter courtyard under the stars, a dainty restaurant with mellow music (zither, oboe, harp) on first floor up, or the giant festival hall (sometimes reserved for events) under a big barrel vault on the top floor. The festival hall has a free folk show every evening from 18:30-22:30.

Except for Weissbier, they only sell beer by the *Mass* (one-liter mug, €7.60)—and they claim to sell 10,000 of these liters every day. The Hofbräuhaus offers regular live oompah music. This music-every-night atmosphere is irresistible, and the fat, shiny-leather bands get even church mice to stand up and conduct three-quarter time with breadsticks (daily 9:00-23:30, music during lunch and dinner only—daily 12:00-16:00 and 18:00-23:30, 5-minute walk from Marienplatz at Platzl 9, tel. 089/2901-3610, www.hofbraeu-haus.de).

Wirtshaus Ayingers, just across the street from the Hofbräu-haus, is good for those who've seen the Hofbräuhaus but would rather eat somewhere less chaotic. It serves quality Bavarian food—especially the schnitzels—and beer from Aying, a village south of Munich. There's lively outside seating on the cobbles facing the touristic chaos or a simple woody interior (€15-18 main courses, daily 11:00-23:30, Platzl 1a, tel. 089/2370-3666, www.ayingers.de).

Haxnbauer is a stark, old, and elegant place filled with locals here for one thing: the best pork knuckle in town. You'll pay a little extra, but it's clearly the place for what looks like pork knee (half *Schweinshaxe*-€18, daily 11:00-23:30, two blocks from Hofbräu-haus at Sparkassenstrasse 6, tel. 089/216-6540).

Jodlerwirt ("Yodeling Innkeeper") is a tiny, cramped, and smart-alecky pub. The food is great, and the ambience is as Bavarian as you'll find. Avoid the basic ground-floor bar and climb the stairs into the action. Even if it's just you and the accordionist, it's fun. Good food and lots of belly laughs...completely incomprehensible to the average tourist (€8-16 main courses, Tue-Sat 19:00-3:00 in the morning, food until 23:00, closed Mon except Oktoberfest and Dec, closed Sun except Oktoberfest, accordion act nightly 20:00-2:00 in the morning, between Hofbräuhaus and Marienplatz at

Altenhofstrasse 4, tel. 089/221-249, www.jodlerwirt-muenchen. net).

Andechser am Dom, at the rear of the twin-domed Frauen-kirche on a breezy square, is a trendy place serving Andechs beer and great food to appreciative regulars. Münchners favor the dark beer (ask for *dunkles*), but I love the light *(helles)*. The €12.50 *Gourmetteller* is a great sampler of their specialties, and the *Rostbrat-wurst* with kraut (€7.50) gives you the virtual *Nürnberger* bratwurst experience with the better Andechs beer (€8-18 main courses, daily 10:00-24:00, Weinstrasse 7a, reserve during peak times, tel. 089/2924-2420, www.andechser-am-dom.de).

Nürnberger Bratwurst Glöckl am Dom, around the corner from Andechser am Dom, is popular with tourists and offers a more traditional, fiercely Bavarian evening. Dine outside under the trees or in the dark, medieval, cozy interior. Enjoy the tasty little *Nürnberger* sausages with kraut (€8-19 main courses, daily 10:00-24:00, Frauenplatz 9, tel. 089/291-9450, www.bratwurst-gloeckl.de).

Altes Hackerhaus is popular with locals for its traditional *Bayerisch* (Bavarian) fare served with a slightly fancier feel in one of the oldest buildings in town. It offers a small courtyard and a fun forest of characteristic nooks festooned with old-time paintings, ads, and posters. This place is much-appreciated for its Hacker-Pschorr beer (€7-10 wurst dishes, €9-25 main courses, daily 10:00-24:00, Sendlinger Strasse 14, tel. 089/260-5026, www.hackerhaus. de).

Munich's **Ratskeller** fills the City Hall's vast cellar, and also has some tables in the courtyard (offering a 360-degree view of the architecture with the sky overhead). Traditionally, City Halls had a fine restaurant in their cellar—a *Rathauskeller.* While touristy, locals still dine here to sit in elegant nooks and enjoy the time-less traditional atmosphere (€14-23 main courses, €13.50 3-course lunches with water, daily 10:00-24:00, Marienplatz 8, tel. 089/219-9890, www.ratskeller.com).

Der Pschorr, an upscale beer hall occupying a former slaugh-terhouse, has a terrace overlooking the Viktualienmarkt and serves a special premium version of what many consider Munich's fin-est beer. With organic "slow food" and chilled glasses, this place mixes modern concepts—no candles, industrial-strength con-viviality—with traditional, quality, classic dishes. They tap classic wooden kegs every few minutes with gusto. The sound of the ham-mer lets patrons know they're getting it good and fresh (€15-18 main courses, €8-9 lunch specials, daily 10:00-24:00, Viktualien-markt 15, at end of Schrannenhalle, tel. 089/442-383-940, www .der-pschorr.de).

Spatenhaus is the opera-goers' beer hall, serving more elegant

Munich's Beer Scene

In Munich's beer halls *(Brauhäuser)* and beer gardens *(Biergartens)*, meals are inexpensive, white radishes are salted and cut in delicate spirals, and surly beer maids pull mustard packets from their cleavage. Unlike with wine, spending more money on beer doesn't get you a better drink. Beer is truly a people's drink, and you'll get the very best here in Munich. The big question among connoisseurs (local and foreign) is, "Which brew today?"

Beer gardens go back to the days when monks brewed their beer and were allowed to sell it directly to the thirsty public. They stored their beer in cellars under courtyards kept cool by the shade of bushy chestnut trees. Eventually, tables were set up, and these convivial eateries evolved. The tradition (complete with chestnut trees) survives, and any real beer garden will keep a few tables (those without tablecloths) available for customers who buy only beer and bring their own food.

Huge liter beers (called *eine Mass* in German, or "*ein* pitcher" in English) cost about €7. (Men's rooms come with vomitoriums.) If you order a half-liter *(eine Halbe)*, the barmaid is likely to say, "Why don't you go home and come back when you are thirsty?" You can order your beer *helles* (light in color but not "lite" in calories), *dunkles* (dark), *Weiss* or *Weizen* ("white" or wheat-based beer—cloudy and sweet), or *Radler* (half lemon soda, half beer).

Most beer gardens have a deposit *(Pfand)* system for their big glass steins: You pay €1 extra, and when you're finished, you can take the mug and your deposit token *(Pfandmarke)* to the return man *(Pfandrückgabe)* for your refund, or leave it on the table and lose your money. If you buy a bottled beer, pour it into the glass before you check out; otherwise you'll pay two deposits

food in a woodsy, traditional setting since 1896—maybe it's not even right to call it a "beer hall." You can also eat outside, on the square facing the opera and palace. It's pricey, but you won't find better-quality Bavarian cuisine. The upstairs restaurant serves a more international cuisine and is dressier—reservations are advised (€15-28 main courses, daily 9:30-24:00, on Max-Joseph-Platz opposite opera, Residenzstrasse 12, tel. 089/290-7050, www.spaten-haus.de).

Heilig-Geist-Stüberl ("Holy Ghost Pub") is a funky, retro little hole-in-the-wall where you are sure to meet locals (the Ger-

(one for the glass, the other for the bottle).

Many beer halls have a cafeteria system. The food is usually *selbstdienst* (self-service)—a sign may say *Bitte bedienen Sie sich selbst* (please serve yourself). If two prices are listed, *Schank* is for self-service, while *Bedienung* is for table service. If you have trouble finding cutlery, ask around for *Besteck*. In addition to the predictable *Wurst* and *Brotzeit* (salads and spreads), look for these heavy specialties:

Fleischpfanzerl (a.k.a. **Fleischklösse** or **Frikadellen**): meatballs

Grosse Brez'n: gigantic pretzel

Hendl (or **Brathähnchen**): roasted chicken

Radi: radish that's thinly spiral-cut and salted

Schweinrollbraten: pork belly

Schweinshax'n (or just **Hax'n**): pork knuckle

Spareribs: spareribs

Steckerlfisch: a whole fish (usually mackerel) herbed and grilled on a stick

At a large *Biergarten*, assemble your dream feast by visiting various counters, marked by type of food (*Bier* or *Bierschänke* for beer, *Bratwürste* for sausages, *Brotzeiten* for lighter fare served cold, and so on). After the meal, reclaim your deposit and bus your dirty dishes *(Geschirr)*—look for *Geschirrrückgabe* or *Geschirrabgabe* signs.

Eating outside is made more pleasant by the *Föhn* (warm winds that come over the Alps from Italy), which gives this part of Germany 30 more days of sunshine than the North—and sometimes even an Italian ambience. (Many natives attribute the city's huge increase in outdoor dining to global warming.)

Beer halls take care of their regular customers. You'll notice many tables marked *Stammtisch* (reserved for regulars and small groups, such as the "Happy Saturday Club"). These have a long tradition of being launch pads for grassroots action. In the days before radio and television, aspiring leaders used beer halls to connect with the public. Hitler hosted numerous political rallies in beer halls, and the Hofbräuhaus was the first place he talked to a big crowd.

man cousins of those who go to Reno because it's cheaper than Vegas, and who consider karaoke high culture). The interior, a 1980s time warp, makes you feel like you're stepping into an alcoholic cuckoo clock. There's no food—just drink here (Mon-Sat 9:00-22:00, Sun 14:00-22:00, just off the Viktualienmarkt at Heiliggeiststrasse 1, tel. 089/297-233).

Near the Train Station

Augustiner Beer Garden is a sprawling haven for local beer lovers on a balmy evening. A true under-the-leaves beer garden packed with Münchners, this is a delight. In fact, most Münchners consider Augustiner the best beer garden in town—which may be why there are 5,000 seats. There's no music, it's away from the tourist hordes, and it serves up great beer, good traditional food, huge portions, reasonable prices, and perfect conviviality. The outdoor self-service ambience is best, making this place ideal on a nice summer evening

(figure €12 for a main course and a drink). Parents with kids can sit at tables adjoining a sizable playground. There's also indoor and outdoor seating at a more expensive restaurant with table service (€12-19 main courses) by the entrance (daily 10:00-24:00, self-service outdoors until 22:00, table service indoors until 23:00, Arnulfstrasse 52, 3 looooong blocks from station going away from the center—or take tram #16/#17 one stop to Hopfenstrasse, taxis always waiting at the gate, tel. 089/594-393, www.augustinerkeller. de).

Park Café, though in a park, is much more than a café. The indoor section is big and bold, with a clean yet rustic ambience, DJs or live music in the late evening, few tourists, and quality food (€9-16 main courses). When it's hot, everyone decamps to the beer garden out back in the Alter Botanischer Garden, where you can order off the menu or from the self-service counters. Don't forget to reclaim the deposit for your plate and mug when you leave (daily 10:00-24:00, beer garden opens at 11:30, a short walk north of the train station at Sophienstrasse 7, tel. 089/5161-7980, www.park-cafe089.de).

In the English Garden

For outdoor ambience and a cheap meal, spend an evening at the English Garden's **Chinese Tower Beer Garden** *(Chinesischer Turm Biergarten)*. You're welcome to B.Y.O. food and grab a table, or buy from the picnic stall *(Brotzeit)* right there. Don't bother to phone ahead—they have 6,000 seats. This is a fine opportunity to try a *Steckerlfisch*, sold for €9 at a separate kiosk (daily, long hours in good weather, usually live music, tel. 089/383-8730, www.chinaturm.de; take tram #18 from main train station or Sendlinger Tor to Tivolistrasse, or U-3 or U-6 to Giselastrasse and then bus #54 or #154 two stops).

Deeper into the English Garden, **Seehaus** is a 10-minute walk past the Chinese Tower. It's famous among Münchners for its idyllic lakeside setting and excellent Mediterranean and traditional cooking. It's dressy and a bit snobbish, and understandably filled with locals who fit the same description. Choose from classy indoor or lakeside seating (€17-27 main courses, daily 10:00-24:00; take U-3 or U-6 to Münchner Freiheit and walk 10 minutes, or get off at Dietlindenstrasse and then take bus #144 one stop to Osterwaldstrasse; Kleinhesselohe 3, tel. 089/381-6130).

Seehaus Beer Garden, adjacent to the fancy Seehaus restaurant, offers the same waterfront atmosphere in a less expensive, more casual setting. There's all the normal wurst, kraut, pretzels, and fine beer at typical prices (daily, long hours from 11:00 when the weather's fine).

Non-Beer Hall Restaurants

Man does not live by beer alone. Well, maybe some do. But for the rest of us, I recommend the following alternatives to the beer-and-wurst circuit.

On and near Marienplatz

Kantine im Rathaus is your solid, fast, economical, and no-nonsense standby in the center. (It's actually the cafeteria for City Hall workers—they get a discount off the listed prices.) The entrance is just behind the New Town Hall tower—go through the arch under the tower into the courtyard and look for the sign on the right. There's seating in the courtyard or inside (€5-10 main courses, Mon-Fri 11:00-18:30, Sat 12:00-16:00, closed Sun, closes at 17:00 on weekdays Jan-April).

Glockenspiel Café is good for a coffee or a meal with a bird's-eye view down on the Marienplatz action—I'd come for the view more than the food. Locals like the open terrace without a view, but regardless of the weather, I grab a seat overlooking Marienplatz (daily 9:00-18:00, ride elevator from Rosenstrasse entrance, opposite glockenspiel at Marienplatz 28, tel. 089/264-256).

The **Hugendubel bookstore** has a Starbucks-style café on the top floor. It's quicker and less crowded than the Glockenspiel Café, and comes with the same great view (self-serve, take the glass elevator, Mon-Sat 9:30-20:00, closed Sun, tel. 089/2601-1987).

Der Kleine Chinese, two blocks downhill from Marienplatz, is popular, with inexpensive Asian standards (€5-7 main courses, order at counter and they'll bring it to your table, daily 11:00-22:00, Im Tal 28, tel. 089/2916-3536).

Blatt Salate is a self-serve salad bar on a side street between the Frauenkirche and the New Town Hall; it's a great little hideaway for a healthy quick lunch. You'll spend €12-14 for a yummy salad with fresh bread and a drink (vegetarian and meat salads and soups, Mon-Fri 11:00-19:00, Sat 11:00-18:00, closed Sun, Schäflerstrasse 5a, tel. 089/2102-0281).

Around the Viktualienmarkt

The small **beer garden** at the center of the Viktualienmarkt taps you into about the best budget eating in town; it's just steps from Marienplatz (Mon-Sat until late, closed Sun). There's table service wherever you see a tablecloth; to picnic, choose a table without one—but you must buy a drink from the counter. Countless stalls surround the beer garden and sell wurst, sandwiches, produce, and so on. This B.Y.O.F. tradition recalls a time when monastery beer gardens served beer but not food. This is a good spot to grab a typical Munich *Weisswurst*—and some beer.

Restaurant Opatija, in the Viktualienmarktpassage a few steps from Marienplatz, is modern and efficient, bringing the Adriatic to Munich with a big, eclectic Italian and Balkan menu, plus traditional German favorites. Choose between the comfortable indoor section and the outdoor seating in a quiet, narrow courtyard. Prices are low, it's family-friendly, and they do takeout (good €7 pizzas, €7 pastas, €9-10 salad plates, €8-12 main courses, daily 11:30-22:30, kitchen closes at 21:30, enter the passage at Viktualienmarkt 6 or Rindermarkt 2, tel. 089/2323-1995).

Die Münchner Suppenküche ("Munich Soup Kitchen"), a self-service soup joint at the Viktualienmarkt, is fine for a small, cozy sit-down lunch at picnic tables under a closed-in awning. The chalkboard lists six soups of the day (€4-6 soup meals, Mon-Fri 10:00-18:00, Sat 9:00-18:00, closed Sun, near corner of Reichenbachstrasse and Frauenstrasse, tel. 089/260-9599).

Stadt Café is a lively café serving healthy fare, with great daily specials (€7-10), an inventive menu of Italian, German, and vegetarian dishes, salads, and a big selection of cakes by the slice. This informal, no-frills restaurant draws newspaper-readers, stroller moms, and tourists, too. Dine in the quiet cobbled courtyard, inside, or outside facing the new synagogue (blackboard has today's specials, daily 10:00-24:00, in same building as Munich City Museum, St.-Jakobs-Platz 1, tel. 089/266-949).

Prinz Myshkin Vegetarian Restaurant is an upscale vegetarian eatery in the old center. The menu is totally meatless and dictated by the season. You'll find a clever, appetizing selection of €14-20 main courses. The decor is modern, the arched ceilings are cool, and the outside seating is on a quiet street. Don't miss the enticing appetizer selection on display as you enter (they do a fine €14 mixed-appetizer plate). They also have vegetarian sushi, pastas, Indian dishes, and their own baker, so they're proud of their sweets

(€7.50 weekday lunch specials, daily 11:30-23:00, Hackenstrasse 2, tel. 089/265-596).

Eateries on Sebastiansplatz: Looking for a no-schnitzel-or-dumplings alternative? Sebastiansplatz is a long, pedestrianized square between the Viktualienmarkt and the synagogue, lined with bistros handy for a healthy and quick lunch. Options range from French to Italian to Asian to salads. All serve €10 main courses on the busy cobbled square or inside—just survey the scene and choose. The **Schrannenhalle,** the former grain exchange over-looking the square, is also busy with creative, modern eateries and gourmet delis.

Near the Train Station

La Vecchia Masseria, between Sendlinger Tor and the train sta-tion hotels, serves Italian food inside amid a cozy Tuscan farmhouse decor, or outside in a beautiful flowery courtyard. Try the €25 tast-ing *menu* (€6-8 pizza or pasta, €14-16 main courses, daily 11:30-23:30, reservations smart, Mathildenstrasse 3, tel. 089/550-9090).

Altin Dilim, a self-service Turkish restaurant, is a standout among the many hole-in-the-wall Middle Eastern places in the ethnic area just near the station. It feels like a trip to Istanbul—complete with a large, attractively displayed selection, ample seat-ing, and a handy pictorial menu which helps you order. Pay at the counter (€3.50 *Döner Kebab*, €8-13 main courses, Mon-Sat 8:00-24:00, Sun 9:00-24:00, Goethestrasse 17, tel. 089/9734-0869).

Picnics

For a truly elegant picnic (costing as much as a restaurant meal), **Dallmayr's** is the place to shop. The crown in their emblem re-flects that no less than the royal family assembled its picnics at this historic and expensive delicatessen. Pretend you're a Bavarian aristocrat—King Ludwig himself, even—and put together a royal spread to munch in the nearby Hofgarten. Or visit the classy but pricey cafés that serve light meals on the ground floor and first floor (Mon-Sat 9:30-19:00, closed Sun, behind New Town Hall, Dienerstrasse 13-15, tel. 089/21350).

A Budget Picnic: To save money, browse at Dallmayr's but buy at a **supermarket.** The ones that hide in the basements of depart-ment stores are on the upscale side: the **Kaufhof** stores at Marien-platz and Karlsplatz (Mon-Sat 9:30-20:00, closed Sun), or the even more upmarket **Karstadt** across from the train station (same hours). Cheaper options include the **REWE** in the basement at Fünf Höfe (Mon-Sat 7:00-20:00, closed Sun, entrance is in Viscardihof) or the **Lidl** at Schwantaler Strasse 31, near the train-station hotels (Mon-Sat 8:00-20:00, closed Sun).

Munich Connections

Munich is a super transportation hub (one reason it was the target of so many WWII bombs), with easy train and bus connections to most Bavarian destinations, as well as international trains.

By Train

For quick help at the main train station, stop by the service counter in front of track 18. For better English and more patience, drop by the EurAide desk at counter #1 in the *Reisezentrum*. Train info: tel. 0180-599-6633, www.bahn.com.

From Munich by Train to: Füssen (hourly, 2 hours, most with easy transfer in Kaufbeuren; for a Neuschwanstein Castle day trip, leave as early as possible), **Reutte,** Austria (every hour, 2.5-3.25 hours, change in **Füssen**), **Oberammergau** (nearly hourly, 1.75 hours, change in Murnau), **Salzburg,** Austria (2/hour, 1.5-2 hours), **Berchtesgaden** (at least hourly, 2.5-3 hours, change in Freilassing or Salzburg), **Nürnberg** (2-3/hour, 1-1.5 hours), **Köln** (2/hour, 4.5 hours, some with 1 change), **Würzburg** (1-2/hour, 2 hours), **Rothenburg** (hourly, 2.5-4 hours, 2-3 changes), **Frankfurt** (hourly, 3.25 hours), **Frankfurt Airport** (1-2/hour, 3.5 hours), **Leipzig** (8/day direct, 5.5 hours; more with change in Nürnberg or Naumburg, 5.5 hours), **Erfurt** (about 2/hour, 4.5-4.75 hours, change in Fulda), **Dresden** (every 2 hours, 6 hours, change in Leipzig or Nürnberg), **Hamburg** (hourly, 6-6.5 hours), **Berlin** (1-2/hour, 6-6.75 hours, some direct, otherwise change in Göttingen), **Vienna** (direct trains every 2 hours, 4.25 hours), **Venice** (every 2 hours, 7-7.5 hours, change in Verona, 1 direct night train, 9 hours), **Paris** (1/day direct, 6 hours, 6/day with transfer, 6-8.5 hours, 1 direct night train, 10.5 hours), **Prague** (2/day direct, 6 hours; better by bus—see below; no night trains), **Zürich** (3/day direct, 4.25 hours). Trains run nightly to Berlin, Vienna, Venice, Florence, Rome, Paris, Amsterdam, and Budapest (at least 6 hours to each city). To use a railpass for a night train to Italy, your pass must include all countries on the train route (i.e., Austria or Switzerland), or you'll have to buy the segment that's not included.

By Bus

The Lufthansa airport bus (described later) as well as Deutsche Bahn buses to **Prague** (only €4 with Eurail Pass, 4/day, 5 hours) leave from the north side of the train station (exit by track 26).

Romantic Road Bus: The **Romantic Road bus** (mid-April-late Oct only) connects Munich's Central Bus Station to Füssen, Dinkelsbühl, Rothenburg, Würzburg, Frankfurt, and other destinations en route. This slower but more scenic alternative to the train allows a glimpse of towns such as Augsburg, Nördlingen, and

Dinkelsbühl (no advance reservations needed, northbound bus departs Munich at 10:30, arrives Rothenburg at 15:50; southbound bus departs Munich at 17:55, arrives Füssen at 20:20).

By Plane

Munich's airport (code: MUC) is an easy 40-minute ride on the S-1 or S-8 **subway,** each of which runs every 20 minutes (starting at 4:00 in the morning and continuing until almost 2:00 in the morning) between the airport and Marienplatz and the train station. While you can buy a single ticket for €10.40, the €11.20 Munich *Gesamtnetz* day pass, which covers public transportation all day, is worth getting if you'll be making just one more public transport journey that same day. Groups of two or more should buy the €20.40 Munich *Gesamtnetz* partner day pass, which gives up to five adults the run of the system for the day. The trip is also free with a validated and dated railpass. The S-8 is a bit quicker and easier, as the S-1 line has two branches and some trains split—if on the S-1 to the airport, be certain your train is going to the *Flughafen*.

Another alternative is the Lufthansa airport bus, which links the airport with the main train station (€10.50, €17 round-trip, 3/ hour, 45 minutes, buses depart train station 5:15-19:55, buy tickets on bus; from inside the station, exit near track 26 and look for yellow Airport Bus signs; www.airportbus-muenchen.de). If you're traveling alone, going round-trip, and not using other public transport the same day, the bus saves a few euros. Avoid taking a taxi from the airport, as it's a long, expensive drive; it's better to take public transport and then switch to a taxi if needed. Airport info: tel. 089/97500, www.munich-airport.de.

BAVARIA AND TIROL

Füssen • King's Castles • Wieskirche • Oberammergau
• Linderhof Castle • Ettal Monastery • Zugspitze
• Reutte, Austria

Two hours south of Munich, in the most picturesque corner of Germany's Bavaria and Austria's Tirol, is a timeless land of fairy-tale castles, painted buildings shared by cows and farmers, and locals who still yodel when they're happy and dress in dirndls and lederhosen.

In southern Bavaria, tour "Mad" King Ludwig II's ornate Neuschwanstein Castle, Europe's most spectacular. Stop by the Wieskirche, a textbook example of Bavarian Rococo bursting with curlicues, and browse through Oberammergau, Germany's woodcarving capital and home of the famous Passion Play (next performed in 2020). Then, just over the border in Austria, explore the ruined Ehrenberg Castle and scream down the mountain on an oversized skateboard. In this chapter, I'll cover Bavaria first, then the area around Reutte in Tirol.

Choosing a Home Base

My hotel recommendations in this chapter cluster in three areas: Füssen, Oberammergau, and Reutte. When selecting a home base, here are a few factors to consider:

Füssen offers the easiest access to the biggest attraction in the region, the "King's Castles," Neuschwanstein and Hohenschwangau. The town itself is a mix of real-world and cutesy-cobbled, and has some of the glitziest hotels in the region (as well as more affordable options). Füssen is also handiest for train travelers.

Oberammergau is the best-known, most touristy, and cutest town of the bunch. World-famous for its once-per-decade Passion Play, it's much sleepier nine years out of ten. Oberammergau offers the easiest access to some of the region's lesser, but still worthwhile, sights: Ettal Monastery, Linderhof Castle, and the German lift to the Zugspitze.

Reutte is the least appealing town, but its surrounding villages are home to some of the coziest, most pleasant rural accommodations in the region—making it a particularly good option for drivers (but less practical for others). It's butted up against the ruined Ehrenberg Castle, and within a 30-minute drive of the King's Castles, Linderhof, and the Austrian approach to the Zugspitze.

For specifics on public-transit logistics from each town, see "By Public Transportation," later.

Planning Your Time and Getting Around Bavaria

While Germans and Austrians vacation here for a week or two at a time, the typical speedy American traveler will find two days' worth of sightseeing. With a car and more time, you could enjoy three or four days, but the basic visit ranges anywhere from a long day trip from Munich to a three-night, two-day stay. If the weather's good and you're not going to Switzerland on your trip, be sure to ride a lift to an alpine peak.

By Car

This region is best by car, and all the sights are within an easy 60-mile loop from Füssen or Reutte. Even if you're doing the rest of your trip by train, consider renting a car for your time here.

Here's a good one-day circular drive from either Füssen or Reutte (from Füssen, you can start about 30 minutes later):

7:00	Breakfast
7:30	Depart hotel
8:00	Arrive at Neuschwanstein to pick up tickets for the two castles (Neuschwanstein and Hohenschwangau)
9:00	Tour Hohenschwangau
11:00	Tour Neuschwanstein
13:00	Drive to Oberammergau, and spend an hour there browsing the carving shops
15:00	Drive to Ettal Monastery for a half-hour stop (if you're not otherwise seeing the Wieskirche), then on to Linderhof Castle
16:00	Tour Linderhof

Füssen & Reutte Area

18:00   Drive along scenic Plansee Lake back to your hotel
19:00   Back at hotel
20:00   Dinner

Off-season (Oct-March), start your day an hour later, since Neuschwanstein and Hohenschwangau tours don't depart until 10:00; and skip Linderhof, which closes at 16:00.

The next morning, you could stroll through Reutte, hike to the Ehrenberg ruins, and ride the luge on your way to Munich, Innsbruck, Switzerland, Venice, or wherever.

If you're based in Oberammergau (rather than Füssen or Reutte), get an early start to hit Neuschwanstein and Hohenschwangau first. If the weather's good, hike to the top of Ehrenberg Castle (in Reutte). Drive along Plansee and tour Linderhof and Ettal Monastery on your way back home.

By Public Transportation

Where you stay determines which sights you can see most easily. Train travelers use **Füssen** as a base, and bus or bike the three miles to Neuschwanstein and the Tegelberg luge or gondola. Staying in **Oberammergau** gives you easy access to Linderhof and Ettal Monastery, and you can day-trip to the top of the Zugspitze via Garmisch. Although **Reutte** is the least convenient base if you're carless, travelers staying there can easily bike or hike to the Ehrenberg ruins, and can reach Neuschwanstein by bus (via Füssen), bike (1.5 hours), or taxi (€35 one-way); if you stay at the recommended Gutshof zum Schluxen hotel (between Reutte and Füssen, in Pinswang, Austria) it's a 1- to 1.5-hour hike through the woods to Neuschwanstein.

Visiting sights farther from your home base is not impossible by local bus, but requires planning. The Deutsche Bahn (German Railway) website at www.bahn.com does a great job of finding bus connections that work, on both sides of the border. (Schedules for each route are available at www.rvo-bus.de, but only in German.) Those staying in **Füssen** can day-trip by bus to Reutte and the Ehrenberg ruins, to the Wieskirche, or, with some effort, to Linderhof via Oberammergau. From **Oberammergau,** you can reach Neuschwanstein and Füssen by bus. From **Reutte,** you can take the train to Ehrwald to reach the Zugspitze from the Austrian side, but side-trips from Reutte to Oberammergau and Linderhof are impractical. More transport details are provided later, under each individual destination.

Hitchhiking, though always risky, is a slow-but-doable way to connect the public-transportation gaps. For example, even reluctant hitchhikers can catch a ride from Linderhof back to Oberammergau, as virtually everyone leaving there is a tourist like you and heading that way.

Staying overnight in this region is magical, but travelers in a hurry can make it a day trip from **Munich.** If you can postpone leaving Munich until after 9:00 on weekday mornings, the **Bayern-Ticket** is a great deal for getting to Füssen or Oberammergau: It covers buses and slower regional trains throughout Bavaria for up to five people at a very low price (€22/day for the first person plus €4 for each additional person). If you're interested only in Ludwig's castles, consider an all-day organized bus tour of the Bavarian biggies as a side-trip from Munich.

By Bike
This is great biking country. Many hotels loan bikes to guests, and shops in Reutte and at the Füssen train station rent bikes for €8-15 per day. The ride from Reutte to Neuschwanstein and the Tegelberg luge (1.5 hours) is a natural.

Helpful Hints
Sightseeing Pass: The Bavarian Palace Department offers a **14-day ticket** (called *Mehrtagesticket*) that covers admission to

---

Bavarian Craftsmanship

The scenes you'll see painted on the sides of houses in Bavaria are called *Lüftlmalerei*. The term came from the name of the house ("Zum Lüftl") owned by a man from Oberammergau who pioneered the practice in the 18th century. As the paintings became popular during the Counter-Reformation Baroque age, themes tended to involve Christian symbols, saints, and stories (such as scenes from the life of Jesus), to reinforce the Catholic Church's authority in the region. Some scenes also depicted an important historical event that took place in that house or town.

Especially in the northern part of this region, you'll see *Fachwerkhäuser*—half-timbered houses. *Fachwerk* means "craftsmanship," as this type of home required a highly skilled master craftsman to create. They are most often found inside fortified cities (such as Rothenberg, Nürnberg, and Dinkelsbühl) that were once strong and semi-independent.

Neuschwanstein (but not Hohenschwangau) and Linderhof; the Residenz, Nymphenburg Palace, and Amalienburg Palace in Munich; the Imperial Palace in Nürnberg; the Residenz and Marienberg Fortress in Würzburg; and many other castles and palaces not mentioned in this book. The one-person pass costs €24, and the family/partner version (up to two adults plus children) costs €40. If you are planning to visit at least three of these sights within a two-week period, the pass will likely pay for itself. (For longer stays, there's also an annual pass available—€45/single, €65/family.) The pass is sold at all covered castles and online. For more information, see www.schloesser.bayern.de. Don't confuse this with the pointless combination ticket for Ludwig II's castles, which costs the same (€24) but only covers three castles—Neuschwanstein, Linderhof, and Herrencheimsee (farther east and not covered in this book).

Local Guest Tax: Hotels and B&Bs in the region are usually required to collect a local tax (called a *Kurtax*) of about €2 per person per night, which is not included in the rates I've listed and will be added to your bill. However, in both Füssen and Ruette, this tax funds a card that provides discounts to attractions and free public transportation; details are in each city's "Tourist Information" section, later.

Visiting Churches: At any type of church, if you'd like to attend a service, look for the *Gottesdienst* schedule. In every small German town in the very Catholic south, when you pass the big town church, look for a sign that says *Heilige Messe*. This is the schedule for holy Mass, usually on Saturday *(Sa.)* or Sunday *(So.)*.

Updates to This Book: For news about changes to this book's coverage since it was published, see www.ricksteves.com/update.

Füssen

Dramatically situated under a renovated castle on the lively Lech River, Füssen (FEW-sehn) has been a strategic stop since ancient times. Its main street sits on the Via Claudia Augusta, which crossed the Alps (over the Brenner Pass) in Roman times. Going north, early traders could follow the Lech River downstream to the  Danube, and then cross over to the Main and Rhine valleys—a route now known to modern travelers as the "Romantic Road." Today, while Füssen is overrun by tourists in the summer, few venture to the back streets...which is where you'll find the real charm. Apart from my self-guided walk and the Füssen Heritage Museum, there's little to do here. It's just a pleasant small town with a big history and lots of hardworking people in the tourist business.

Halfway between Füssen and the border (as you drive, or a woodsy walk from the town) is the **Lechfall,** a thunderous waterfall (with a handy WC).

Orientation to Füssen

Füssen's roughly circular old town huddles around its castle and monastery, along the Lech River. From here, roads spin off in all directions. The train station is a few blocks from the TI, the town center (a cobbled shopping mall), and all my hotel listings.

Tourist Information

The TI is in the center of town (July-mid-Sept Mon-Fri 9:00-18:00, Sat 10:00-14:00, Sun 10:00-12:00; mid-Sept-June Mon-Fri 9:00-17:00, Sat 10:00-14:00, closed Sun; one Internet terminal, free with Füssen Card—described next, 3 blocks down Bahnhofstrasse from station at Kaiser-Maximilian-Platz 1, tel. 08362/93850, www.fuessen.de). If necessary, the TI can help you find a room. After hours, the little self-service info pavilion near the front of the TI features an automated room-finding service with a phone to call hotels.

Be sure to ask your hotel for a **Füssen Card**, which you're entitled to if you're sleeping even just one night in town. This card, paid for by your hotel tax, gives you free use of public transportation in the immediate region (including the bus to Neuschwanstein), as well as discounts to major attractions: €1 each on Neuschwanstein, Hohenschwangau, the Museum of the Bavarian Kings, and the Forggensee boat trip, and €2 on the Füssen Heritage Museum (plus discounts on the Tegelberg gondola, the Royal Crystal Baths, and the Hahnenkammbahn cable car near Reutte). Using this card will more than pay for your hotel tax.

Arrival in Füssen

From the train station (lockers available, €2-3), exit to the left and walk a few short blocks to reach the center of town and the TI. Buses to Neuschwanstein, Reutte, and elsewhere leave from a parking lot next to the station.

Helpful Hints

Internet Access: ICS Internet Café has four computers and decent prices (€1.50/hour, daily 9:00-24:00, Luitpoldstrasse 8, tel. 08362/883-7073). The **city library** (Stadtbibliothek), inside the same monastery complex that houses the Füssen Heritage Museum, has Wi-Fi (€1/30 minutes, free with Füssen Card; Tue-Wed 13:00-17:00, Thu 13:00-19:00, Fri 10:00-17:00, closed Mon, Lechhalde 3).

Bike Rental: Fahrrad-Station, sitting right where the train tracks end, outfits sightseers with good bikes and tips on two-wheeled fun in the area (prices per 24 hours: €10-city bike, €15-sport bike, €20-electric bike; March-Oct Mon-Fri 9:00-12:00 & 14:00-18:00, Sat 9:00-13:00, Sun 10:00-12:00, closed Nov-Feb, tel. 08362/505-9155, mobile 0176-2205-3080, www.ski-sport-luggi.de).

Car Rental: Peter Schlichtling is in the town center (Mon-Fri 8:00-18:00, Sat 9:00-12:00, closed Sun, Kemptener Strasse 26, tel. 08362/922-122, www.schlichtling.de); **Auto Osterried/Europcar** rents at similar prices, but is an €8 taxi ride away from the train station (daily 8:00-19:00, past waterfall on road to Austria, Tiroler Strasse 65, tel. 08362/6381).

Local Guide: Silvia Beyer speaks English, knows the region very well, and can even drive you to sights that are hard to reach by train (€30/hour, mobile 0160-901-13431, silliby@web.de).

Self-Guided Walk

Welcome to Füssen

For most, Füssen is just a home base for visiting Ludwig's famous castles. But the town has a rich history and hides some evocative corners, as you'll see when you follow this orientation walk. This 45-minute stroll is designed to get you out of the cutesy old cobbled core where most tourists spend their time. Throughout the town, "City Tour" information plaques explain points of interest in English (in more detail than I've provided).

• *Begin at the square in front of the TI, three blocks from the train station.*

❶ **Kaiser-Maximilian-Platz:** The entertaining "Seven Stones" fountain on this square, by sculptor Christian Tobin, was built in 1995 to celebrate Füssen's 700th birthday. The stones symbolize community, groups of people gathering, conviviality...each is different, with "heads" nodding and talking. It's granite on granite. The moving heads are not connected, and nod only with waterpower. While frozen in winter, it's a popular and splashy play zone for kids on hot summer days.

• *Walk half a block down the busy street (to the left, with the TI at your back). You'll soon see...*

❷ **Hotel Hirsch and Medieval Towers:** Recent renovations have restored some of the original Art Nouveau flavor to Hotel Hirsch, which opened in 1904. In those days, aristocratic tourists came here to appreciate the castles and natural wonders of the Alps. Across the busy street stands one of two surviving towers from Füssen's medieval town wall (c. 1515), and next to it is a passageway into the old town.

• *Walk 50 yards farther down the busy street to another tower. Just before it, you'll see an information plaque and an archway where a small street called Klosterstrasse emerges through a surviving piece of the old town wall. Step through the smaller pedestrian archway, walk along Klosterstrasse for a few yards, and turn left through the gate into the...*

❸ **Historic Cemetery of St. Sebastian (Alter Friedhof):** This peaceful oasis of Füssen history, established in the 16th century, fills a corner between the town wall and the Franciscan monastery. It's technically full, and only members of great and venerable Füssen

BAVARIA & TIROL

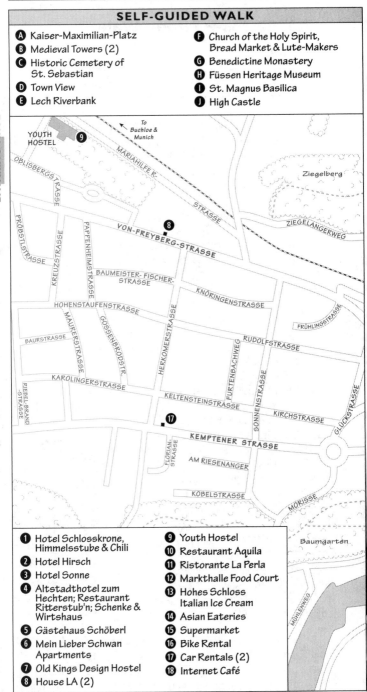

SELF-GUIDED WALK

- **A** Kaiser-Maximilian-Platz
- **B** Medieval Towers (2)
- **C** Historic Cemetery of St. Sebastian
- **D** Town View
- **E** Lech Riverbank
- **F** Church of the Holy Spirit, Bread Market & Lute-Makers
- **G** Benedictine Monastery
- **H** Füssen Heritage Museum
- **I** St. Magnus Basilica
- **J** High Castle

- **1** Hotel Schlosskrone, Himmelsstube & Chili
- **2** Hotel Hirsch
- **3** Hotel Sonne
- **4** Altstadthotel zum Hechten; Restaurant Ritterstub'n; Schenke & Wirtshaus
- **5** Gästehaus Schöberl
- **6** Mein Lieber Schwan Apartments
- **7** Old Kings Design Hostel
- **8** House LA (2)
- **9** Youth Hostel
- **10** Restaurant Aquila
- **11** Ristorante La Perla
- **12** Markthalle Food Court
- **13** Hohes Schloss Italian Ice Cream
- **14** Asian Eateries
- **15** Supermarket
- **16** Bike Rental
- **17** Car Rentals (2)
- **18** Internet Café

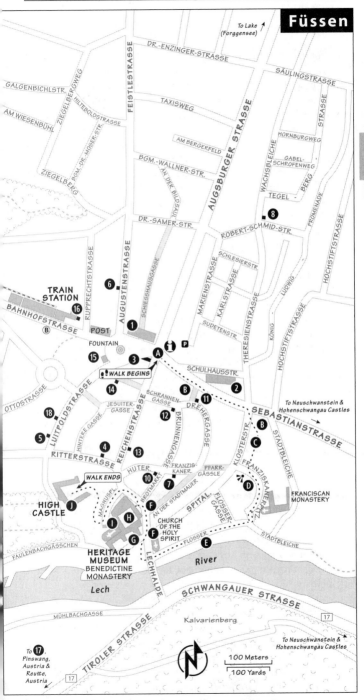

Füssen

To Lake (Forggensee)

DR.-ENZINGER-STRASSE

FEISTLESTRASSE

SÄULINGSTRASSE

GALGENBICHLSTR.

AM WIESENBÜHL

ZIEGELBERGWEG

HILTEBOLDSTRASSE

BGM.-DR.-MODER-STR.

ZIEGELBERG

TAXISWEG

AM BERGERFELD

BGM.-WALLNER-STR.

AN DER BILDSÄUL

DR.-SAMER-STR.

AUGSBURGER STRASSE

HÖRNBURGWEG

GABEL-SCHROFENWEG

WACHSBLEICHE

BERG

TEGEL

STRASSE

PROMENADE

LUDWIG

HOCHSTIFTSTRASSE

ROBERT-SCHMID-STR. **8**

SCHLESIERSTR.

MARIENSTRASSE

KARLSTRASSE

THERESIENSTRASSE

KÖNIG

HOCHSTIFTSTRASSE

SUDETENSTR.

RUPPRECHTSTRASSE

AUGUSTENSTRASSE

SCHIESSHAUSGASSE

TRAIN STATION

16

6

POST **B**

BAHNHOFSTRASSE

FOUNTAIN

15

3 **A** **i** **P**

1

SCHULHAUSSTR.

WALK BEGINS

14

2

JESUITER-GASSE

SCHRANNEN-GASSE

B

11

To Neuschwanstein & Hohenschwangau Castles

OTTOSTRASSE

LUITPOLDSTRASSE

HINTERE GASSE

REICHENSTRASSE

12

BRUNNENGASSE

DREHERGASSE

SEBASTIANSTRASSE

B

18

5

RITTERSTRASSE

4

13

HUTER-

FRANZIS-KANER.

PFARR-GASSLE

KLOSTERSTR.

FRANZISKANERPL.

STADTBLEICHE

C

WALK ENDS

10

7

BROTMARKT

AN DER STADTMAUER

SPITAL

FLOSSER-GASSE

D

FRANCISCAN MONASTERY

HIGH CASTLE

J

MAGNUSPL.

I **H**

F

CHURCH OF THE HOLY SPIRIT

F

STADTBLEICHE

FAULENBACHGÄSSCHEN

G

HERITAGE MUSEUM

BENEDICTINE MONASTERY

LECHHALDE

E

FLOSSER

River

Lech

MÜHLBACHGASSE

SCHWANGAUER STRASSE

Kalvarienberg

17

To **17**, Pinswang, Austria & Reutte, Austria

TIROLER STRASSE

17

To Neuschwanstein & Hohenschwangau Castles

N

100 Meters

100 Yards

families (who already own plots here) can join those who are buried (free, daily April-Sept 7:30-19:00, Oct-March 8:00-17:00).

Immediately inside the gate and on the right is the tomb of Domenico Quaglio, who painted the Romantic scenes decorating the walls of Hohenschwangau Castle in 1835. Across the cemetery, on the old city wall (beyond the church), is the World War I memorial, listing all the names of men from this small town killed in that devastating conflict (along with each one's rank and place of death). A bit to the right, also along the old wall, is a statue of the hand of God holding a fetus—a place to remember babies who died before being born. And in the corner, farther to the right, is a gated area with the simple wooden crosses of Franciscans who lived just over the wall in the monastery. Strolling the rest of the grounds, note the fine tomb art from many ages collected here, and the loving care this community gives its cemetery.

• *Exit on the far side, just past the dead Franciscans, and continue toward the big church.*

❿ **Town View from Franciscan Monastery (Franziskanerkloster):** From the Franciscan Monastery (which still has big responsibilities, but only a handful of monks in residence), there's a fine view over the medieval town with an alpine backdrop. The Church of St. Magnus and the High Castle (the former summer residence of the Bishops of Augsburg) break the horizon. The tall, skinny smokestack (c. 1886) and workers' housing on the left are reminders that when Ludwig built Neuschwanstein, the textile industry (linen and flax) was very big here. Walk all the way to the far end of the monastery chapel and peek around the corner, where you'll see a gate that proclaims the *Ende der romantischen Strasse* (end of the Romantic Road).

• *Now go down the stairway and turn left, through the medieval "Bleachers' Gate" (marked 5½) to the...*

⓫ **Lech Riverbank:** This low end of town, the flood zone, was the home of those whose work depended on the river—bleachers, rafters, and fishermen. In its heyday, the Lech River was an expressway to Augsburg (about 70 miles to the north). Around the year 1500, the rafters established the first professional guild in Füssen. As Füssen was on the Via Claudia, cargo from Italy passed here en route to big German cities farther north. Rafters would assemble rafts and pile them high with goods—or with people needing a lift. If the water was high, they could float all the way to Augsburg in as little as one day. There they'd disassemble their raft and sell off the lumber along with the goods they'd carried, then make their way home to raft again. Today you'll see no modern-day rafters here, as there's a hydroelectric plant just downstream.

• *Walk upstream a bit, appreciating the river's milky color, and head inland (turn right) immediately after crossing under the bridge.*

⊕ Church of the Holy Spirit, Bread Market, and Lute-Makers: Climbing uphill, you pass the colorful Church of the

Holy Spirit (Heilig-Geist-Spitalkirche) on the right. As this was the church of the rafters, their patron, St. Christopher (with the Baby Jesus on his shoulder), is prominent on the facade. Today it's the church of Füssen's old folks' home (it's adjacent—notice the easy-access skyway).

Farther up the hill on the right (almost opposite an archway into a big courtyard) is Bread Market Square (Brotmarkt), with a fountain honoring the famous 16th-century lute-making family, the Tieffenbruckers. In its day, Füssen was a huge center of violin- and lute-making, with about 200 workshops. Today only three survive.

• *Backtrack and go through the archway into the courtyard of the former...*

⊕ Benedictine Monastery (Kloster St. Mang): From 1717 until secularization in 1802, this was the powerful center of town. Today the courtyard is popular for concerts, and the building houses the City Hall and Füssen Heritage Museum (and a public WC).

⊕ Füssen Heritage Museum: This is Füssen's one must-see sight (€6, €7 combo-ticket includes painting gallery and castle

tower; April-Oct Tue-Sun 11:00-17:00, closed Mon; Nov-March Fri-Sun 13:00-16:00, closed Mon-Thu; tel. 08362/903-146, www.museum.fuessen.de). Pick up the loaner English translations and follow the one-way route. In the St. Anna Chapel, you'll see the famous *Dance of Death*. This was painted shortly after a plague devastated the community in 1590. It shows 20 social classes, each dancing with the Grim Reaper—starting with the pope and the emperor. The words above say, essentially, "You can say yes or you can say no, but you must ultimately dance with death." Leaving the chapel, you walk over the metal lid of the crypt. Upstairs, exhibits illustrate the rafting trade and violin- and lute-making (with a complete workshop). The museum also includes an exquisite *Kaisersaal* (main festival hall), an old library, an exhibition on textile production, and a King Ludwig-style "castle dream room."

• *Leaving the courtyard, hook left around the old monastery and go uphill. The square tower marks...*

⊕ St. Magnus Basilica (Basilika St. Mang): St. Mang (or

Magnus) is Füssen's favorite saint. In the eighth century, he worked miracles all over the area with his holy rod. For centuries, pilgrims came from far and wide to enjoy art depicting the great works of St. Magnus. Above the altar dangles a glass cross containing his relics (including that holy stick). Just inside the door is a chapel remembering a much more modern saint—Franz Seelos (1819-1867), the local boy who went to America (Pittsburgh and New Orleans) and lived such a righteous life that in 2000 he was beatified by Pope John Paul II. If you're in need of a miracle, fill out a request card next to the candles.

• *From the church, a lane leads high above, into the courtyard of the...*

❶ **High Castle (Hohes Schloss):** This castle, long the summer residence of the Bishop of Augsburg, houses a painting gallery (the upper floor is labeled in English) and a tower with a view over the town and lake (included in the €7 Füssen Heritage Museum combo-ticket, otherwise €6, same hours as museum). Its courtyard is interesting for the striking perspective tricks painted onto its flat walls.

From below the castle, the city's main drag (once the Roman Via Claudia, and now Reichenstrasse) leads from a grand statue of St. Magnus past lots of shops, cafés, and strolling people to Kaiser-Maximilian-Platz and the TI...where you began.

Sleeping in Füssen

(country code: 49, area code: 08362)

Convenient Füssen·is just three miles from Ludwig's castles and offers a cobbled, riverside retreat. All recommended accommodations are within a few handy blocks of the train station and the town center. Parking is easy at the station, and some hotels also have their own lot or garage. Prices listed are for one-night stays; most hotels give about 5-10 percent off for two-night stays—always request this discount. Competition is fierce, and off-season prices are soft. High season is mid-June-September. Rooms are generally 10-15 percent less in shoulder season and much cheaper off-season. Be sure to ask your hotelier for a Füssen Card.

Big, Fancy Hotels in the Center of Town

$$$ Hotel Schlosskrone, with 64 rooms and all the amenities, is just a block from the station. It also runs two restaurants and a fine pastry shop—you'll notice at breakfast (Sb-€99-109, standard Db-€129-149, bigger Db-€149-169, Db with balcony-€155-175,

---

Sleep Code

(€1 = about $1.30)
S = Single, **D** = Double/Twin, **T** = Triple, **Q** = Quad, **b** = bathroom, **s** = shower only. Unless otherwise noted, credit cards are accepted, English is spoken, and breakfast is included.

To help you sort easily through these listings, I've divided the accommodations into three categories, based on the price for a standard double room with bath:

$$$ **Higher Priced**—Most rooms €100 or more.
$$ **Moderately Priced**—Most rooms between €60-100.
$ **Lower Priced**—Most rooms €60 or less.

Prices can change without notice; verify the hotel's current rates online or by email. For the best prices, always book direct.

Tb-€159-179, Qb-€169-189, lower prices are for Oct-April, various pricey suites also available, air-con in a few suites only, elevator, free Wi-Fi, free sauna and fitness center, parking-€9/day, Prinzregentenplatz 2-4, tel. 08362/930-180, www.schlosskrone.com, rezeption@schlosskrone.com, Norbert Schöll and family).

$$$ Hotel Hirsch is a romantic, well-maintained, family-run, 53-room, old-style hotel that takes pride in tradition. Their standard rooms are fine, and their rooms with historical and landscape themes are a fun splurge (Sb-€80-90, standard Db-€125-145, theme Db-€165-185, price depends on demand, cheaper Nov-March and during slow times, family rooms, elevator, pay guest computer, free Wi-Fi, free parking, Kaiser-Maximilian-Platz 7, tel. 08362/93980, www.hotelfuessen.de, info@hotelhirsch.de).

$$$ Hotel Sonne, in the heart of town, has a modern lobby and takes pride in decorating (some would say overdecorating) its 50 stylish rooms (Sb-€89-109, Db-€111-135, bigger Db-€155-185, Tb-€149, bigger Tb-€169-199, Qb-€189-219, lower prices are for Nov-March, 5 percent discount if you book on their website, elevator, guest computer, free Wi-Fi, free laundry machine-€3 for soap, free sauna and fitness center, parking-€6-8/day, kitty-corner from TI at Prinzregentenplatz 1, on GPS you may need to enter Reichenstrasse 37, tel. 08362/9080, www.hotel-sonne.de, info@hotel-sonne.de).

Smaller, Mid-Priced Hotels and Pensions

$$ Altstadthotel zum Hechten offers 34 modern and nicely renovated rooms in a friendly, traditional building right under Füssen Castle in the old-town pedestrian zone. It's a good value, with lots of extras (laundry-€10-20/load, travel resource/game room with maps and books, borrowable hiking gear, fun miniature bowling alley in basement, recommended restaurant, electric-bike rental-€20/day), a family-run feel, and borderline-kitschy decor (Sb-€62-72, Db-€92-124, extra bed-€35-47, price depends on season and length of stay, ask when you reserve for 5 percent off these prices with this book, also mention if you're very tall as most beds can be short, non-smoking, lots of stairs, free guest computer in lounge, free Wi-Fi, parking-€4/day on-site—or free a 5-minute walk away, in the heart of the old town at Ritterstrasse 6, tel. 08362/91600, www.hotel-hechten.com, info@hotel-hechten.com, Pfeiffer and Tramp families).

$$ Gästehaus Schöberl, run by the head cook at Altstadthotel zum Hechten, rents six attentively furnished, modern rooms a five-minute walk from the train station. One room is in the owners' house, and the rest are in the building next door (Sb-€40-55, Db-€70-80, Tb-€85-95, Qb-€100-120, lower prices are for Jan-Feb and Nov or for longer stays, cash only, free Wi-Fi, free parking, Luitpoldstrasse 14-16, tel. 08362/922-411, www.schoeberl-fuessen.de, info@schoeberl-fuessen.de, Pia and Georg Schöberl).

$$ Mein Lieber Schwan, a block from the train station, is a former private house with four superbly outfitted apartments, each with a double bed, sofa bed, kitchen, and antique furnishings. The catch is the three-night minimum stay in high season (Sb-€68-79, Db-€78-89, Tb-€88-99, Qb-€98-109, price depends on season and apartment size, cash or PayPal only, no breakfast, free Wi-Fi, free parking, laundry facilities, garden, from station turn left at traffic circle to Augustenstrasse 3, tel. 08362/509-980, www.meinlieberschwan.de, fewo@meinlieberschwan.de, Herr Bletschacher).

Budget Beds

$ Old Kings Design Hostel shoehorns five boldly modern, themed rooms (three doubles and two eight-person dorms) into an old townhouse buried deep in the pedestrian zone. While the quarters are tight (all the rooms share two bathrooms), the Old World location and reasonable prices are enticing (dorm bed-€18, D-€55, breakfast-€5, free Wi-Fi, Franziskanergasse 2, tel. 08362/883-7385, www.oldkingshostel.com, info@oldkingshostel.com).

$ House LA, run by energetic mason Lahdo Algül and hardworking Agata, has two branches. The backpacker house has 11 basic, clean four-bed dorm rooms at rock-bottom prices about a 10-minute walk from the station (€18/bed, D-€45, breakfast-€3, pay guest computer, free Wi-Fi, free parking, Wachsbleiche 2). A second building has five family apartments with kitchen and bath, each sleeping four to six people (apartment-€60-90, depends on number of people and season—mention Rick Steves for best price, breakfast-€3, free Wi-Fi, free parking, 6-minute walk back along tracks from station to von Freybergstrasse 26; contact info for both: tel. 08362/607-366, mobile 0170-624-8610, www.housela. de, info@housela.de). Both branches rent bikes (€8/day) and have laundry facilities (€7/load).

$ Füssen Youth Hostel, with 138 beds in 32 institutional rooms, occupies a pleasant modern building in a grassy setting an easy walk from the center. There are ping-pong tables and a basketball net out front, but few other extras (bed in 2- to 6-bed dorm rooms-€22, bunk-bed Db-€50, €3 more for nonmembers, €2 extra for one-night stays, includes breakfast and sheets, laundry-€4/load, dinner-€5, office open daily 8:00-12:00 & 17:00-22:00, lockers, free Wi-Fi, free parking, from station backtrack 10 minutes along tracks, Mariahilfer Strasse 5, tel. 08362/7754, www.fuessen. jugendherberge.de, fuessen@jugendherberge.de).

Eating in Füssen

Restaurant Aquila serves modern international dishes in a simple, traditional *Gasthaus* setting with great seating outside on the delightful little Brotmarkt square (€10-17 main courses, serious €9-10 salads, Wed-Mon 11:30-21:30, closed Tue, Brotmarkt 9, tel. 08362/6253).

Restaurant Ritterstub'n offers delicious, reasonably priced German grub, fish, salads, veggie plates, gluten-free options, and a fun kids' menu. They have three eating zones: modern decor in front, traditional Bavarian in back, and a courtyard. Demure Gabi serves while her husband cooks standard Bavarian fare (€8-12 main courses, smaller portions available for less, €6.50 lunch specials, €19 three-course fixed-price dinners, Tue-Sun 11:30-14:30 & 17:30-23:00, closed Mon, Ritterstrasse 4, tel. 08362/7759).

Schenke & Wirtshaus (inside the recommended Altstadthotel zum Hechten) dishes up hearty, traditional Bavarian dishes in a cozy setting. They specialize in pike *(Hecht)* pulled from the Lech River, served with a tasty fresh-herb sauce (€8-14 main courses, salad bar, daily 11:00-22:00, Ritterstrasse 6, tel. 0836/91600).

The **Himmelsstube** ("Heaven's Lounge," inside Hotel Schlosskrone, right on Füssen's main traffic circle) boasts good weekly specials and live Bavarian zither music most Fridays during dinner. Choose between a traditional dining room and a pastel winter garden (both feel quite formal). If your pension doesn't offer breakfast, consider their €13 "American-style" breakfast or huge €16 Sunday spread (at lunch and dinner: €10-19 main dishes, open daily 7:30-10:30 & 11:30-14:30 & 18:00-22:00, Prinzregentenplatz 2-4, tel. 08362/930-180). The hotel's second restaurant, **Chili,** serves Mediterranean dishes.

Ristorante La Perla is the place to sate your Italian-food cravings, with friendly staff and fair prices. Sit either in the classic interior, or in one of two delightful outside areas: streetside seating, or the more peaceful back courtyard (€7-11 pizzas and pastas, €11-22 meat and fish dishes, daily 11:00-22:00, in winter closed 14:30-17:30 and all day Mon, Drehergasse 44, tel. 08362/7155).

The **Markthalle** is a fun food court offering a wide selection of reasonably priced, wurst-free food. Located in an old warehouse from 1483, it's now home to a fishmonger, deli counters, a fruit stand, a bakery, and a wine bar. Buy your food from one of the vendors, park yourself at any one of the tables, then look up and admire the Renaissance ceiling (Mon-Fri 7:30-20:00, Sat 7:30-15:00, closed Sun, corner of Schrannengasse and Brunnengasse).

Brewpub near the Castles: If you have a car, consider heading to **Schloss Brauhaus,** in the village of Schwangau.

Gelato: Hohes Schloss Italian Ice Cream is a good *gelateria* on the main drag and has an inviting people-watching perch for coffee or dessert (Reichenstrasse 14).

Asian Food: You'll find inexpensive Thai, Indian, and Chinese restaurants in the Luitpold-Passage at Reichenstrasse 33.

Picnic Supplies: Bakeries and *Metzger*s (butcher shops) abound and frequently have ready-made sandwiches. For groceries, try the underground **Netto** supermarket at Prinzregentenplatz, the roundabout on your way into town from the train station (Mon-Sat 7:00-20:00, closed Sun).

Füssen Connections

From Füssen to: Neuschwanstein (bus #73 or #78, departs from train station, most continue to Tegelberg lift station after castles, 1/hour, 10 minutes, €2.10 one-way, buses #9606 and #9651 also make the trip; taxis cost €10 one-way); **Oberammergau** (one direct bus #9606 daily, leaves around midday; otherwise bus #73 to Echelsbacher Brücke, change there to bus #9606—likely marked *Garmisch,* confirm with driver that bus will stop in Oberammergau; in summer 3/day, 1.5 hours total, bus continues to **Garmisch,** where you can connect to the **Zugspitze**)—from Oberammergau, you can connect to **Linderhof Castle** or **Ettal Monastery; Reutte** (bus #74; Mon-Fri almost hourly, last bus 19:00; Sat-Sun every 2 hours, last bus 18:00; 45 minutes, €4.20 one-way; taxis cost €35 one-way); **Wieskirche** (bus #73 or #9606, 4-5/day, 40-50 minutes each way, a few more options with a transfer in Steingaden; or take Romantic Road bus—see next); **Munich** (hourly trains, 2 hours, some change in Buchloe); **Innsbruck** (take bus #74 to Reutte, then train from Reutte to

Innsbruck via Garmisch, about every 2 hours, 3.5 hours); **Salzburg** (hourly via Munich, 4 hours, 1-2 changes); **Rothenburg ob der Tauber** (hourly, 5 hours, look for connections with only 2-3 changes—often in Augsburg, Treuchtlingen, and Steinach); **Frankfurt** (hourly, 5-6 hours, 1-2 changes). Train info: tel. 0180-599-6633, www.bahn.com.

Romantic Road Buses: The northbound Romantic Road bus departs Füssen at 8:00; the southbound bus arrives in Füssen at 20:20 (daily, mid-April-late Oct only, bus stop is at train station, www.romanticroadcoach.de). A railpass gets you a 20 percent discount on the Romantic Road bus (without using up a day of a flexipass). The northbound bus arrives in Munich at 10:30 and in Rothenburg at 15:45. The bus is much slower than the train, especially to Rothenburg; the only reason to take the bus is that it gives you the briefest glimpse of the Wieskirche and other sights along the way, and requires no changes. Note that the northbound bus stops at the **Wieskirche** for 20 minutes, while the southbound bus stops there for 15 minutes—but after the church has closed.

Best of Bavaria

Within a short drive of Füssen and Reutte, you'll find some of the most enjoyable—and most tourist-filled—sights in Germany. The otherworldly "King's Castles" of Neuschwanstein and Hohenschwangau capture romantics' imaginations, the ornately decorated Wieskirche puts the faithful in a heavenly mood, and the little town of Oberammergau overwhelms visitors with cuteness. Yet another impressive castle (Linderhof), another fancy church (Ettal), and a sky-high viewpoint (the Zugspitze) round out southern Bavaria's top attractions.

The King's Castles: Neuschwanstein and Hohenschwangau

The most popular tourist destinations in southern Bavaria are the two "King's Castles" (Königsschlösser) near Füssen. The older Hohenschwangau, King Ludwig's boyhood home, is less famous but more historic. The more dramatic Neuschwanstein, which inspired Walt Disney, is the one everyone visits. I'd recommend visiting both, and planning some time to hike above Neuschwanstein to Mary's Bridge—and, if you enjoy romantic hikes, down through the gorge below. Reservations are a magic wand to smooth out your visit. With fairy-tale turrets in a fairy-tale alpine setting built by a fairy-tale king, these castles are understandably a huge hit.

Getting There

If arriving by **car,** note that road signs in the region refer to the sight as *Königsschlösser,* not Neuschwanstein. There's plenty of parking (all lots–€5). The first lots require more walking. Drive right through Touristville and past the ticket center, and park in lot #4 by the lake *(Parkplatz am Alpsee)* for the same price.

From **Füssen,** those without cars can catch **bus** #73 or #78 (hourly, generally departs Füssen's train station at :05 past the hour, €2.10 each way, 10 minutes, extra buses often run when crowded; a few additional departures of #9606 and #9651 also make this trip), take a **taxi** (€10 one-way), ride a rental **bike** (two level miles), or—if you're in a pinch—**walk** (less than an hour). The bus drops you at the tourist office; it's a one-minute walk from there to the ticket office. When returning, note that buses #73 and #78 pointing left (with your back to the TI) are headed to Füssen, while the same numbers pointing right are going elsewhere.

From **Reutte,** take bus #74 to the Füssen train station, then hop on bus #73 or #78 to the castles. Or pay €35 for a taxi right to the castles.

Orientation to the King's Castles

Cost: Neuschwanstein and Hohenschwangau cost €12 apiece. A "Königsticket" combo-ticket for both castles costs €23, and a "Schwanenticket," which also covers the Museum of the Bavarian Kings costs €29.50. Children under 18 (accompanied by an adult) are admitted free. Neuschwanstein, but not Hohenschwangau, is covered by Bavaria's 14-day ticket (Mehrtagesticket). If you have the pass, note this in the "message" field when making an online reservation.

Hours: The ticket center, located at street level between the two castles, is open daily April-Sept 8:00-17:30, Oct-March 9:00-15:30. The first castle tour of the day departs an hour after the ticket office opens and the last departs 30 minutes after it closes: April-Sept at 9:00 and 18:00, Oct-March at 10:00 and 16:00.

Getting Tickets for the Castles: Every tour bus in Bavaria converges on Neuschwanstein, and tourists flush in each morning from Munich. A handy reservation system sorts out the chaos for smart travelers. (One out of every three castle tickets is reserved. Look left. Look right. If you want to be smarter than these two people, prebook.) Tickets, whether reserved in

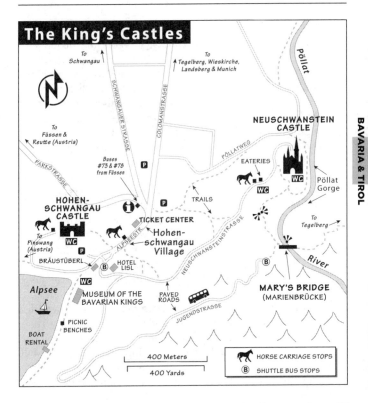

advance or bought on the spot, come with admission times. If you miss your appointed tour time, you can't get in. To tour both castles, you must do Hohenschwangau first (logical, since this gives a better introduction to King Ludwig's short life). You'll get two tour times: Hohenschwangau and then, two hours later, Neuschwanstein.

Arrival: Make the **ticket center** your first stop. If you have a reservation, stand in the short line for picking up tickets. If you don't have a reservation...welcome to the very long line. Arrive by 8:00 in summer, and you'll likely be touring at 9:00. During August, the busiest month, tickets for English tours can run out by around noon. Because day-trippers from Munich tend to take the 8:52 train—with a bus connection arriving at the castles at 11:13—if you need to buy a ticket on the spot, you'll be wise to try to make it here by 11:00; a few minutes later, and the line grows quickly.

Reservations: It's smart to reserve in peak season (June-early Oct—especially in July-Aug, when slots can book up several days in advance). Reservations cost €1.80 per person per castle, and must be made no later than 17:00 on the previous day. It works best to book online (www.ticket-center-hohen-schwangau.de); you can also reserve by phone (tel. 08362/930-830) or email (info@ticket-center-hohenschwangau.de). A few hotels can book these tickets for you with enough notice (ask). You must pick up reserved tickets an hour before the appointed entry time, as it takes a while to walk up to the castles. (It doesn't usually take an hour, though—so this might be a good time to pull out a sandwich or a snack.) Show up late and they may have given your slot to someone else (but then they'll likely help you make another reservation). If you know a couple of hours in advance that you're running late and can call the office, they'll likely rebook you at no charge.

Tips for Day-Tripping from Munich: Rather than buy point-to-point train tickets, it's a no-brainer to buy the Bayern-Ticket; not only is it cheaper, but it also covers the bus between Füssen and the castles (the only catch is that on weekdays, the pass isn't valid before 9:00). If coming by train, make a castle tour reservation and take a train leaving at least four hours before your reserved castle entry. (The train to Füssen takes over two hours, getting from Füssen to the castle ticket office by bus takes another half-hour, and you must be there an hour before your tour.) Trains from Munich leave hourly at :52 past the hour. So, if you take the 9:52 train, you can make a 14:00 castle tour. If you reserve a castle tour for 11:00, you'll need to pack breakfast and take the 6:52 train (confirm train times in advance).

Getting Up to the Castles: From the ticket booth, Hohen-schwangau is an easy 10-minute climb (just zigzag up to the big yellow castle, following the signs), while Neuschwanstein is a moderately steep 30-minute hike in the other direction (also well-signed—the most direct and least steep approach begins across the street from the ticket center).

To minimize hiking to Neuschwanstein, you can take a **shuttle bus** (leaves every few minutes from in front of Hotel Lisl, just above ticket office and to the left) or a horse-drawn carriage (in front of Hotel Müller, just above ticket office and to the right), but neither gets you to the castle doorstep. The shuttle bus drops you off near Mary's Bridge (Marienbrücke), leaving you a steep, 10-minute downhill walk to the castle—so be sure to see the view from Mary's Bridge *before* hiking down (€1.80 one-way, the €2.60 round-trip is not worth it since you have to hike uphill to the bus stop for your return trip). **Horse-drawn carriages** (€6 up, €3 down) are slower than walking and stop below Neuschwanstein, leaving you a five-minute uphill hike. Here's the most economical and least strenuous plan: Ride the bus to Mary's Bridge for the view, hike down to Neuschwanstein, and then catch the horse carriage from the castle back down to the parking lot (total round-trip cost: €4.80). Carriages also run to Hohenschwangau (€4 up, €2 down).

Warning: Both the shuttle bus and the carriage can have long lines at peak times—especially if it's raining. You might wait up to 45 minutes for the bus, making it slower than walking. If you're cutting it close to your appointed time, you may need to hoof it.

Entry Procedure: For each castle, tourists jumble at the entry, waiting for their ticket number to light up on the board. When it does, power through the mob (most waiting there are holding higher numbers) and go to the turnstile. Warning: You must use your ticket while your number is still on the board. If you space out while waiting for a polite welcome, you'll miss your entry window and never get in.

Services: A TI (run by helpful Thomas), bus stop, ATM, WC (€0.50), lockers (€1), coin-op Internet terminal, and telephones cluster around the main intersection a couple hundred yards before you get to the ticket office (TI open daily April-mid-Oct 10:00-17:30, mid-Oct-March generally 10:00-16:00, tel. 08362/81980, www.schwangau.de). While the bathrooms inside the castles themselves are free, you'll pay €0.30-0.50 to use the freestanding ones elsewhere in the area.

Bike Rental: The easiest place to rent a bike is at Füssen's train station. Near the castles, rentals are available in Schwangau (the next village over) at **Todos** (€8/day, €18/day-electric bike, daily 9:30-18:30, on the main street at Füssener Strasse 13, tel. 08362/987-888).

Best Views: In the morning, the light comes in just above the mountains—making your initial view of Neuschwanstein hazy and disappointing (though views from the ticket center up to Hohenschwangau are nice). Later in the day, the sun drops down into the pasture, lighting up Neuschwanstein magnificently. Regardless of time of day, the best accessible Neuschwanstein view is from Mary's Bridge (or, for the bold, from the little bluff just above it)—an easy 10-minute hike from the castle. (Many of the postcards and posters you'll see are photographed from high in the hills, best left to avid hikers.)

Eating: Bring a packed lunch. The park by the Alpsee (the nearby lake) is ideal for a picnic, although you're not allowed to sit on the grass—only on the benches (you could also eat out on the lake in one of the old-fashioned rowboats, rented by the hour in summer). The restaurants in the "village" at the foot of Europe's Disney castle are mediocre and overpriced, feeding off the endless droves of hungry, shop-happy tourists. There are no grocery shops near the castles, but you can buy sandwiches and hot dogs across from the TI, and at the *Imbiss* (take-out window) next to Hotel Alpenstuben (between the TI and ticket center). For a sit-down meal, the **Bräustüberl cafeteria** serves the cheapest grub, but isn't likely to be a highlight of your visit (€6-7 gut-bomb grill meals, often with live folk music, daily 10:00-17:00, close to end of road and lake). Up near Neuschwanstein itself (near the horse carriage drop-off) is another cluster of overpriced eateries.

After Your Castle Visit: If you follow my advice, you could be done with your castle tours in the early afternoon. With a car, you could try to squeeze in a nearby sight (such as Linderhof Castle, Ehrenberg Castle ruins, or Wieskirche). If you'd rather stick closer to this area, here are some ideas: The hike from Neuschwanstein up to **Mary's Bridge** is easy and rewarding; the hike back down to the valley through the **Pollät Gorge** is also highly recommended. With a **bike**, you could pedal through the mostly flat countryside that spreads out in front of Neuschwanstein (perhaps partway around Forggensee). And nearby—an easy drive or bus ride away—the Tegelberg area has both a high-mountain **cable car** and a fun **luge** ride. All of these options are described later in this chapter. Yet another option is to walk all the way around Alpsee, the lake below Hohenschwangau (about 1.5 hours, some steps).

Sights at the King's Castles

The two castles complement each other perfectly. But if you have to choose one, Neuschwanstein's wow factor—inside and out—is undeniable.

▲▲▲Hohenschwangau Castle

Standing quietly below Neuschwanstein, the big, yellow Hohenschwangau Castle was Ludwig's boyhood home. Originally built in the 12th century, it was ruined by Napoleon. Ludwig's father, King Maximilian II, rebuilt it in 1830. Hohenschwangau (hoh-en-SH-VAHN-gow, loosely translated as "High Swanland") was used by the royal family as a summer hunting lodge until 1912. The Wittelsbach family (which ruled Bavaria for nearly seven centuries) still owns the place (and lived in the annex—today's shop—until the 1970s).

"Mad" King Ludwig (1845-1886)

A tragic figure, Ludwig II (a.k.a. "Mad" King Ludwig) ruled Bavaria for 22 years until his death in 1886 at the age of 40. Bavaria was weak. Politically, Ludwig's reality was to "rule" either as a pawn of Prussia or a pawn of Austria. Rather than deal with politics in Bavaria's capital, Munich, Ludwig frittered away most of his time at his family's hunting palace, Hohenschwangau. He spent much of his adult life constructing his fanciful Neuschwanstein Castle—like a kid builds a tree house—on a neighboring hill upon the scant ruins of a medieval castle. Here and in his other projects (such as Linderhof Castle and the never-built Falkenstein Castle), even as he strove to evoke medieval grandeur, he embraced the state-of-the-art technology of the Industrial Age in which he lived. Neuschwanstein had electricity, running water, and a telephone (but no Wi-Fi).

Ludwig was a true romantic living in a Romantic age. His best friends were artists, poets, and composers such as Richard Wagner. His palaces are wallpapered with misty medieval themes—especially those from Wagnerian operas.

Although Ludwig spent 17 years building Neuschwanstein, he lived in it only 172 days. Soon after he moved in (and before his vision for the castle was completed), Ludwig was declared mentally unfit to rule Bavaria and taken away. Two days after this eviction, Ludwig was found dead in a lake. To this day, people debate whether the king was murdered or committed suicide.

The interior decor (mostly Neo-Gothic, like the castle itself) is harmonious, cohesive, and original—all done in 1835, with paintings inspired by Romantic themes. As you tour the castle, imagine how the paintings must have inspired young Ludwig. For 17 years, he lived here at his dad's place and followed the construction of his dream castle across the way—you'll see the telescope still set up and directed at Neuschwanstein.

The excellent 30-minute tours give a better glimpse of Ludwig's life than the more-visited and famous Neuschwanstein Castle tour. Tours here are smaller (35 people rather than 60) and more relaxed. You'll explore rooms on two floors—the queen's rooms, and then, upstairs, the king's. (Conveniently, their bedrooms were connected by a secret passage.) You'll see photos and busts of Ludwig and his little brother, Otto; some Turkish-style flourishes (to please the king, who had been impressed after a visit to the Orient); more than 25 different depictions of swans (honoring the Knights of Schwangau, whose legacy the Wittelsbachs inherited); over-the-top gifts the Wittelsbachs received from their adoring subjects; and paintings of VIGs (very important Germans, including Martin

Luther—who may or may not have visited here—and an infant Charlemagne).

One of the most impressive rooms is the Banquet Hall (also known as the Hall of Heroes); one vivid wall mural depicts a savage, yet bloodless, fifth-century barbarian battle. Just as the castle itself had running water and electricity despite its historic appearance, its Romantic decor presents a sanitized version of the medieval past, glossing over inconvenient details. You'll also see Ludwig's bedroom, which he inherited from his father. He kept most of the decor (including the nude nymphs frolicking over his bed), but painted the ceiling black and installed transparent stars that could be lit from the floor above to create the illusion of a night sky.

▲▲▲Neuschwanstein Castle

Imagine "Mad" King Ludwig as a boy, climbing the hills above his dad's castle, Hohenschwangau, dreaming up the ultimate

fairy-tale castle. Inheriting the throne at the young age of 18, he had the power to make his dream concrete and stucco. Neuschwanstein (noy-SHVAHN-shtine, roughly "New Swanstone") was designed first by a theater-set designer...then by an architect. While it was built upon the ruins of an old castle and looks medieval, Neuschwanstein is modern iron-and-brick construction with a sandstone veneer—only about as old as the Eiffel Tower. It feels like something you'd see at a home show for 19th-century royalty. Built from 1869 to 1886, it's the epitome of the Romanticism popular in 19th-century Europe. Construction stopped with Ludwig's death (only a third of the interior was finished), and within six weeks, tourists were paying to go through it.

During World War II, the castle took on a sinister role. The Nazis used Neuschwanstein as one of their primary secret storehouses for stolen art. After the war, Allied authorities spent a year sorting through and redistributing the art, which filled 49 rail cars from this one location alone. It was the only time the unfinished rooms were put to use.

Today, guides herd groups of 60 through the castle, giving an interesting—if rushed—30-minute tour. (While you're waiting for your tour time to pop up on the board, climb the stairs up to the upper courtyard to see more of the exterior, which isn't covered on your tour.) Once inside, you'll go up and down more than 300 steps, visiting 15 lavish rooms with their original furnishings and fanciful wall paintings—mostly based on Wagnerian opera themes.

Ludwig's extravagant throne room, modeled in a Neo-Byzantine style to emphasize his royal status, celebrates six valiant Christian kings (whose mantle Ludwig clearly believed he had donned) under a huge gilded-bronze chandelier. The exquisite two-million-stone mosaic floor is a visual encyclopedia of animals and plant life. The most memorable stop may be the king's gilded-lily bedroom, with his elaborately carved canopy bed (with a forest of Gothic church spires on top), washstand (filled with water piped in from the Alps), and personal chapel. After passing through Ludwig's living room (decorated with more than 150 swans) and a faux grotto, you'll climb to the fourth floor for the grand finale: the Singers' Hall, an ornately decorated space filled with murals depicting the story of Parzival, the legendary medieval figure Ludwig identified with.

After the tour, before you descend to the king's kitchen, see the 13-minute video (runs continuously, English subtitles). This uses historical drawings and modern digital modeling to tell the story of how the castle was built, and illustrates all of the unfinished parts of Ludwig's vision (more prickly towers, a central chapel, a fancy view terrace, an ornate bathhouse, and more). Finally you'll see a digital model of Falkenstein—a whimsical, over-the-top, never-built castle that makes Neuschwanstein look stubby. Falkenstein occupied Ludwig's fantasies the year he died.

After the kitchen (state of the art for this high-tech king in its day), you'll see a room lined with fascinating drawings (described in English) of the castle plans, as well as a large castle model.

Near the Castles

These activities are within a short walk of the castles—an easy way to round out your day if you have extra time and lack a car.

Near Neuschwanstein

▲▲Mary's Bridge (Marienbrücke)

Before or after the Neuschwanstein tour, climb up to Mary's Bridge to marvel at Ludwig's castle, just as Ludwig did. Jockey with a United Nations of tourists for the best angle. This bridge was quite an engineering accomplishment 100 years ago. (Access to the bridge is closed in bad winter weather, but many travelers walk around the barriers to get there—at their own risk, of course.)

For an even more glorious castle view, the frisky can hike even higher: After crossing the bridge, you'll see very rough, steep, unofficial trails crisscrossing the hillside on your left. If you're willing to

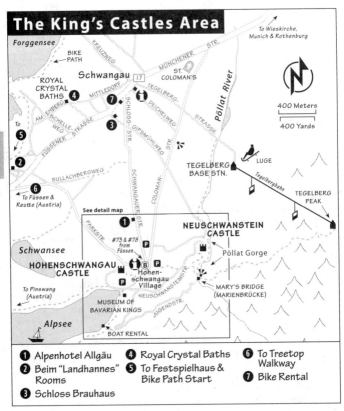

The King's Castles Area

BAVARIA & TIROL

- ❶ Alpenhotel Allgäu
- ❷ Beim "Landhannes" Rooms
- ❸ Schloss Brauhaus
- ❹ Royal Crystal Baths
- ❺ To Festspielhaus & Bike Path Start
- ❻ To Treetop Walkway
- ❼ Bike Rental

ignore the *Lebensgefahr* (danger of death) signs, you can scamper up to the bluff just over the bridge.

The trail connecting Neuschwanstein to Mary's Bridge is also scenic, with views back on Neuschwanstein's facade in one direction, and classic views of Hohenschwangau—perched on its little hill between lakes, with cut-glass peaks on the horizon—in the other.

▲Pöllat Gorge (Pöllatschlucht)

The river gorge that slices into the rock just behind Neuschwanstein's lofty perch is a more interesting and scenic—and less crowded—alternative to shuffling back down the main road. While it takes an extra 15 minutes or so, it's well worth it. You'll find the trailhead just above the Neuschwanstein exit, on the path toward Mary's Bridge (look for *Pöllatschlucht* signs; gorge trail closed in winter).

You'll begin by walking down a steep, well-maintained set of concrete stairs, with Germany's finest castle looming through the trees. Then you'll pop out along the river, passing a little beach (with neatly stacked stones) offering a view up at the grand waterfall that gushes beneath Mary's Bridge. From here, follow the river as it goes over several smaller waterfalls—and for a while stroll along steel walkways and railings that help make this slippery area safer. After passing an old wooden channel used to harness the power of all that water, you'll hit level ground; turn left and walk through a pleasantly untouristy residential settlement back toward the TI.

Near Hohenschwangau

Museum of the Bavarian Kings (Museum der Bayerischen Könige)

About a five-minute walk from the castles' ticket center, in a former grand hotel on the shore of the Alpsee, this modern, well-presented exhibit documents the history of the Wittelsbachs, Bavaria's royal family. On display are plenty of family portraits and busts, as well as treasures including Ludwig II's outlandish royal robe and elaborately decorated fairy-tale sword, and the impressive dining set given as a golden-anniversary present to his cousin Ludwig III and his wife, the last reigning Wittelsbachs. A free, dry audioguide lends some context to the family's history, in more detail than most casual visitors want. The museum is worth the price only if you're captivated by this clan and have some time to kill. (But trying to squeeze it between your two castle visits is a bit too brief—especially if you like to linger.)

Cost and Hours: €29.50 "Schwanenticket" combo-ticket covers this museum as well as both castles, otherwise €9.50; no reservations required, includes audioguide, guided tour can be reserved ahead for €1.50 extra, daily April-Sept 9:00-19:00, Oct-March 10:00-18:00, mandatory lockers with refundable €1 deposit, Alpseestrasse 27, tel. 08362/926-4640, www.museumderbayerischen-koenige.de).

Also Nearby

If you have a car or bike (or are willing to hop a bus), here are a few more attractions that lie within a few miles of Neuschwanstein.

▲Tegelberg Gondola

Just north of Neuschwanstein is a fun play zone around the mighty Tegelberg Gondola, a scenic ride to the mountain's 5,500-foot summit. On a clear day, you get great views of the Alps and Bavaria and the vicarious thrill of watching hang gliders and paragliders leap into airborne ecstasy. Weather permitting, scores of adventurous Germans line up and leap from the launch ramp at the top of the lift. With someone leaving every two or three minutes, it's great for spectators. Thrill-seekers with exceptional social skills may talk themselves into a tandem ride with a paraglider. From the top of Tegelberg, it's a steep and demanding 2.5-hour hike down to Ludwig's castle. (Avoid the treacherous trail directly below the gondola.) At the base of the gondola, you'll find a playground, a cheery eatery, the stubby remains of an ancient Roman villa, and a summer luge ride (described next).

Cost and Hours: €18.40 round-trip, €11.80 one-way, daily 9:00-17:00, closed Nov, 4/hour, last ride at 16:45, 5-minute ride to the top, in bad weather call first to confirm, tel. 08362/98360, www.tegelbergbahn.de. Most buses #73 and #78 from Füssen continue from the castles to Tegelberg.

▲Tegelberg Luge

Next to the Tegelberg Gondola is a summer luge course. A summer luge is like a bobsled on wheels. This course's stainless-steel track is heated, so it's often dry and open even when drizzly weather shuts down the concrete luges. A funky cable system pulls riders (in their sleds) to the top without a ski lift. It's not as long, fast, or scenic as Austria's Biberwier luge, but it's handy, harder to get hurt on, and half the price.

Cost and Hours: €3.40/ride, 6-ride shareable card-€13.60, July-Sept daily 10:00-18:00, otherwise same hours as gondola, in winter sometimes opens late if track is wet, in bad weather call first to confirm, waits can be long in good weather, no children under 3, ages 3-8 may ride with an adult, tel. 08362/98360, www.tegelberg-bahn.de.

▲Royal Crystal Baths (Königliche Kristall-Therme)

This pool/sauna complex just outside Füssen is the perfect way to relax on a rainy day, or to cool off on a hot one. The main part of the complex (downstairs), called the *Therme*, contains two heated indoor pools and a café; outside you'll find a shallow kiddie pool, a lap pool, a heated *Kristallbad* with massage jets and a whirlpool, and a salty mineral bath. The extensive saunas upstairs are well worth the few extra euros, as long as you're OK with nudity. (Swimsuits are required in the downstairs pools, but *verboten* in the upstairs saunas.) You'll see pool and sauna rules in German all over, but don't worry—just follow the locals' lead.

To enter the baths, first choose the length of your visit and your focus (big outdoor pool only, all ground-floor pools but not the saunas, or the whole enchilada—a flier explains all the prices in English). You'll get a wristband and a credit-card-sized ticket with a bar code. Insert that ticket into the entry gate, and keep it—you'll need it to get out. Enter through the yellow changing stalls—where you'll change into your bathing suit—then choose a storage locker (€1 coin deposit). When it's time to leave, reinsert your ticket in the gate—if you've gone over the time limit, feed extra euros into the machine.

Cost and Hours: Baths only-€10.40/2 hours, €15.90/4 hours, €19.80/all day; saunas-about €5-6 extra, towel rental-€3, bathrobe rental-€5, bathing suits sold but not rented, Sun-Thu 9:00-22:00, Fri-Sat until 23:00, nude swimming everywhere Tue and Fri after 19:00; from Füssen, drive, bike, or walk across the river, turn left toward Schwangau, and then, about a mile later, turn left at signs for *Kristall-Therme,* Am Ehberg 16; tel. 08362/819-630, www. kristalltherme-schwangau.de.

Bike Ride Around the Forggensee

On a beautiful day, nothing beats a bike ride around the bright-turquoise Forggensee, a nearby lake. This 20-mile ride is exclusively on bike paths (give it a half-day; it's tight to squeeze it in the afternoon after a morning of castle visits, but possible with an early start). Locals swear that going clockwise is less work, but either way has a couple of strenuous uphill parts. Still, the amazing views of the surrounding Alps will distract you from your churning legs—so this is still a great way to spend the afternoon. Rent a bike, pack a picnic lunch, and figure about a three-hour round-trip. From Füssen, follow *Festspielhaus* signs; once you reach the theater, follow *Forggensee Rundweg* signs.

From the theater, you can also take a **boat ride** on the Forggensee (€8/50-minute cruise, 6/day; €11/2-hour cruise, 3/day; runs daily June-mid-Oct, possible but unlikely off-season, tel. 08362/921-363, www.stadt-fuessen.de—click on "Forggensee - Schiffahrt"). Unless it's very crowded in the summer, you can bring your bike onto the boat and get off across the lake—shortening the total loop.

Treetop Walkway
(Baumkronenweg Ziegelwies)

This brand-new elevated wooden "treetop path" lets you stroll for a third of a mile high in the trees above the Lech River just outside Füssen. It's on the road to Reutte, just before the Austrian border.

Cost and Hours: €4, April-Oct daily 11:00-17:00, closed off-season, tel. 08362/938-7550, www.walderlebniszentrum.eu.

Sleeping near the King's Castles

(country code: 49, area code: 08362)

Inexpensive farmhouse B&Bs abound in the Bavarian countryside around Neuschwanstein, offering drivers a decent value. Look for *Zimmer Frei* signs ("room free"/vacancy). The going rate is about €50-65 for a double, including breakfast. Though a bit inconvenient for those without a car, my listings here are a quick taxi ride from the Füssen train station and also close to local bus stops.

$$ Alpenhotel Allgäu is a small, family-run hotel with 18 rooms in a bucolic setting. It's a 15-minute walk from the castle ticket office, not far beyond the humongous parking lot (small Sb without balcony-€48, Sb-€58, perfectly fine older Db-€85, newer Db-€93, Tb-€135, ask about discount with cash and this book—but only if you book direct, all rooms except one single have porches or balconies—some with castle views, family rooms, free Wi-Fi, elevator, free parking, just before tennis courts at Schwangauer Strasse 37 in the town of Schwangau—don't let your GPS take you to Schwangauer Strasse 37 in Füssen, tel. 08362/81152, www.alpenhotel-allgaeu.de, info@alpenhotel-allgaeu.de, Frau Reiss).

$ Beim "Landhannes," a 200-year-old working dairy farm run by Conny Schön, is a great value for drivers. They rent three creaky but sunny rooms, and keep flowers on the balconies, big bells and antlers in the halls, and cows in the yard (Sb-€30, Db-€60, €5 less per person for 3 or more nights, also rents apartments with kitchen with a 5-night minimum, cash only, free Wi-Fi, free parking, nearby bike rental, poorly signed in the village of Horn on the Füssen side of Schwangau, look for the farm down a tiny lane through the grass 100 yards in front of Hotel Kleiner König, Am Lechrain 22, tel. 08362/8349, www.landhannes.de, info@landhannes.de).

Eating near the King's Castles

For pointers on quick, functional eateries in the immediate castle area, see "Orientation to the King's Castles," earlier.

For something more memorable, consider **Schloss Brauhaus,** a big, new brewpub in the village of Schwangau, about 1.5 miles away from the castles. They brew five types of beer (dark, light, wheat, and two seasonal brews) and serve classic German fare (€10-19 hearty meals). Choose between the woody-industrial interior—with big copper vats, or the outdoor *Biergarten*, with distant views of Neuschwanstein (food served Mon-Thu 14:00-21:00, Fri-Sun 11:00-21:00, longer hours for beer; Gipsmühlweg 5 in Schwangau—watch for signs on the main street, Füssener Strasse, coming in from Füssen; tel. 08362/926-4680).

Wieskirche

Germany's greatest Rococo-style church, this "Church in the Meadow"—worth ▲▲—looks as brilliant as the day it floated

down from heaven. Overripe with decoration but bright and bursting with beauty, this church is a divine droplet, a curly curlicue, the final flowering of the Baroque movement.

Cost and Hours: Donation requested, daily April-Oct 8:00-20:00, Nov-March 8:00-18:00. The interior is closed to sightseers for about an hour during services: Sun at 8:30 and 11:00; Tue, Wed, and Sat at 10:00; and Fri at 19:00 (17:00 in winter). Tel. 08862/932-930, www.wieskirche.de.

Getting There: The Wieskirche is a 30-minute drive north of Neuschwanstein. The Romantic Road bus tour stops here for 20 minutes on the northbound route to Frankfurt. Southbound buses stop here for 15 minutes, but it's after the church has closed for the day. (If you're heading from Wieskirche directly to Munich, Füssen is out of your way; it's much faster to take bus #9651 to Weilheim—2/day Mon-Sat, 1/day Sun, 1 hour—and train to Munich from there.) By car, head north from Füssen, turn right at Steingaden, and follow the brown signs. Lots of trinket shops and snack stands (one sells freshly made doughnuts) clog the parking area in front of the church; take a commune-with-nature-and-smell-the-farm detour back through the meadow to the parking lot (€2/2 hours minimum).

❷ Self-Guided Tour: This pilgrimage church is built around the much-venerated statue of a scourged (or whipped) Christ, which supposedly wept in 1738. The carving—too graphic to be accepted by that generation's Church—was the focus of worship in a peasant's barn. Miraculously, it shed tears—empathizing with all those who suffer. Pilgrims came from all around. A tiny and humble chapel was built to house the statue in 1739. (You can see it where the lane to the church leaves the parking lot.) Bigger and bigger crowds came. Two of Bavaria's top Rococo architects, the Zimmermann brothers (Johann Baptist and Dominikus), were commissioned to build the Wieskirche that stands here today.

Follow the theological sweep from the altar to the ceiling: Jesus whipped, chained, and then killed (notice the pelican above the altar—recalling a pre-Christian story of a bird that opened its breast to feed its young with its own blood); the painting of Baby

Jesus posed as if on the cross; the golden sacrificial lamb; and finally, high on the ceiling, the resurrected Christ before the Last Judgment. This is the most positive depiction of the Last Judgment around. Jesus, rather than sitting on the throne to judge, rides high on a rainbow—a symbol of forgiveness—giving any sinner the feeling that there is still time to repent, with plenty of mercy on hand. In the back, above the pipe organ, notice the closed door to paradise, and at the opposite end (above the main altar), the empty throne—waiting for Judgment Day.

Above the doors flanking the altar are murky glass cases with 18th-century handkerchiefs. People wept, came here, were healed, and no longer needed their hankies. Walk through either of these doors and up an aisle flanking the high altar to see votives—requests and thanks to God (for happy, healthy babies, and so on). Notice how the kneelers are positioned so that worshippers can meditate on scenes of biblical miracles painted high on the ceiling and visible through the ornate tunnel frames. A priest here once told me that faith, architecture, light, and music all combine to create the harmony of the Wieskirche.

Two paintings flank the door at the rear of the church. The one on the right shows the ceremonial parade in 1749 when the white-clad monks of Steingaden carried the carved statue of Christ from the tiny church to its new big one. The second painting (on the left), from 1757, is a votive from one of the Zimmermann brothers, the artists and architects who built this church. He is giving thanks for the successful construction of the new church.

If you can't visit the Wieskirche, visit one of the other churches that came out of the same heavenly spray can: Oberammergau's church, Munich's Asamkirche, Würzburg's Hofkirche Chapel (at the Residenz), the splendid Ettal Monastery (free and near Oberammergau), and, on a lesser scale, Füssen's basilica.

Route Tips for Drivers: If you're driving from Wieskirche to Oberammergau, you'll cross the **Echelsbacher Bridge,** which arches 230 feet over the Pöllat Gorge. Thoughtful drivers let their passengers walk across to enjoy the views, then meet them at the other side. Any kayakers? Notice the painting of the traditional village woodcarver (who used to walk from town to town with his art on his back) on the first big house on the Oberammergau side. It holds the Almdorf Ammertal shop, with a huge selection of over-priced carvings and commission-hungry tour guides.

Oberammergau

The Shirley Temple of Bavarian villages, and exploited to the hilt by the tourist trade, Oberammergau wears too much makeup.

During its famous Passion Play (every 10 years, next in 2020), the crush is unbearable—and the prices at the hotels and restaurants can be as well. The village has about 1,200 beds for the 5,000 playgoers coming daily. But the rest of the time, Oberammergau—while hardly "undiscovered"—is a pleasant, and at times even sleepy,

Bavarian village. If you're passing through, Oberammergau is a ▲ sight—worth a wander among the half-timbered *Lüftlmalerei* houses frescoed with biblical scenes and famous fairy-tale characters. It's also a relatively convenient home base for visiting Linderhof Castle, Ettal Monastery, and the Zugspitze (via Garmisch). A smaller (and less conveniently located) alternative to Füssen and Reutte, it's worth considering for drivers who want to linger in the area. A day trip to Neuschwanstein from Oberammergau is manageable if you have a car, but train travelers do better to stay in Füssen.

Getting There

Trains run from Munich to Oberammergau (nearly hourly, 1.75 hours, change in Murnau). From Füssen to Oberammergau, **buses** run daily (in summer 1/day direct, otherwise 3/day with change at Echelsbacher Brücke, 1.5 hours). Leaving town (to Linderhof or Reutte), head out past the church and turn toward Ettal on Road 23. You're 20 miles from Reutte via the scenic Plansee. If heading to Munich, Road 23 takes you to the autobahn, which gets you there in less than an hour.

Orientation to Oberammergau

This village of about 5,000 feels even smaller, thanks to its remote location and lack of Reutte-like sprawl. The downtown core, huddled around the onion-domed church, is compact and invites strolling; all of my recommended sights, hotels, and restaurants are within about a 10-minute walk of each other. (While the name sounds like a mouthful, it just means, roughly, "Upper Water District.")

BAVARIA & TIROL

Oberammergau

1 Hotel Fux
2 Gasthof zur Rose & Gästehaus Magold
3 Pension Zwink
4 Youth Hostel
5 Ammergauer Maxbräu
6 s' Wirtshaus
7 Wanninger
8 El Puente
9 Eis Café Paradiso
10 To Sommerrodelbahn Steckenberg (Summer Luge)
11 Internet Café

Tourist Information: The helpful, well-organized TI provides a wide range of glossy brochures, including maps and English information on area hikes (Mon-Fri 9:00-18:00, Sat 9:00-13:00, closed Sun—except open 9:00-13:00 mid-July-mid-Sept, closed Sat-Sun in winter, Eugen-Papst-Strasse 9A, tel. 08822/922-740, www.ammergauer-alpen.de).

Internet Access: The only Internet café in this small town is at **Hotel Alte Post,** right in the heart of town. At the reception desk, pay for access, then either use Wi-Fi or the terminals in the little room at the right end of the building (€3/hour, €5/day, daily 7:00-21:00, Dorfstrasse 19).

Arrival in Oberammergau

The town's **train** station is a short walk from the center: Turn left, cross the bridge, and you're already downtown.

If you're **driving,** you'll find that there are two exits from the main road into Oberammergau—at the north and south ends. Either way, make your way to the free lot between the TI and the

Woodcarving in Oberammergau

The Ammergau region is relatively poor, with no appreciable industry and no agriculture, save for some dairy farming. What they *do* have is wood. Carving religious and secular themes became a lucrative way for the locals to make some money, especially when confined to the house during the long, cold winter. And with a major pilgrimage site—Ettal Monastery—just down the road, there was a built-in consumer base eager to buy hand-carved crucifixes and other souvenirs. Carvers from Oberammergau peddled their wares across Europe, carrying them on their backs (on distinctive wooden backpack-racks called *Kraxe*) as far away as Rome.

Today, the Oberammergau Carving School (founded in 1887) is a famous institution that takes only 20 students per year out of 450 applicants. Their graduates do important restoration work throughout Europe. For example, much of the work on Dresden's Frauenkirche was done by these artists.

river. While there's ample street parking in town, most is time-limited and/or requires payment—be sure to read signs carefully. Hotels and sights are well-signed in the town.

Sights in Oberammergau

Oberammergau Church

Visit the town church, which is typically Bavarian Baroque—but a poor cousin of the one at Wies. Being in a woodcarving center, it's only logical that all the statues are made of wood, and then stuccoed and gilded to look like marble or gold. Saints Peter and Paul flank the altar, where the central painting can be raised to reveal a small stage decorated to celebrate special times during the church calendar. In the central dome, a touching painting shows Peter and Paul bidding each other farewell (with the city of Rome as a backdrop) on the day of their execution—the same day, in the year A.D. 67. On the left, Peter is crucified upside-down. On the right, Paul is beheaded with a sword. (A fine little €3 booklet explains it all.)

Wander through the lovingly maintained **graveyard**, noticing the wide variety in headstones. A towering stone WWI memorial at the gate has an imposing look and sternly worded celebrations of the "heroes" of that war. But around the other side, below it on the outer fence, find the newer glass panel that modifies the sentiment: "We honor and remember the victims of the violence that our land gave the world."

Local Arts and Crafts

The town's best sights are its woodcarving shops *(Holzschnizerei)*. Browse through these small art galleries filled with very expensive whittled works. The beautifully frescoed **Pilatus House** at Ludwig-Thoma-Strasse 10 has an open workshop where you can watch woodcarvers and painters at work (free; mid-May–mid-Oct Tue-Sat 13:00-18:00, closed Sun-Mon; open two weeks after Christmas 11:00-17:00; closed rest of year, tel. 08822/949-511).

▲Oberammergau Museum

Oberammergau's only real sight comes in three parts, all well-presented. The **main branch** (at Dorfstrasse 8) showcases local woodcarving, with good English explanations. The ground floor has a small exhibit of nativity scenes (*Krippe*—made of wood, of course, but also paper); in the back, find the small theater, where you can watch an interesting film in English about the 2010 Passion Play. Upstairs is a small Passion Play exhibit, a replica of a woodcarver's workshop, and an extensive collection of the wood carvings that helped put Oberammergau on the map. The top floor has temporary exhibits.

Your ticket also lets you into the lobby of the **Passion Play Theater** *(Festspielhaus)*, which houses a modest exhibition on the history of the performances. A long wall of photographs of past performers shows the many generations of Oberammergauers who have participated in this sacred tradition. Climb the stairs and peek into the indoor/outdoor audience hall, with a real-life alpine backdrop.

Finally, the **Pilatus House** (mentioned earlier) has a small upstairs exhibit of "reverse glass" paintings *(églomisé)*. While this technique has been popular in many parts of Europe—mostly among poorer people (since glass is a much cheaper and more forgiving medium than canvas)—an Oberammergau collector fell in with the famous, Munich-based Expressionistic Blaue Reiter (Blue Rider) movement, which was inspired to bring glass art to the mainstream. The museum also organizes guided tours of the theater (see next).

Cost and Hours: €6 includes all three parts; museum and theater lobby open Easter-Oct and Dec-mid-Jan Tue-Sun 10:00-17:00; Pilatus House exhibit open same days 15:00-17:00; all three closed Mon, Nov, and mid-Jan-Easter; tel. 08822/94136, www.oberammergaumuseum.de.

Passion Play Theater

Back in 1633, in the midst of the bloody Thirty Years' War and with horrifying plagues devastating entire cities, the people of Oberammergau promised God that if they were spared from extinction, they'd "perform a play depicting the suffering, death, and resurrection of our Lord Jesus Christ" every decade thereafter. The town survived, and, heading into its 41st decade, the people of Oberammergau are still making good on the deal. For 100 days every 10 years (most recently in 2010), about half of the town's population (a cast of 2,000) are involved in the production of this extravagant five-hour Passion Play—telling the story of Jesus' entry into Jerusalem, Crucifixion, and Resurrection.

Until the next show in 2020, you'll have to settle for reading the book, seeing Nicodemus tool around town in his VW, or taking a quick look at the theater, a block from the center of town. The only way to see the theater hall itself is on a 45-minute guided tour organized by the Oberammergau Museum.

Cost and Hours: €6-theater tour only, €8-includes Oberammergau Museum and Pilatus House exhibit; you can see the exhibit in the lobby and peek into the audience hall with the €6 ticket; April-Oct Tue-Sun at 11:00 in English, at 10:00 and 14:00 in German; no tours off-season, tel. 08822/94136, www.oberammergaumuseum.de.

Activities Just Outside of Town

Mountain Lifts

Oberammergau has two mountain lifts of its own. At the east end of town is the **Laber Bergbahn**, a gondola that lifts you up to fine views over the town (www.laber-bergbahn.de). Across town to the west is the **Klobensattel** chairlift—popular for skiers in winter and hikers in summer (www.kolbensattel.de). From the top, you can hike along the ridge to a series of mountain huts: In about 1.5 hours, you'll reach Pürschling; two hours later is Brunnenkopf (from which you could hike down to Linderhof Castle). Get tips and maps from the TI before doing any of these hikes. Also in the works at Klobensattel is an "AlpinCoaster"—similar to a luge, but fixed to a track—which promises to be the longest in Bavaria.

Swimming Pool

Near the Laber Bergbahn lift, at the eastern edge of town, is WellenBerg, a sprawling complex of indoor and outdoor pools and saunas (€7/3 hours, €12/day, €4 extra for sauna, daily 10:00-21:00, Himmelreich 52, tel. 08822/92360, www.wellenberg-oberammergau.de).

Sommerrodelbahn Steckenberg

The next town over, Unterammergau, hosts a stainless-steel summer luge track that's faster than the Tegelberg luge, but not quite as wicked as the one in Biberwier. This one has double-decker seats (allowing a parent to accompany a child) and two sticks—one for each hand; be careful of your elbows. On your way down, enjoy the views of Unterammergau.

Cost and Hours: €3/ride, €12/6 rides, May-Oct daily 8:30-17:00, closed when wet, Liftweg 1 in Unterammergau, clearly marked and easy 2.5-mile bike ride to Unterammergau along Bahnhofstrasse/Rottenbucherstrasse, take the first left when entering Unterammergau, tel. 08822/4027, www.steckenberg.de.

Sleeping in Oberammergau

(country code: 49, area code: 08822)

Accommodations in Oberammergau tend to be affordable and friendly. All offer free parking.

$$ Hotel Fux—quiet, romantic, and well-run—rents eight large rooms and six apartments decorated in the Bavarian *Landhaus* style (Sb-€65, Db-€84; apartment prices without breakfast: Sb-€68, Db-€78, larger apartments-€89-120; cheaper Nov-April, guest computer, free Wi-Fi, Mannagasse 2a, tel. 08822/93093, www.hotel-in-oberammergau.de, info@firmafux.de).

$$ Gasthof zur Rose is a big, central, classic, family-run place with 19 mostly small but comfortable rooms, with tiny bathrooms. At the reception desk, look at the several decades-worth of photos showing the family performing in the Passion Play (Sb-€60, Db-€80, Tb-€90, Qb-€100, guest computer, free Wi-Fi, sauna, indoor playground, Dedlerstrasse 9, tel. 08822/4706, www.rose-oberammergau.de, info@rose-oberammergau.de, Frank family).

$$ Pension Zwink offers 10 small, quiet, woody rooms in a residential-feeling neighborhood just across the street from the town center (Sb-€36, Db-€64, free Wi-Fi, Daisenbergerstrasse 10, tel. 08822/923-753, www.pension-oberammergau.de, info@pension-oberammergau.de).

$ Gästehaus Magold, homey and family-friendly, has three bright and spacious rooms—twice as nice as the cheap hotel rooms in town, and for much less money (Db-€60, cash only, non-smoking, free Wi-Fi, also has two family apartments—but these generally have a one-week minimum in summer, immediately behind Gasthof zur Rose at Kleppergasse 1, tel. 08822/4340, www.gaestehaus-magold.de, info@gaestehaus-magold.de, Christine).

$ Oberammergau Youth Hostel, on the river, is a short walk from the center. A planned renovation may add amenities...and cost (€21/bed, includes breakfast and sheets, €3 extra for nonmembers, €2 extra for one-night stays, reception open 8:00-10:00 & 17:00-19:00, closed mid-Nov-Dec, Malensteinweg 10, tel. 08822/4114, www.oberammergau.jugendherberge.de, oberammergau@jugendherberge.de).

Eating in Oberammergau

With relatively few restaurants—and most of them quite similar—Oberammergau isn't a place for high cuisine (though Maxbräu comes close). If you want basic Germanic grub, just find a woody ambience or pleasant patio that appeals; most of the big hotels in town (including the recommended Gasthof zur Rose—restaurant closed Mon) have sprawling restaurants with serviceable meals. The options below are for those who want to try something a little different.

Ammergauer Maxbräu serves high-quality, thoughtfully presented Bavarian fare with a modern, international twist. The rustic-yet-mod interior—with big copper vats where they brew their own beer—is cozy on a rainy day. And in nice weather, locals fill its serene beer garden out front. The food is a bit pricey, but worth paying for if you want to go beyond the predictable *Wurst und Kraut* (€11-17 main dishes, daily 11:00-22:00, right behind the church, Ettaler Strasse 5, tel. 08822/948-740).

s' Wirtshaus has an all-over-the-place menu (Bavarian classics, Italian pasta, and a few Asian dishes) served in a modern space in the heart of town (€12-18 main dishes, Tue-Sun 11:00-21:00, Mon 17:00-21:00, Dorfstrasse 28, tel. 08822/948-770).

Wanninger is a café by day (coffee, cakes, €10 lunch special, €12-14 lunch dishes) and a steakhouse by night (€13-24 steaks, €11-14 main dishes). The atmosphere is nondescript modern (daily 12:00-22:00, dinner after 18:00, Dorfstrasse 22, tel. 08822/836).

El Puente may vex Mexican food purists, but it's the most hopping place in town, with €7.50 cocktails attracting young locals and tourists alike. Come not for the burritos and enchiladas, but for the bustling energy (€12-17 dishes, Mon-Sat 18:00-23:30, closed Sun, Daisenbergerstrasse 3, tel. 08822/945-777).

And for Dessert: **Eis Café Paradiso** serves up good Italian-style gelato along the main street; in nice weather, Germans sunbathe with their big sundaes on the generous patio out front (daily until 22:00, Dorfstrasse 4, tel. 08822/6279).

Oberammergau Connections

From Oberammergau to: Linderhof Castle (bus #9622, 8/day Mon-Fri, 4/day Sat-Sun, 30 minutes; many of these also stop at **Ettal Monastery**), **Füssen** (in summer 1 direct bus/day, departs Oberammergau at 10:25; otherwise 3/day with transfer to #73 at Echelsbacher Brücke and stop also at **Hohenschwangau** for Neuschwanstein, 1.5 hours total; both of these originate in Oberammergau as #9606, so confirm with driver whether you need to change to reach Füssen), **Garmisch** (nearly hourly buses,

#9606, better frequency in morning, 40 minutes; also possible—but much longer—by train with a transfer in Murnau, 1.5 hours; from Garmisch, you can ascend the **Zugspitze**), **Munich** (nearly hourly trains, 1.75 hours, change in Murnau). Train info: tel. 0180-599-6633, www.bahn.com.

Linderhof Castle

This homiest of "Mad" King Ludwig's castles is a small, comfortably exquisite mini-Versailles—good enough for a minor god, and worth ▲▲. Set in the woods 15 minutes from Oberammergau and surrounded by fountains and sculpted, Italian-style gardens, it's the only palace I've toured that actually had me feeling envious.

Cost and Hours: €8.50, covered by Bavaria's 14-day ticket (Mehrtagesticket), €5 for grotto only, daily April-mid-Oct 9:00-18:00, mid-Oct-March 10:00-16:00, last tour 30 minutes before closing, tel. 08822/92030, www.linderhof.de.

Getting There: Without a car, getting to (and back from) Linderhof is a royal headache, unless you're staying in Oberammergau. Buses from Oberammergau take 30 minutes (#9622, 6/day Mon-Fri, 4/day Sat-Sun). If you're driving, park near the ticket office (€2.50). Driving from Reutte, take the scenic Plansee route.

Crowd-Beating Tips: July and August crowds can mean an hour's wait between when you buy your ticket and when you start your tour. It's most crowded in the late morning. During this period, you're wise to arrive after 15:00. Any other time of year, you should get your palace tour time shortly after you arrive. If you do wind up with time to kill, consider it a blessing—the gardens are fun to explore, and some of the smaller buildings can be seen quickly while you're waiting for your appointment. While it's possible to reserve ahead by fax or email for 10 percent extra (see the website for details), it's generally not necessary.

Sightseeing Tips and Procedure: The complex sits isolated in natural splendor. Plan for lots of walking and a two-hour stop to fully enjoy this royal park. Bring raingear in iffy weather. Your ticket comes with an entry time to tour the palace, which is a 10-minute walk from the ticket office. At the palace entrance, wait in line at the turnstile listed on your ticket (A through D) to take the required 30-minute English tour. Afterwards, explore the rest of the park; be sure not to miss the grotto (10-minute uphill hike from palace, brief but interesting free tour in English, no appointments—the board out front lists the time of the next tour). Then see the other royal buildings dotting the king's playground if you like. You can eat lunch at a café across from the ticket office.

Visiting the Castle and Grounds: The main attraction here is the **palace** itself. While Neuschwanstein is Neo-Gothic—romanticizing the medieval glory days of Bavaria—Linderhof is Baroque and Rococo, the frilly, overly ornamented styles more associated with Louis XIV, the "Sun King" of France. And, while Neuschwanstein is full of swans, here you'll see fleur-de-lis (the symbol of French royalty) and multiple portraits of Louis XIV, Louis XV, Madame Pompadour, and other pre-Revolutionary French elites. Though they lived a century apart, Ludwig and Louis were spiritual contemporaries: Both clung to the notion of absolute monarchy, despite the realities of the changing world around them. Capping the palace roofline is one of Ludwig's favorite symbols: Atlas, with the weight of the world literally on his shoulders. Oh, those poor, overburdened, misunderstood absolute monarchs!

Ludwig was king for 22 of his 40 years. He lived much of his last 8 years here—the only one of his castles that was finished in his lifetime. Frustrated by the limits of being a "constitutional monarch," he retreated to Linderhof, inhabiting a private fantasy world where extravagant castles glorified his otherwise weakened kingship. You'll notice that the castle is small—designed for a single occupant. Ludwig, who never married or had children, lived here as a royal hermit.

The castle tour includes 10 rooms on the upper floor. (The downstairs, where the servants lived and worked, now houses the gift shop.) You'll see room after room exquisitely carved with Rococo curlicues, wrapped in gold leaf. Up above, the ceiling paintings have 3-D legs sticking out of the frame. Clearly inspired by Versailles, Linderhof even has its own (much smaller) hall of mirrors—decorated with over a hundred Nymphenburg porcelain vases and a priceless ivory chandelier. The bedroom features an oversized crystal chandelier, delicate Meissen porcelain flowers framing the mirrors, and a literally king-size bed—a two-story canopy affair draped in blue velvet. Perhaps the most poignant sight, a sad commentary on Ludwig's tragically solitary lifestyle, is his dinner table—preset with dishes and food—which could rise from the kitchen below into his dining room so he could eat alone. (Examine the incredibly delicate flowers in the Meissen porcelain centerpiece.)

The palace is flanked on both sides with grand, terraced **fountains** (peopled by gleaming golden gods) that erupt at the top and bottom of each hour. If you're waiting for your palace tour to begin, hike up to the top of either of these terraces for a fine photo-op. (The green gazebo, on the hillside between the grotto and the palace, provides Linderhof's best view.)

The other must-see sight at Linderhof is Ludwig's **grotto.** Exiting the gift shop behind the palace, turn right, then cut left through the garden to climb up the hill. You'll wait out front for the next tour (the time is posted on the board), then head inside. Inspired by Wagner's *Tannhäuser* opera, this artificial cave (300 feet long and 70 feet tall) is actually a performance space. Its rocky walls are made of cement poured over an iron frame. (While Ludwig exalted the distant past, he took full advantage of then-cutting-edge technology to bring his fantasies to life.) The grotto provided a private theater for the reclusive king to enjoy his beloved Wagnerian operas—he was usually the sole member of the audience. The grotto features a waterfall, fake stalactites, and a swan boat floating on an artificial lake (which could be heated for swimming). Brick ovens hidden in the walls could be used to heat the huge space. The first electricity in Bavaria was generated here, to change the colors of the stage lights and to power Ludwig's fountain and wave machine.

Several other, smaller buildings are scattered around the grounds; look for posted maps and directional signs to track them down. Most interesting are the **Moroccan House** and **Moorish Kiosk.** With over-the-top decor seemingly designed by a sultan's decorator on acid, these allowed Ludwig to "travel" to exotic lands without leaving the comfort of Bavaria. (The Moorish Kiosk is more interesting; look for its gilded dome in the woods beyond the grotto.) At the far edge of the property is **Hunding's Hut,** inspired by Wagner's *The Valkyrie*—a rustic-cottage stage-set with a giant fake "tree" growing inside of it. And closer to the entrance—along the path between the ticket booth and the palace—is the **King's Cottage,** used for special exhibitions (often with an extra charge).

Ettal Monastery and Pilgrimage Church

In 1328, the Holy Roman Emperor was returning from Rome with what was considered a miraculous statue of Mary and Jesus. He was

in political and financial trouble, so to please God, he founded a monastery with this statue as its centerpiece. The monastery was located here because it was suitably off the beaten path, but today Ettal is on one of the most-traveled tourist routes in Bavaria.

20 + C + M + B + 14

All over Germany (and much of Catholic Europe), you'll likely see written on doorways a mysterious message: "20 + C + M + B + 14." This is marked in chalk on Epiphany (Jan 6), the Christian holiday celebrating the arrival of the Magi to adore the newborn Baby Jesus. In addition to being the initials of the three wise men (Caspar, Melchior, and Balthazar), the letters also stand for the Latin phrase *Christus mansionem benedicat*— "May Christ bless the house." The little crosses separating the letters remind all who enter that the house has been blessed in this year (20+14). Epiphany is a bigger deal in Catholic Europe than in the US. The holiday includes gift-giving, feasting, and caroling door to door—often collecting for a charity organization. Those who donate get their doors chalked up in thanks, and these marks are left on the door through the year.

Stopping here (free and easy for drivers) offers a convenient peek at a splendid Baroque church. Restaurants across the road serve lunch. A visit is worth ▲.

Cost and Hours: Free, daily 8:00-19:45 in summer, until 18:00 off-season, tel. 08822/740, www.kloster-ettal.de. If you're moved to make a donation, you can use the self-serve credit-card machine (to the right as you enter)...or drop a coin in one of the old-fashioned collection boxes.

Getting There: Ettal Monastery dominates the village of Ettal—you can't miss it. Ettal is a few minutes' **drive** (or a delightful **bike** ride) from Oberammergau. Just park (€1/4 hours in larger lots; free in small, crowded lot near the *Klosterladen*, alongside the building) and wander in. Some Oberammergau-to-Linderhof **buses** stop here (see "Oberammergau Connections," earlier).

⊙ **Self-Guided Tour:** As you enter the more than 1,000-square-foot **courtyard,** imagine the 14th-century Benedictine abbey, an independent religious community. It produced everything it needed right here. In the late Middle Ages, abbeys like this had jurisdiction over the legal system, administration, and taxation of their district. Since then,

the monastery has had its ups and downs. Secularized during the French Revolution and Napoleonic age, the Benedictines' property was confiscated by the state and sold. Religious life returned a century later. Today the abbey survives, with 50 or 60 monks. It remains a self-contained community, with living quarters for the monks, workshops, and guests' quarters. Along with their religious responsibilities, the brothers make their famous liqueur, brew beer, run a hotel, and educate 380 students in their private high school. The monks' wares are for sale at two shops (look for the *Klosterladen* by the courtyard or the *Kloster-Markt* across the street).

After entering the outer door, notice the **tympanum** over the inner door dating from 1350. It shows the founding couple, Emperor Louis the Bavarian and his wife Margaret, directing our attention to the crucified Lord and inviting us to enter the church contemplatively.

Stepping inside, the light draws our eyes to the **dome** (it's a double-shell design, 230 feet high) rather than to the high altar. Illusions—with the dome opening right to the sky—merge heaven and earth. The dome fresco shows hundreds of Benedictines worshipping the Holy Trinity...the glory of the Benedictine Order. This is classic "south-German Baroque."

Statues of the **saints** on the altars are either engaged in a holy conversation with each other or singing the praises of God. Broken shell-style patterns seem to create constant movement, with cherubs adding to the energy. Side altars and confessionals seem to grow out of the architectural structure; its decorations and furnishings become part of an organic whole. Imagine how 18th-century farmers and woodcutters, who never traveled, would step in here on Sunday and be inspired to praise their God.

The origin of the monastery is shown over the **choir arch:** An angel wearing the robe of a Benedictine monk presents the emperor with a marble Madonna and commissions him to found this monastery. (In reality, the statue was made in Pisa, circa 1300, and given to the emperor in Italy.)

Dwarfed by all the magnificence and framed by a monumental tabernacle is that tiny, most precious statue of the abbey—the miraculous **statue of Mary and the Baby Jesus.**

Nearby: The fragrant **demonstration dairy** *(Schaukäserei)* about a five-minute walk behind the monastery is worth a quick look. The farmhouse displays all the steps in the production line, starting with the cows themselves (next to the house), to the factory staff hard at work, and through to the end products, which you can sample in the shop (try the beer cheese). Better yet, enjoy a snack on the deck while listening to the sweet music/incessant clanging of cowbells (free; daily 10:00-17:00—but to see the most cheese-making action, come in the morning, ideally between 10:00-11:00;

BAVARIA & TIROL

Mandlweg 1, tel. 08822/923-926, www.schaukaeserei-ettal.de). To walk there from the monastery's exit, take a left and go through the passageway; take another left when you get to the road, then yet another left at the first street (you'll see it up the road, directly behind the abbey).

Zugspitze

The tallest point in Germany, worth ▲▲ in clear weather, is also a border crossing. Lifts from both Austria and Germany meet at

the 9,700-foot summit of the Zugspitze (TSOOG-shpit-seh). You can straddle the border between two great nations while enjoying an incredible view. Restaurants, shops, and telescopes await you at the summit.

German Approach: There are several ways to ascend, but they all cost the same (€50 round-trip, €40 in winter, tel. 08821/7970, www.zugspitze.de). If relying on public transit, you'll first head to Garmisch. From there, you'll ride a train to Eibsee (30 minutes, hourly departures daily 8:15-14:15), at which point you can choose: Walk across the parking lot and zip up to the top in a cable car (10 minutes, daily 8:00-14:15, departs at least every 30 minutes; in busy times departs every 10 minutes, but since each car fits only 35—which the electronic board suspensefully counts down as each passenger goes through the turnstile—you may have to wait to board), or transfer to a cogwheel train (45 minutes to the top, departs about hourly—coordinated with Garmisch train; once up top, you'll transfer from the train to a short cable car for the quick, 3-minute ascent to the summit).

Drivers can go straight to Eibsee (about 10 minutes beyond Garmisch—head through town following signs for *Fernpass/Reutte*, and watch for the Zugspitze turnoff on the left); once there, you have the same cable car vs. cog railway choice. (Even though they're not taking the train from Garmisch, drivers pay the same—€50 round-trip, plus another €3 for parking.)

You can choose how you want to go up and down at the spur of the moment: both ways by cable car, both by cog train, or mix and match. Although the train ride takes longer, many travelers enjoy the more involved cog-railway experience—at least one way. The disadvantage of the train is that more than half of the trip is through dark tunnels deep in the mountains; aside from a few fleeting glimpses of the Eibsee sparkling below, it's not very scenic.

Arriving at the top, you'll want to head up to the third floor (elevators recommended, given the high altitude)—follow signs for *Gipfel* (summit).

To get back down to Eibsee, the last cable car departs the summit at 16:45, and the last cogwheel train at 16:30. On busy days, you may have to reserve a return time once you reach the top—if it's crowded, look for signs and prebook your return to avoid getting stuck up top longer than you want. In general, allow plenty of time for afternoon descents: If bad weather hits in the late afternoon, cable cars can be delayed at the summit, causing tourists to miss their train connection from Eibsee back to Garmisch.

Hikers can enjoy the easy six-mile walk around the lovely Eibsee (start 5 minutes downhill from cable-car station).

Austrian Approach: The Tiroler Zugspitzbahn ascent is less crowded and cheaper than the Bavarian one. Departing from

above the village of Ehrwald (a 30-minute train trip from Reutte, runs almost hourly), the lift zips you to the top in 10 minutes (€37.50 round-trip, departures in each direction at :00, :20, and :40 past the hour, daily 8:40-16:40 except closed late April-mid-May and most of Nov, last ascent at 16:00,

drivers follow signs for *Tiroler Zugspitzbahn*, free parking, Austrian tel. 05673/2309, www.zugspitze.at). While those without a car will find the German ascent from Garmisch easier, the Austrian ascent is also doable: Either hop the bus from the Ehrwald train station to the Austrian lift (departures nearly hourly), or pay €8 for the five-minute taxi ride from Ehrwald train station.

☉ Self-Guided Tour: Whether you've ascended from the Austrian or German side, you're high enough now to enjoy a little tour of the summit. The two terraces—Bavarian and Tirolean—are connected by a narrow walkway, which was the border station before Germany and Austria opened their borders. The Austrian (Tirolean) side was higher until the Germans blew its top off in World War II to make a flak tower, so let's start there.

Tirolean Terrace: Before you stretches the Zugspitzplatt glacier. Each summer, a 65,000-square-foot reflector is spread over the ice to try to slow the shrinking. Since metal ski-lift towers collect heat, they, too, are wrapped to try to save the glacier. Many ski lifts fan out here, as if reaching for a ridge that defines the border between Germany and Austria. The circular metal building is the top of the cog-railway line that the Germans cut through the mountains in 1931. Just above that, find a small square building—the *Hochzeitskapelle* (wedding chapel) consecrated in 1981 by Cardinal Joseph Ratzinger (now Pope Benedict XVI).

Both Germany and Austria use this rocky pinnacle for communication purposes. The square box on the Tirolean Terrace provides the Innsbruck airport with air-traffic control, and a tower nearby is for the German *Kathastrophenfunk* (civil defense network).

This highest point in Germany (there are many higher points in Austria) was first climbed in 1820. The Austrians built a cable car that nearly reached the summit in 1926. (You can see it just over the ridge on the Austrian side—look for the ghostly, abandoned concrete station.) In 1964, the final leg, a new lift, was built connecting that 1926 station to the actual summit, where you stand now. Before then, people needed to hike the last 650 feet to the top. Today's lift dates from 1980, but was renovated after a 2003 fire. The Austrian station, which is much nicer than the German station, has a fine little museum—free with Austrian ticket, €2.50 if you came up from Germany—that shows three interesting videos (6-minute 3-D mountain show, 30-minute making-of-the-lift documentary, and 45-minute look at the nature, sport, and culture of the region).

Looking up the valley from the Tirolean Terrace, you can see the towns of Ehrwald and Lermoos in the distance, and the valley that leads to Reutte. Looking farther clockwise, you'll see Eibsee Lake below. Hell's Valley, stretching to the right of Eibsee, seems to merit its name.

Bavarian Terrace: The narrow passage connecting the two terraces used to be a big deal—you'd show your passport here at the little blue house and shift from Austrian shillings to German marks. Notice the regional pride here: no German or Austrian national banners, but regional ones instead—*Freistaat Bayern* (Bavaria) and *Land Tirol*.

The German side features a golden cross marking the summit...the highest point in Germany. A priest and his friends hauled it up in 1851. The historic original was shot up by American soldiers using it for target practice in the late 1940s, so what you see today is a modern replacement. In the summer, it's easy to "summit" the Zugspitze, as there are steps and handholds all the way to the top. Or you can just stay behind and feed the birds. The yellow-beaked ravens get chummy with those who share a little pretzel or bread. Below the terrace, notice the restaurant that claims—irrefutably— to be the "highest Biergarten in Deustchland."

The oldest building up here is the rustic tin-and-wood weather tower near the border crossing, erected in 1900 by the *Deutscher Wetterdienst* (German weather service). The first mountaineers' hut, built in 1897, didn't last. The existing one—entwined with mighty cables that cinch it down—dates from 1914. In 1985, observers clocked 200-mph winds up here—those cables were necessary. Step inside the restaurant to enjoy museum-like photos and paintings on the wall (including a look at the team who hiked up with the golden cross in 1851).

Near the waiting area for the cable cars and cogwheel train is a little museum (in German only) that's worth a look if you have some time to kill before heading back down. If you're going down on the German side, remember you must choose between the cable car (look for the *Eibsee* signs) or cog railway (look for *Talfahrt/Descent*, with a picture of a train; you'll board a smaller cable car for the quick trip to the train station.

Reutte, Austria

Reutte (ROY-teh, with a rolled *r*), a relaxed Austrian town of 5,700, is located 20 minutes across the border from Füssen. While overlooked by the international tourist crowd, it's popular with Germans and Austrians for its climate. Doctors recommend its "grade 1" air.

Although its setting—surrounded by alpine peaks—is striking, the town itself is pretty unexceptional. But that's the point. I enjoy Reutte for the opportunity it offers to simply be in a real community. As an example of how the town is committed to its character, real estate can be sold only to those using it as a primary residence. (Many formerly vibrant alpine towns made a pile of money but lost their sense of community by becoming resorts. They allowed  wealthy foreigners—who just drop in for a week or two a year—to buy up all the land, and are now shuttered up and dead most of the time.)

Reutte has one claim to fame among Americans: As Nazi Germany was falling in 1945, Hitler's top rocket scientist, Werner von Braun, joined the Americans (rather than the Russians) in Reutte. You could say that the American space program began here.

Reutte isn't featured in any other American guidebook. The town center can be congested and confusing, and its charms are subtle. It was never rich or important. Its castle is ruined, its buildings have painted-on "carvings," its churches are full, its men yodel for each other on birthdays, and its energy is spent soaking its

Austrian and German guests in *Gemütlichkeit*. Most guests stay for a week, so the town's attractions are more time-consuming than thrilling.

Some travelers tell me this town is over-Reutte-d. Füssen's tidy pedestrian core and glitzy hotels make it an easier home base. But in my view, Reutte's two big trump cards are its fine countryside accommodations (the farther from the town center, the more rustic, authentic, and relaxing) and its proximity to one of my favorite ruined castles in Europe, Ehrenberg. As both of these pluses are most easily appreciated with a car, drivers will have the best Reutte experience.

Orientation to Reutte

Little Reutte, with about 6,000 people, sprawls into several surrounding villages—creating a thriving community that fills a basin hemmed in by mountains and cut through by the Lech River. The town center is a tangle of crisscrossing roads that's bewildering for drivers; know where you're going and follow signs (to your point of interest, hotel, or neighboring village) to stay on track. While strolling through Reutte can be enjoyable, ultimately it's a workaday burg.

The area's real charm lies in the abutting hamlets, and that's where my favorite hotels and restaurants are located: **Breitenwang**, flowing directly from Reutte to the east, marked by its pointy steeple; **Ehenbichl**, a stand-alone, time-warp farming village cuddled up against the mountains to the south; **Höfen**, squeezed between an airstrip and a cable-car station, just across the river from Ehenbichl; and remote **Pinswang**, stranded in a forgotten valley halfway to Germany, just over the mountain from Neuschwanstein. Watching over it all to the south are the **Ehrenberg Castle** ruins—viewable from just about everywhere (and evocatively floodlit at night), but most easily conquered by foot from the Klause Valley (two miles out of town on the main Innsbruck road).

Remember, Reutte is in a different country. While Austrians use the same euro currency the Germans do, postage stamps and phone cards only work in the country where you buy them. If you have a German SIM card in your mobile phone, you're roaming (and paying higher rates) in Reutte.

To **telephone** from Germany to Austria, dial 00-43 and then the number listed in this section (omitting the initial zero). To call from Austria to Germany, dial 00-49 and then the number (again, omitting the initial zero).

Tourist Information

Reutte's TI is a block in front of the train station (Mon-Fri 8:00-12:00 & 14:00-17:00, no midday break July-Aug, Sat 8:30-12:00, closed Sun, Untermarkt 34, tel. 05672/62336, www.reutte.com). Go over your sightseeing plans, ask about a folk evening, and pick up city and biking/hiking maps, bus schedules, the *Sommerprogramm* events schedule (in German only), and a free town info booklet (with a good self-guided walk).

Guests staying in the Reutte area (and, therefore, paying local hotel tax) are entitled to an **Aktiv-Card**—be sure to ask your hotel for one. The TI has a brochure explaining all of the perks of this card, including free travel on local buses (including the Reutte-Füssen route—but not Füssen-Neuschwanstein) and free admission to some otherwise very pricey attractions, including the recommended Klause Valley Fort Museum, the Hahnenkammbahn mountain lift (summer only), and the Alpentherme bath complex (2 hours free each day). Also included are various guided hikes in the surrounding mountains (get schedule from TI), and discounts on mountain-bike tours, rafting trips, and paragliding. If you know what's covered and ask for these discounts, the value of this card is far more than the modest tax (€2/person per day).

Arrival in Reutte

By Car: If you're coming by car from Germany, skip the north *(Nord)* exit and take the south *(Süd)* exit into town. For parking in town, blue lines denote pay-and-display spots (if you're staying more than 30 minutes, pay at the meter, then put the receipt in your windshield). There are a few spaces just outside the TI that are free for up to 30 minutes—handy for stopping by with a few questions en route to your out-of-town hotel. For longer stays, there's a free lot (P-1) just past the train station on Muhlerstrasse (about a 10-minute walk from the town center and TI).

While Austria requires a **toll sticker** *(Vignette)* for driving on its expressways (€8.30/10 days, buy at the border, gas stations, car-rental agencies, or *Tabak* shops), those just dipping into Tirol from Bavaria don't need one—even on the expressway-like bypass around Reutte.

By Train or Bus: From Reutte's tidy little train station (no baggage storage), exit straight ahead and walk three minutes straight up Bahnhofstrasse. After the park on your left, you'll see the TI; my recommended town-center hotels are down the street just beyond the TI and its parking lot.

Helpful Hints

Laundry: There isn't an actual launderette in town, but the recommended Hotel Maximilian lets non-guests use its laundry service (wash, dry, and fold—€16/load; hotel guests pay €12).

Bike Rental: Try **Intersport** (€15/day, Mon-Fri 9:00-18:00, Sat 9:00-17:00, closed Sun, Lindenstrasse 25, tel. 05672/62352), or check at the recommended Hotel Maximilian.

Taxi: **STM Shuttle Service** promises 24-hour service (mobile 0664-113-3277).

"Nightlife": Reutte is pretty quiet. For any action at all, there's a strip of bars, dance clubs, and Italian restaurants on Lindenstrasse.

Sights in and near Reutte

▲▲Ehrenberg Castle Ensemble (Festungsensemble Ehrenberg)

If Neuschwanstein was the medieval castle dream, Ehrenburg is the medieval castle reality. Once the largest fortification in Tirol,

its brooding ruins lie about two miles outside Reutte. Ehrenburg is actually an "ensemble" of four castles, built to defend against the Bavarians and to bottle up the strategic Via Claudia trade route, which cut through the Alps as it connected Italy and Germany. Today, these castles have become a European "castle museum," showing off 500 years of military architecture in one swoop. The European Union is helping fund the project (paying a third of its €9 million cost) because it promotes the heritage of a multinational region—Tirol—rather than a country.

The four parts of the complex are the fortified Klause toll booth on the valley floor, the oldest castle on the first hill above (Ehrenberg), a mighty and more modern castle high above (Schlosskopf, built in the age when cannon positioned there made the original castle vulnerable), and a smaller fourth castle across the valley (Fort Claudia, an hour's hike away). All four were once a single complex connected by walls. Signs posted throughout the site help visitors find their way and explain some background on the region's history, geology, flora, and fauna—along with some colorful, fun boards that relate local folktales regarding the castle. (While the castles are free and open all the time, the museum and multimedia show at the fort's parking lot charge admission; they also may begin charging for parking in 2014—likely €2/day.)

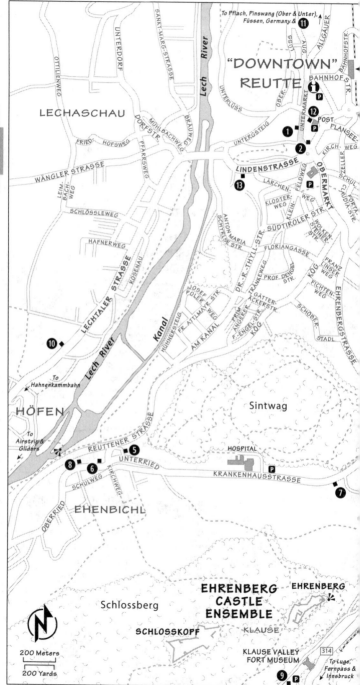

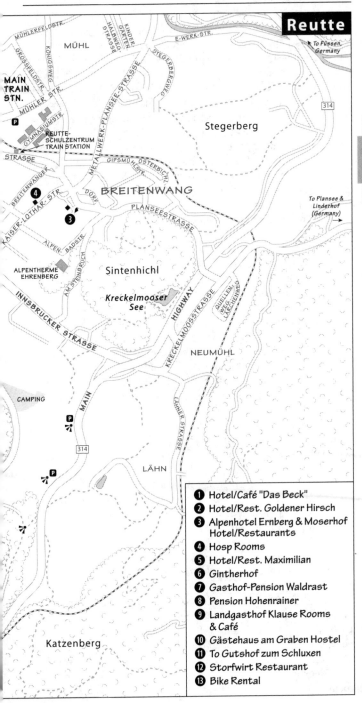

Reutte

To Füssen, Germany

BAVARIA & TIROL

MÜHLERFELDSTR.

MÜHL

E-WERK-STR.

KÖNIGSWEG

GROSSFELDSTR.

KINDER GARTEN

HALLWEG

HALLWEG

STRASSE

STEGERBERGWEG

MAIN TRAIN STN.

Stegerberg

MÜHLER STR.

GYMNASIUMSTR.

314

REUTTE-SCHULZENTRUM TRAIN STATION

STRASSE

METZ WERK-PLANSEE-STRASSE

GIPSMÜHLSTR.

OSTERBICHL

BREITENWÄNGER

DORF

BREITENWANG

BREITENWANGER

KAISER-LOTHAR-STR.

PLANSEESTRASSE

To Plansee & Linderhof (Germany)

ALPEN. BADSTR.

AM STEINBRUCH

ALPENTHERME EHRENBERG

Sintenhichl

Kreckelmooser See

HIGHWAY

KRECKELMOOSSTRASSE

QUELLEN WEG

LÄRCHENWEG

INNSBRUCKER STRASSE

NEUMÜHL

CAMPING

MAIN

LÄHNER STRASSE

314

LÄHN

Katzenberg

① Hotel/Café "Das Beck"
② Hotel/Rest. Goldener Hirsch
③ Alpenhotel Ernberg & Moserhof Hotel/Restaurants
④ Hosp Rooms
⑤ Hotel/Rest. Maximilian
⑥ Gintherhof
⑦ Gasthof-Pension Waldrast
⑧ Pension Hohenrainer
⑨ Landgasthof Klause Rooms & Café
⑩ Gästehaus am Graben Hostel
⑪ To Gutshof zum Schluxen
⑫ Storfwirt Restaurant
⑬ Bike Rental

Getting to the Castle Ensemble: The Klause, Ehrenberg, and Schlosskopf castles are on the road to Lermoos and Innsbruck. These are a pleasant 30- to 45-minute walk or a short bike ride from Reutte; bikers can use the *Radwanderweg* along the Lech River (the TI has a good map). Local bus #5 runs from Reutte's main train station to Ehrenberg sporadically (usually 3-4/day; see www.vvt.at for schedules—the stop name is "Ehrenberger Klause").

▲Klause Valley Fort Museum

Historians estimate that about 10,000 tons of precious salt passed through this valley (along the route of Rome's Via Claudia) each year in medieval times, so it's no wonder the locals built this complex of fortresses and castles. Beginning in the 14th century, the fort controlled traffic and levied tolls on all who passed. Today, these scant remains hold a museum and a theater with a multimedia show.

While there are no real artifacts here (other than the sword used in A.D. 2008 to make me the honorary First Knight of Ehrenberg), the clever, kid-friendly **museum** takes one 14th-century decade (1360-1370) and attempts to bring it to life. It's a hands-on experience, well-described in English. You can try on a set of armor (and then weigh yourself), see the limited vision knights had to put up with when wearing their helmet, learn about everyday medieval life, empathize with victims of the plague, join a Crusade, and play soccer with gigantic stone balls once tossed by a catapult. In the armory section, you can heft replica weapons from the period. Several videos and soundtracks spring to life if you press a button (select *E* for English).

The **multimedia show** takes you on a 30-minute spin (in German) through the 2,000-year history of this valley's fortresses, with images projected on the old stone walls and modern screens (50-minute English version runs Mon-Fri at 13:00 with a minimum of 5 people, or sometimes by request).

Cost and Hours: €7.50, €3 more to include multimedia show, €17.80 family pass (€20.80 with multimedia show) for 2 adults and any number of kids, daily 10:00-17:00, closed Nov-mid-Dec, tel. 05672/62007, www.ehrenberg.at.

Information: The museum's atrium stays open (until 22:00) after the museum itself closes; you can come in and help yourself to brochures on the local area.

Eating: Next to the museum, the **Landgasthof Klause** serves typical Tirolean meals (€10-16 main courses, late June-mid-Sept daily 10:00-20:00 or later, off-season closed Mon and generally shorter hours, closed Nov and early Jan, tel. 05672/62213). They also rent a few rooms if you'd like to stay right at Ehrenberg.

Nearby: A local group plans to open a new exhibition nearby, focusing on the nature park for the Lech River Valley. The new exhibit may be part of a combo-ticket with the castle museum; ask for details.

▲▲Ehrenberg Ruins

Ehrenberg, a 13th-century rock pile, provides a super opportunity to let your imagination off its leash. Hike up 30 minutes from the

parking lot of the Klause Valley Fort Museum for a great view from your own private ruins (you'll likely have to pay €2 for parking). The trail is well-marked and has well-groomed gravel, but it's quite steep, and once you reach the castle itself, you'll want good shoes to scramble over the uneven stairs.

BAVARIA & TIROL

● **Self-Guided Tour:** From the parking lot, follow yellow signs up into the woods, tracking *Ruine Ehrenberg* or *Bergruine Ehrenberg*. At the top of the first switchback, notice the option to turn left and hike 45 minutes up to Schlosskopf, the higher castle (described next; this is an easier ascent than the very steep route you can take from closer to Ehrenberg). But we'll head right and continue up the path through the lower entrance bastion of Ehrenberg.

Emerging from the woods, you'll pop out at a saddle of land between two steep hills. As you face Reutte, the hill on the left is Schlosskopf (notice the steeper ascent here to reach the top), and to the right is Ehrenberg. Ehrenberg (which means "Mountain of Honor") was the first castle here, built in 1296. Thirteenth-century castles were designed to stand boastfully tall. Later, with the advent of gunpowder, castles dug in. (Notice the 18th-century ramparts around the castle.)

Now continue twisting up the path to Ehrenberg Castle. As you approach its outer gate, look for the small **door** to the left. It's the night entrance (tight and awkward, and therefore safer against a surprise attack). But we'll head through the **main gate**—actually, two of them. Castles were designed with layered defenses—outer bastion down below, outer gate here, inner gate deeper within—which allowed step-by-step retreat, giving defenders time to regroup and fight back against invading forces.

After you pass through the outer gate, but before climbing to the top of the castle, follow the path around to the right to a big, grassy courtyard with commanding views and a fat, restored **turret.** This stored gunpowder and held a big cannon that enjoyed a clear view of the valley below. In medieval times, all the trees approaching the castle were cleared to keep an unobstructed view.

Look out over the valley. The pointy spire marks **Breitenwang,** which was a stop on the ancient Via Claudia. In A.D. 46, there was a Roman camp there. In 1489, after Reutte's bridge crossed the Lech

River, Reutte (marked by the onion-domed church) was made a market town and eclipsed Breitenwang in importance. Any gliders circling? They launch from just over the river in Höfen.

For centuries, this castle was the seat of government—ruling an area called the "judgment of Ehrenberg" (roughly the same as today's "district of Reutte"). When the emperor came by, he stayed here. In 1604, the ruler moved downtown into more comfortable quarters, and the castle was no longer a palace.

Now climb to the top of Ehrenberg Castle. Take the high ground. There was no water supply here—just kegs of wine, beer, and a cistern to collect rain. Up at the top, appreciate how strategic this lofty position is—with commanding views over Reutte, the entire valley, and the narrow side-valley with today's highway to Innsbruck (and yesterday's important Via Claudia trading route through the Alps). But also notice that you're sandwiched between two higher hilltops: Schlosskopf in one direction, and Falkenberg (across the narrow valley) in the other. In the days before gunpowder, these positions offered no real threat; but in the age of cannonballs, Ehrenberg was suddenly very vulnerable...and very obsolete.

Ehrenberg repelled 16,000 Swedish soldiers in the defense of Catholicism in 1632. Ehrenberg saw three or four other battles, but its end was not glorious. In the 1780s, a local businessman bought the castle in order to sell off its parts. Later, in the late 19th century, when vagabonds moved in, the roof was removed to make squatting miserable. With the roof gone, deterioration quickened, leaving only this evocative shell and a whiff of history.

Scramble around the ruined walls a bit—nocking imaginary arrows—and head back down through the main gate, returning to the valley the way you came. If you have more energy and castle curiosity, you could try conquering the next castle over: Schlosskopf.

▲Schlosskopf

When the Bavarians captured Ehrenberg in 1703, the Tiroleans climbed up to the bluff above it to rain cannonballs down on their former fortress. In 1740, a mighty new castle—designed to defend against modern artillery—was built on this sky-high strategic location: Schlosskopf ("Castle Head"). By the end of the 20th century, the castle was completely overgrown with trees—you literally couldn't see it from Reutte. But today the trees have been shaved away, and the castle has been excavated. In 2008, the Castle Ensemble project, led by local architect Armin Walch, opened the site with English descriptions and view platforms. One spot gives spectacular views of the strategic valley. The other looks down on the older Ehrenberg Castle ruins, illustrating the strategic problems presented with the advent of cannon.

Getting There: There are two routes to Schlosskopf, both steep and time-consuming. The steeper of the two (about 30 minutes straight up) starts at the little saddle of land between the two castles (described earlier). The second, which curls around the back of the hill, is less steep but takes longer (45-60 minutes); this one begins from partway down the gravel switchbacks between Ehrenberg and the valley floor—just watch for *Schlosskopf* signs.

In the Town

Reutte Museum (Museum Grünes Haus)

Reutte's cute city museum offers a quick look at the local folk culture and the story of the castles. There are exhibits on Ehrenberg and the Via Claudia, local painters, and more—ask to borrow the English translations.

Cost and Hours: €3; May-Oct Tue-Sat 13:00-17:00, closed Sun-Mon; early Dec-Easter Wed-Sat 14:00-17:00, closed Sun-Tue; closed Easter-end of April and Nov-early Dec; in the bright-green building at Untermarkt 25, around corner from Hotel Goldener Hirsch, tel. 05672/72304, www.museum-reutte.at.

▲▲Tirolean Folk Evening

Ask the TI or your hotel if there's a Tirolean folk evening scheduled. During the summer (July-Aug), nearby towns (such as Höfen on Tuesdays) occasionally put on an evening of yodeling, slap dancing, and Tirolean frolic. These are generally free and worth the short drive. Off-season, you'll have to do your own yodeling. There are also weekly folk concerts featuring the local choir or brass band in Reutte's Zeiller Platz, as well as various groups in the surrounding communities (free, July-Aug only, ask at TI). For listings of these and other local events, pick up a copy of the German-only *Sommerprogramm* schedule at the TI.

Alpentherme Ehrenberg

This new, extensive swimming pool and sauna complex, near Breitenwang on the eastern edge of Reutte, is a tempting retreat on a hot day. The Badewelt section features two indoor pools and a big saltwater outdoor pool, as well as two waterslides. The Saunaparadies section (where customers go naked—no kids under 16 allowed) consists of three indoor saunas, three freestanding outdoor saunas, and a big outdoor swimming pool. They'll issue you a wristband that lets you access your locker and buy snacks on credit without needing a key or money. This is particularly worth considering if you're staying in the Reutte area, since you can access the pools for two hours free with an Aktiv-Card (see "Tourist Information," earlier); it's a nice way to relax after hiking castles all day.

Cost and Hours: Pools only-€9/2 hours, €11/4 hours, €13/day; sauna and pools-€17/3 hours, €23/day; towel rental-€3, robe rental-€5, swimsuits sold but not rented; daily 10:00-21:00, sauna until 22:00, Thermenstrasse 10, tel. 05672/72222, www.alpentherme-ehrenberg.at.

Across the River, in Höfen

Just over the Lech River are two very different ways to reach high-altitude views. To get here from Reutte, head up Lindenstrasse (where the cobbled Obermarkt ends), cross the bridge, and turn left down Lechtaler Strasse; as you enter the village of Höfen, you'll see the cable car to your right, and the airstrip to your left.

▲Scenic Flights

For a major thrill on a sunny day, drop by the tiny airport in Höfen and fly. You have two options: prop planes and gliders. Small **single-prop planes,** which take three passengers, can buzz the Zugspitze and Ludwig's castles and give you a bird's-eye peek at Reutte's Ehrenberg ruins (€90/30 minutes, €180/1 hour, these prices for 2 passengers, tel. 05672/632-0729, www.flugsportverein-reutte.at).

Or, to try something more angelic, how about **gliding** *(Segelfliegen)*? For a modest price, you and a pilot get 30 minutes in a two-seat glider. Just watching the towrope launch the graceful glider like a giant slow-motion rubber-band gun is exhilarating (€40/30 minutes, €65/1 hour, May-mid-Sept 12:00-19:00 in good but breezy weather only, tel. 05672/64010, mobile 0676-945-1288, www.segelflugverein-ausserfern.at).

While I've listed phone numbers, those phones are often not answered, and English is limited. Your best bet is to show up at the airstrip on a good-weather afternoon and ask around for somebody in the know. The prop planes and gliders are based out of two different restaurants that face the airstrip. From the main road, watch for the big building marked *Flugplatz* down below. The contact for the prop-plane pilots is the Fliegerklause café; for the gliders, head 100 yards farther down the road to the Thermic Ranch.

Hahnenkammbahn

This mountain lift swoops you high above the tree line to an attractive restaurant and starting point for several hikes. In the alpine flower park, special paths lead you past countless varieties of local flora. Unique to this lift is a barefoot hiking trail *(Barfusswanderweg)*, designed to be walked without shoes—no joke.

Cost and Hours: €11 one-way, €15.50 round-trip, flowers best in late July, runs July-Sept daily 9:00-16:30, also in good weather late May-June and Oct-early Nov, base station across the river in Höfen, tel. 05672/62420, www.reuttener-seilbahnen.at.

Near Reutte

Lechweg

The Lech River begins high in the Alps and meanders 75 miles (including right past Reutte) on its way to the Lechfall, where it becomes navigable, near Füssen. This stretch of the Lech River Valley (Lechtal) has been developed for nature pilgrims as a popular hiking trail, called the Lechweg, divided into 15 stages *(Strecken)*; part

Luge Lesson

Taking a wild ride on a summer luge (pronounced "loozh") is a quintessential alpine experience. In German, it's called a *Sommerrodelbahn* ("summer toboggan run"). To try one of Europe's great accessible thrills (€3-8), take the lift up to the top of a mountain, grab a wheeled sled-like go-cart, and scream back down the mountainside on a banked course. Then take the lift back up and start all over again.

Luge courses are highly weather-dependent, and can close at the slightest hint of rain. If the weather's questionable, call ahead to confirm that your preferred luge is open. Stainless-steel courses are more likely than concrete ones to stay open in drizzly weather.

Operating the sled is simple: Push the stick forward to go faster, pull back to apply brakes. Even a novice can go very, very fast. Most are cautious on their first run, speed demons on their second...and bruised and bloody on their third. A woman once showed me her travel journal illustrated with her husband's dried five-inch-long luge scab. He had disobeyed the only essential rule of luging: Keep both hands on your stick. To avoid getting into a bumper-to-bumper traffic jam, let the person in front of you get way ahead before you start. You'll emerge from the course with a windblown hairdo and a smile-creased face.

Here are a few key luge terms:

Lenkstange	lever
drücken / schneller fahren	push / go faster
ziehen / bremsen	pull / brake
Schürfwunde	scrape
Schorf	scab

of the area has also been designated as a nature park. A variety of glossy brochures—mostly in German and available at local TIs and hotels—explain the importance of the Lech to local culture, and outline some enticing hikes.

Bird Lookout Tower

Between Reutte and Füssen is a pristine (once you get past the small local industrial park) nature preserve, the Tiroler Lech Nature Park, with an impressive wooden tower from which to appreciate the vibrant bird life in the wetlands along the Lech River. Look for *Vogelerlebnispfad* signs as you're driving through the village of Pflach (on the road between Reutte and Füssen). The EU gave half the money needed to preserve this natural area—home to 110 different species of birds that nest here. The best action is early in the day. Be quiet, as eggs are being laid.

Between Reutte and Innsbruck or the Zugspitze
▲▲Biberwier Luge Course
Near Lermoos, on the road toward Innsbruck, you'll find the Biberwier *Sommerrodelbahn*. At 4,250 feet, it's the longest summer luge in Tirol. The only drawbacks are its brief season, short hours, and a proclivity for shutting down sporadically—even at the slightest bit of rain. If you don't have a car, this is not worth the trouble; consider the luge near Neuschwanstein instead. The ugly cube-shaped building marring the countryside near the luge course is a hotel for outdoor adventure enthusiasts. You can ride your mountain bike right into your room, or skip the elevator by using its indoor climbing wall.

Cost and Hours: €7.40/ride, less for 3-, 5-, and 10-ride tickets, early May-early Oct daily 9:00-16:30, closed off-season, tel. 05673/2323, www.bergbahnen-langes.at. It's 20 minutes from Reutte on the main road toward Innsbruck; Biberwier is the first exit after a long tunnel.

High in the Mountains, South of Reutte
▲Fallerschein
Easy for drivers and a special treat for those who may have been Kit Carson in a previous life, this extremely remote log-cabin village is a 4,000-foot-high flower-speckled world of serene slopes and cowbells. Thunderstorms roll down the valley like it's God's bowling alley, but the pint-size church on the high ground, blissfully simple in a land of Baroque, seems to promise that this huddle of houses will survive, and the river and breeze will just keep flowing. The couples sitting on benches are mostly Austrian vacationers who've rented cabins here. Some of them, appreciating the remoteness of Fallerschein, are having affairs.

Getting to Fallerschein: From Reutte, it's a 45-minute drive. Take road 198 to Stanzach (passing Weisenbach am Loch, then Forchach), then turn left toward Namlos. Follow the L-21 Berwang road for about five miles to a parking lot. From there, it's a two-mile walk down a drivable but technically closed one-lane road. Those driving in do so at their own risk.

Sleeping in Fallerschein: **$ Michl's Fallerscheiner Stube** is a family-friendly mountain-hut restaurant with a low-ceilinged attic space that has basic beds for up to 17 sleepy hikers. The accommodations aren't fancy, but if you're looking for remote, this is it (dorm bed-€19, cheaper without breakfast, dinner-€11, sheets-€4, open May-Oct only, wildlife viewing deck, mobile 0676-727-9681, www.alpe-fallerschein.at, michaelknitel@mountainmichl.at, Knitel family).

Sleeping in and near Reutte

(country code: 43, area code: 05672)

Reutte is a mellow Füssen with fewer crowds and easygoing locals with a contagious love of life. Come here for a good dose of Austrian ambience and lower prices. While it's not impossible by public transport, staying here makes most sense for those with a car. Reutte is popular with Austrians and Germans, who come here year after year for one- or two-week vacations. The hotels are big, elegant, and full of comfy carved furnishings and creative ways to spend lots of time in one spot. All include a great breakfast. They take great pride in their restaurants, and the owners send their children away to hotel-management schools. Most hotels give a small discount for stays of two nights or longer. Remember to ask for the Aktiv-Card, which is covered by your hotel tax and includes lots of freebies during your time here.

The Reutte TI has a list of 50 private homes that rent out generally good rooms *(Zimmer)* with facilities down the hall, pleasant communal living rooms, and breakfast. Most charge €20 per person per night, and the owners speak little or no English. As these are family-run places, it is especially important to cancel in advance if your plans change. I've listed a few favorites in this section, but the TI can always find you a room when you arrive. All of the accommodations here offer free parking.

Reutte is surrounded by several distinct "villages" that basically feel like suburbs—many of them, such as Breitenwang, within easy walking distance of the Reutte town center. If you want to hike through the woods to Neuschwanstein Castle, stay at Gutshof zum Schluxen. To locate these accommodations, see the Reutte map. Remember, to call Reutte from Germany, dial 00-43- and then the number (minus the initial zero).

In Central Reutte

These two hotels are the most practical if you're traveling by train or bus.

$$ Hotel "Das Beck" offers 17 clean, sunny rooms (many with balconies) filling a modern building in the heart of town close to the train station. It's a great value, and guests are personally taken care of by Hans, Inge, Tamara, and Birgit. Their small café offers tasty snacks and specializes in Austrian and Italian wines. Expect good conversation overseen by Hans (Sb-€48-55, Db-€72-78, Tb-€96-99, price depends on room—more for a balcony; family suites: Db-€90, Tb-€108, Qb-€125; these prices with this book in 2014 if you book direct, non-smoking, guest computer, free Wi-Fi with this book, Untermarkt 11, tel. 05672/62522, www.hotel-das-beck.at, info@hotel-das-beck.at).

$$ Hotel Goldener Hirsch, also in the center of Reutte just two blocks from the station, is a grand old hotel with 52 dated, faded rooms and one lonely set of antlers (Sb-€60-68, Db-€90-102, Tb-€135, Qb-€156, less for 2 nights, elevator, free Wi-Fi, restaurant, Mühlerstrasse 1, tel. 05672/62508, www.goldener-hirsch. at, info@goldener-hirsch.at; Monika, Helmut, and daughters Vanessa and Nina).

In Breitenwang

Now basically a part of Reutte, the older and quieter village of Breitenwang has good *Zimmer* and a fine bakery. It's a 20-minute walk from the Reutte train station: From the post office, follow Planseestrasse past the onion-dome church to the pointy straight-dome church near the two hotels. The Hosps—as well as other B&Bs—are along Kaiser-Lothar-Strasse, the first right past this church. If your train stops at the tiny Reutte-Schulzentrum station, hop out here—you're just a five-minute walk from Breitenwang.

$$ Alpenhotel Ernberg's 26 fresh rooms (most with terraces) are run with great care by friendly Hermann, who combines Old World elegance with modern touches. Nestle in for some serious coziness among the carved-wood eating nooks, tiled stoves, and family-friendly backyard (Sb-€55-65, Db-€90-100, price depends on demand, less for 2 nights, free Wi-Fi, popular restaurant, Planseestrasse 50, tel. 05672/71912, www.ernberg.at, info@ernberg.at).

$$ Moserhof Hotel has 40 new-feeling rooms plus an elegant dining room (Sb-€61, Db-€99, larger Db-€109, these special rates promised in 2014 if you ask for the Rick Steves discount when you reserve and pay cash, extra bed-€35, most rooms have balconies, elevator, free Wi-Fi, restaurant, sauna and whirlpool, Planseestrasse 44, tel. 05672/62020, www.hotel-moserhof.at, info@hotel-moserhof.at, Hosp family).

$ Walter and Emilie Hosp rent three simple rooms sharing one bathroom in a comfortable, quiet, and modern house two blocks from the Breitenwang church steeple. You'll feel like you're staying at Grandma's (S-€26, D-€42, T-€60, Q-€80, cash only, Kaiser-Lothar-Strasse 29, tel. 05672/65377).

In Ehenbichl, near the Ehrenberg Ruins

The next listings are a bit farther from central Reutte, a couple of miles upriver in the village of Ehenbichl (under the Ehrenberg ruins). From central Reutte, go south on Obermarkt and turn right on Kög, which becomes Reuttener Strasse, following signs to Ehenbichl. These listings are best for car travelers—if you arrive by train you'll need to take a taxi (or brave the infrequent local buses; see www.vvt.at for schedules).

$$ Hotel Maximilian offers 30 rooms at a great value. It includes table tennis, play areas for children (indoors and out), a pool table, and the friendly service of Gabi, Monika, and the rest of the Koch family. They host many special events, and their hotel has lots of wonderful extras such as a sauna and a piano (Sb-€60, Db-€80-90, ask for these special Rick Steves prices when you book direct, family deals, elevator, guest computer, free Wi-Fi in common areas, pay Wi-Fi in rooms, laundry service-€12/load—non-guests pay €16, good restaurant, Reuttener Strasse 1, tel. 05672/62585, www.maxihotel.com, info@hotelmaximilian.at). They rent cars to guests only (€0.72/km, automatic transmission, book in advance) and bikes to anyone (€5/half-day, €10/day; or, for non-guests, €6/half-day, €12/day).

$$ Gintherhof is a working dairy farm that provides its guests with fresh milk, butter, and bacon. Kind, hardworking Annelies Paulweber offers a warm welcome, geranium-covered balconies, six cozy and well-appointed rooms with carved-wood ceilings, and a Madonna in every corner (Db-€70, Db suite-€75, €3/person less if you stay three nights or more, cash only, free Wi-Fi, Unterried 7, just up the road behind Hotel Maximilian, tel. 05672/67697, www.gintherhof.com, info@gintherhof.com).

$$ Gasthof-Pension Waldrast, separating a forest and a meadow, is run by the farming Huter family and their dog, Picasso. The place feels hauntingly quiet and has no restaurant, but it's inexpensive and offers 10 older rooms with generous sitting areas and castle-view balconies. They've also restored a nearly 500-year-old mill on their property; they rent rustic rooms in that building, as well, and can show you the mill if you ask (Sb-€42, Db-€72, Tb-€91, Qb-€108, 5 percent off second night or longer with this book, cash only, non-smoking, free Wi-Fi; about a mile from Reutte, just off main drag toward Innsbruck, past campground and under castle ruins on Ehrenbergstrasse; tel. 05672/62443, www.waldrasttirol.com, info@waldrasttirol.com, Gerd).

$$ Pension Hohenrainer, a big, quiet, no-frills place, has 12 rooms past their prime, with some castle-view balconies (Sb-€35, Db-€70, €1.50/person less for 2 nights, €3/person less for 3 nights, lower prices are for April-June and Sept-Oct, cash only, family rooms, non-smoking rooms, guest computer, free Wi-Fi, swimming pool, free parking, restaurant and reception in Gasthof Schlosswirt across the street and through the field, follow signs up the road behind Hotel Maximilian into village of Ehenbichl, Unterried 3, tel. 05672/62544 or 05672/63262, mobile 0676-799-6902, www.hohenrainer.at, hohenrainer@aon.at).

At the Ehrenberg Ruins

$$ Landgasthof Klause café, just below the Ehrenberg ruins and next to the castle museum, rents 14 non-smoking, sleek, and modern rooms with balconies, as well as six apartments. The downside is that the café closes a little early (at 20:00, likely later in peak season), and you'll need a car to get anywhere besides Ehrenberg (Sb-€40-45, Db-€80-88, Tb-€111, price depends on season, ask for Rick Steves discount when you book, discount for 2 or more nights, free Wi-Fi, apartments available, closed Nov and Jan, tel. 05672/62213, www.gasthof-klause.com, gasthof-klause@gmx.at).

Across the River, in Höfen

$ The homey **Gästehaus am Graben** is a hotel masquerading as a hostel; only a handful of its 50 beds are in six-bed dorms, while the rest are in private two- to four-bed rooms. It's lovingly run by the Reyman family—Frau Reyman, Rudi, and Gabi keep the place traditional, clean, and friendly. This is a super value less than two miles from Reutte, with fine castle views. If you've never hosteled and are curious (and have a car or don't mind a bus ride), try it. If traveling with kids, this is a great choice. The double rooms are hotel-grade, and they accept nonmembers of any age (dorm bed-€28, Db-€78, includes breakfast and sheets, cash only, non-smoking, expensive guest computer and Wi-Fi, laundry service-€9, no curfew, closed April and Nov-mid-Dec; from downtown Reutte, cross bridge and follow main road left along river, or take the bus—hourly until 19:30, ask for Graben stop; Graben 1, tel. 05672/626-440, www.hoefen.at, info@hoefen.at).

In Pinswang

The village of Pinswang is closer to Füssen (and Ludwig's castles), but still in Austria.

$$ Gutshof zum Schluxen gets the "Remote Old Hotel in an Idyllic Setting" award. This family-friendly farm, with 34 rooms, offers rustic elegance draped in goose down and pastels, and splashed with colorful modern art. Its picturesque meadow setting will turn you into a dandelion-picker, and its proximity to Neuschwanstein will turn you into a hiker—the castle is just an hour's walk away (Sb-€53, Db-€91-99, extra person-€31, these prices with this book in 2014, €3 extra per person for one-night stays in June-Sept, about 5-10 percent cheaper Nov-March, 5 percent discount for stays of three or more nights, free Wi-Fi in common areas, laundry-€9, mountain-bike rental-€10/day or €6/half-day, electric bike rental-€20/day or €12/half-day, restaurant, fun bar, between Reutte and Füssen in village of Pinswang, tel. 05677/89030, www.schluxen.at, info@schluxen.at). While this hotel works best for drivers, it is reachable by yellow post bus from the Füssen train station (every 2 hours, 14 minutes, get off at Pinswang Gemeindeamt stop, verify details with hotel).

To reach Neuschwanstein from this hotel by foot or bike, follow the dirt road up the hill behind the hotel. When the road forks at the top of the hill, go right (downhill), cross the Austria-Germany border (marked by a sign and deserted hut), and follow the narrow paved road to the castles. It's a 1- to 1.5-hour hike or a great circular bike trip (allow 30 minutes; cyclists can return to Schluxen from the castles on a different 30-minute bike route via Füssen).

Eating in Reutte

The hotels here take great pride in serving local cuisine at reasonable prices to their guests and the public. Rather than go to a cheap restaurant, eat at one of the Reutte hotels recommended earlier: **Alpenhotel Ernberg, Moserhof Hotel, Hotel Maximilian,** or **Hotel Goldener Hirsch.** Hotels typically serve €10-15 dinners from 18:00 to 21:00 and are closed one night a week.

Storfwirt is *the* place for a quick and cheap weekday lunch. The giant yet rustic cafeteria serves some 300 happy eaters every day. You can get the usual sausages here, as well as baked potatoes and salads (€6-10 daily specials, salad bar, always something for vegetarians, Mon-Fri 9:00-14:30, closed Sat-Sun). Their adjacent **deli** is a great place to shop for a Tirolean picnic; from the glass case, choose from local meats, cheeses, and prepared salads, and they'll even make you a sandwich to order (deli Mon-Fri 7:00-18:00, Sat 7:00-12:00, closed Sun; Schrettergasse 15 but facing Tauschergasse—roughly next door to the big Müller pharmacy and post office, tel. 05672/62640, helpful manager Rainer).

Across the street from the Hotel Goldener Hirsch on Mühlerstrasse is a *Bauernladen* (farmer's shop) with rustic sandwiches and meals prepared from local ingredients (Wed-Fri 9:00-18:00, Sat 9:00-12:00, closed Sun-Tue, mobile 0676-575-4588).

Picnic Supplies: **Billa** supermarket has everything you'll need (across from TI, Mon-Fri 7:15-19:30, Sat 7:15-18:00, closed Sun).

Reutte Connections

From Reutte by Train to: Ehrwald (at base of Zugspitze lift, every 2 hours, 30 minutes), **Garmisch** (same train, every 2 hours, 1 hour), **Innsbruck** (every 2 hours, 2.5 hours, change in Garmisch), **Munich** (every 2 hours, 2.5 hours, change in Garmisch), **Salzburg** (every 2 hours, 4.5-5.5 hours, quickest with changes in Garmisch and Munich). Train info: tel. 0180-599-6633, www.bahn.com.

By Bus to: Füssen (post bus #4258, Mon-Fri almost hourly, last bus 18:10; Sat-Sun every 2 hours, last bus 17:10; 45 minutes, €4.20 one-way, buses depart from train station, pay driver).

Taxis cost about €35 one-way to Füssen or the King's Castles.

Route Tips for Drivers

From downtown Reutte, *Fernpass* signs lead you out to the main Innsbruck road, which is also the best way to reach the Ehrenberg ruins. To reach the Ehrenberg Castle ruins, the Biberwier luge, the Zugspitze (either the Austrian ascent at Ehrwald or the German ascent at Garmisch), or Innsbruck, turn right for the on-ramp (marked Fernpass and Innsbruck) to highway 179. But if you're headed for Germany via scenic Plansee Lake, Linderhof Castle, Ettal Monastery, or Oberammergau, continue straight (bypassing the highway on-ramp).

SALZBURG AND BERCHTESGADEN

Salzburg, just over the Austrian border, makes a fun day trip from Munich (1.5 hours by direct train). Thanks to its charmingly preserved Old Town, splendid gardens, Baroque churches, and Europe's largest intact medieval fortress, Salzburg feels made for tourism. As a musical mecca, the city puts on a huge annual festival, as well as constant concerts, and its residents—or at least those in its tourism industry—are forever smiling to the tunes of Mozart and *The Sound of Music*. It's a city with class. Vagabonds visiting here wish they had nicer clothes.

In the mountains just outside Salzburg is Berchtesgaden, a German alpine town that was once a favorite of Adolf Hitler's, but thrills a better class of nature-lover today.

Planning Your Time

While Salzburg's sights are, frankly, mediocre, the town itself is a Baroque museum of cobbled streets and elegant buildings—simply a touristy stroller's delight. Even if your time is short, consider allowing half a day for the *Sound of Music* tour. The *S.O.M.* bus tour kills a nest of sightseeing birds with one ticket (city overview, *S.O.M.* sights, and a fine drive by the lakes).

You'd probably enjoy at least two nights in Salzburg—nights are important for swilling beer in atmospheric local gardens and attending concerts in Baroque halls and chapels. Seriously consider one of Salzburg's many evening musical events (a few are free, some are as cheap as €12, and most average €40).

To get away from it all, bike down the river or hike across the Mönchsberg cliffs that rise directly from the middle of town. Or consider swinging by Berchtesgaden, just 15 miles away, in Germany. A direct bus gets you there from Salzburg in 45 minutes.

Salzburg, Austria

Even without Mozart and the von Trapps, Salzburg is steeped in history. In about A.D. 700, Bavaria gave Salzburg to Bishop Rupert

in return for his promise to Christianize the area. Salzburg remained an independent city (belonging to no state) until Napoleon came in the early 1800s. Thanks in part to its formidable fortress, Salzburg managed to avoid the ravages of war for 1,200 years...until World War II. Much of the city was destroyed by WWII bombs (mostly around the train station), but the historic Old Town survived.

Eight million tourists crawl its cobbles each year. That's a lot of Mozart balls—and all that popularity has led to a glut of businesses hoping to catch the tourist dollar. Still, Salzburg is both a must and a joy.

Orientation to Salzburg

Salzburg, a city of 150,000 (Austria's fourth-largest), is divided into old and new. The Old Town (Altstadt), sitting between the Salzach River and its mini-mountain (Mönchsberg), holds nearly all the charm and most of the tourists. The New Town (Neustadt), across the river, has the train station, a few sights and museums, and some good accommodations.

Welcome to Austria: Austria uses the same euro currency as Germany, but postage stamps and phone cards only work in the country where you buy them.

To **telephone** from Germany to Austria, dial 00-43 and then the number listed in this section (omitting the initial zero). To call from Austria to Germany, dial 00-49 and then the number (again, omitting the initial zero).

While Austria requires a **toll sticker** *(Vignette)* for driving on its expressways (€8.30/10 days, buy at the border, gas stations, car-rental agencies, or *Tabak* shops), those just dipping into Salzburg from Bavaria don't need one (you'll also be fine without one on a drive to Hallstatt, provided you stick to the most direct route, which isn't on the *Autobahn*).

Note that **Berchtesgaden**—also covered in this chapter—is in Germany, not Austria.

Tourist Information

Salzburg has three helpful TIs (main tel. 0662/889-870, www. salzburg.info): at the **train station** (daily May-Sept 9:00-19:00, Oct-April 9:00-18:00, tel. 0662/8898-7340); on **Mozartplatz** in the old center (daily 9:00-18:00, July-Aug until 19:00, closed Sun mid-Jan-Easter and Sept-mid-Nov, tel. 0662/889-870); and at the **Salzburg Süd park-and-**

ride (April-Sept generally Tue-Sat 10:00-16:30 but sometimes longer hours, closed Sun-Mon and all of Oct-March, tel. 0662/8898-7360).

At any TI, you can pick up a free city-center map (the €0.70 map has a broader coverage and more information on sights, and is particularly worthwhile if biking out of town), the Salzburg Card brochure (listing sights with current hours and prices), and a bimonthly events guide. The TIs also book rooms (€2.20 fee and 12 percent deposit). Inside the Mozartplatz TI is the privately run Salzburg Ticket Service counter, where you can book concert tickets.

Salzburg Card: The TIs sell the Salzburg Card, which covers all your public transportation (including the Mönchsberg elevator and funicular to the fortress) and admission to all the city sights (including Hellbrunn Palace and a river cruise). The card is pricey, but if you'd like to pop into all the sights, it can save money and enhance your experience (€26/24 hours, €35/48 hours, €41/72 hours). To analyze your potential savings, here are the major sights and what you'd pay without the card: Hohensalzburg Fortress and funicular-€11; Mozart's Birthplace and Residence-€17; Hellbrunn Palace-€10.50; Salzburg Panorama 1829-€3; Salzach River cruise-€15; 24-hour transit pass-€4.20. Busy sightseers can save plenty. Get this card, feel the financial pain once, and the city will be all yours.

Arrival in Salzburg

By Train: The Salzburg station is a gleaming commercial center with all the services you need: train information, tourist information, luggage lockers, and a handy Spar supermarket (daily 6:00-

23:00)—plus a popular shopping mall that's open on weekends. The transit info desk down the stairs from bus platform C has information on local buses.

Getting downtown from the station is a snap. Simply step outside, find **bus platform C** (labeled *Zentrum-Altstadt*), buy a ticket

from the machine, and hop on the next bus. Buses #1, #3, #5, #6, and #25 all do the same route into the city center before diverging at the far end of town. For most sights and city-center hotels, get off just after the bridge, at the fifth stop. For my recommended New Town

hotels, get off at Makartplatz (the fourth stop), just before the bridge.

Taxis don't make much sense to get from the train station into town, as they're expensive for short rides (€2.50 drop charge, about €8 for most rides in town).

To **walk** downtown (15 minutes), turn left as you leave the station, and walk straight down Rainerstrasse, which leads under the tracks past Mirabellplatz, turning into Dreifaltigkeitsgasse. From here, you can turn left onto Linzergasse for many of my recommended hotels, or cross the river to the Old Town. For a slightly longer but more dramatic approach, leave the station the same way but follow the tracks to the river, turn left, and walk the riverside path toward the fortress.

By Car: Mozart never drove in Salzburg's Old Town, and neither should you. The best place to park is the **Salzburg Süd park-and-ride** lot. Coming on A-8 from Munich, cross the border into Austria. Take A-10 toward Hallein, and then take the next exit (Salzburg Süd) in the direction of Anif, and look for signs for the park-and-ride. Park your car (€5/24 hours), get sightseeing information and transit tickets from the TI, and catch bus #3 or #8 into town (€1.90 single-ride ticket or €4.20 *Tageskarte* 24-hour pass, more expensive if you buy tickets on board, every 5 minutes). If traveling with more than one other person, take advantage of a park-and-ride combo-ticket: For €13 (€10 July-Aug), you get 24 hours of parking and a 24-hour bus pass for up to five people.

If you don't believe in park-and-rides, head to the easiest, cheapest, most central parking lot—the 1,500-car Altstadtgarage, in the tunnel under the Mönchsberg (€18/day, note your slot number and which of the twin lots you're in, tel. 0662/846-434). Your hotel may provide discounted parking passes. If staying in Salzburg's New Town, the Mirabell-Congress garage makes more sense than the Altstadtgarage.

By Air: Salzburg's airport is easily reached by regular city buses #2, #8, and #27 (airport code: SZG, tel. 0662/85800, www. salzburg-airport.com).

Helpful Hints

Recommendations Skewed by Kickbacks: Salzburg is addicted to the tourist dollar, and it can never get enough. Virtually all hotels are on the take when it comes to concert and tour recommendations, influenced more by their potential kickback than by what's best for you. Take any tour or concert advice with a grain of salt.

Music Festival: The Salzburg Festival (Salzburger Festspiele) runs each year from late July to the end of August.

Internet Access: A small Internet café is next to the base of the Mönchsberg elevator (€2/hour, daily 10:00-22:00, Gstättengasse 11). The city has several free Wi-Fi hotspots (one is in the Mirabell Gardens, another at Mozartplatz; info at www. salzburg-surft.at). Travelers with this book can get free Wi-Fi or use a computer for a few minutes (long enough to check email) at the Panorama Tours terminal on Mirabellplatz (daily 8:00-18:00).

Post Office: A full-service post office is located in the heart of town, in the New Residenz (Mon-Fri 8:00-18:00, Sat 9:00-12:00, closed Sun).

Laundry: A handy launderette is at Paris-Lodron-Strasse 16, at the corner of Wolf-Dietrich-Strasse, near my recommended Linzergasse hotels (€10 self-service, €15 same-day full-service, Mon-Fri 7:30-18:00, Sat 8:00-12:00, closed Sun, tel. 0662/876-381).

Cinema: Das Kino is an art-house movie theater that plays films in their original language (a block off the river and Linzergasse on Steingasse, tel. 0662/873-100, www.daskino.at).

Smoking Policies: Unlike Germany, which can implement sweeping reforms overnight, conservative Austria has been slow to embrace the smoke-free movement. By law, big restaurants must offer smoke-free zones (and smoking zones, if they choose). Smaller places choose to be either smoking or nonsmoking, indicated by red or green stickers on the door.

Market Days: Popular farmer's markets pop up at Universitätsplatz in the Old Town on Saturdays and around the Andräkirche in the New Town on Thursdays. On summer weekends, a string of craft booths with fun goodies for sale stretches along the river.

Morning Joggers: Salzburg is a great place for jogging. Within minutes you can be huffing and puffing "The hills are alive..." in green meadows outside of town. The obvious best bets in

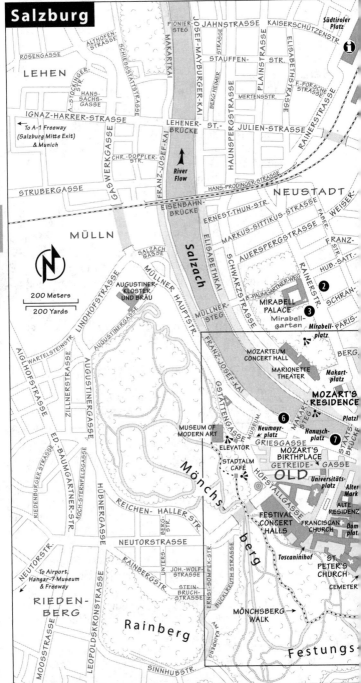

Salzburg

ROSENGASSE

LEHEN

PIONIER-STEG

JOSEF-MAYBURGER-KAI

JAHNSTRASSE

KAISERSCHÜTZENSTR.

Südtiroler Platz

ALTHOFEN-STRASSE

MAKARTKAI

STAUFFEN-

PLAINSTRASSE

ELISABETHSTR.

F-PORSCHE-STRASSE

SCHIESSSTATTSTRASSE

A-STOCKINGER

BERG HEIMER STRASSE

HANS-SACHS-GASSE

IGNAZ-HARRER-STRASSE

← To A-1 Freeway
(Salzburg Mitte Exit)
& Munich

LEHENER-BRÜCKE

ST.-

HAUNSPERGSTRASSE

MERTENSSTR.

JULIEN-STRASSE

RAINERSTRASSE

CHR.-DOPPLER-STR.

GASWERKGASSE

FRANZ-JOSEF-KAI

River Flow

HANS-PRODINGER-STRASSE

NEUSTADT

STRUBERGASSE

EISENBAHN-BRÜCKE

ERNEST-THUN-STR.

WEISER-

MÜLLN

SALZACHGASSE

Salzach

ELISABETHKAI

MARKUS-SITTIKUS-STRASSE

AUERSPERGSTRASSE

FABER-

FRANZ-

MÜLLNER HAUPTSTR.

SCHWARZSTRASSE

RAINERSTR.

HUB.-SATT.

SCHRAN-

AUGUSTINER-KLOSTER UND BRÄU

MÜLLNER-STEG

B.-PAUMGARTNER-WEG

❷

MIRABELL PALACE

❸

N

200 Meters
200 Yards

LINDHOFSTRASSE

AUGUSTINERGASSE

Mirabell-garten

Mirabell-Platz

PARIS-

WARTELSTEINSTR.

AIGLHOFSTRASSE

ZILLNERSTRASSE

FRANZ-JOSEF-KAI

GSTÄTTENGASSE

MOZARTEUM CONCERT HALL

MARIONETTE THEATER

BERG

Makart-platz

MOZART'S RESIDENCE

Mönchsberg

MUSEUM OF MODERN ART

Museum

Neumayr-platz

Makart-steg

Platzl

ED.-BAUMGARTNER-STR.

RIEDENBURGER STRASSE

HÜBNERGASSE

MOCH-STERNFELDGASSE

ELEVATOR

STADTALM CAFÉ

GRIESGASSE

Hanusch-platz

STAATS-BRÜCKE

❻

❼

MOZART'S BIRTHPLACE

GETREIDE-GASSE

OLD

Universitäts-platz

Alter Mark

REICHEN-HALLER-STR.

BERG-STR.

HOFSTALLGASSE

ALTE RESIDENZ

NEUTORSTRASSE

RAINBERGSTR.

FESTIVAL CONCERT HALLS

FRANCISCAN CHURCH

Dom-plat.

INTERS...

JOH.-WOLF-STRASSE

ERNST-SOMPEK-STR.

BÜCKLREUTH STRASSE

Toscaninihof

ST. PETER'S CHURCH

← To Airport,
Hangar-7 Museum
& Freeway

NEUTORSTR.

LEOPOLDSKRONSTRASSE

STEIN-BRUCH-STRASSE

CEMETER

RIEDEN-BERG

MOOSSTRASSE

Rainberg

MÖNCHSBERG WALK →

Festungs-

SINNHUBSTR.

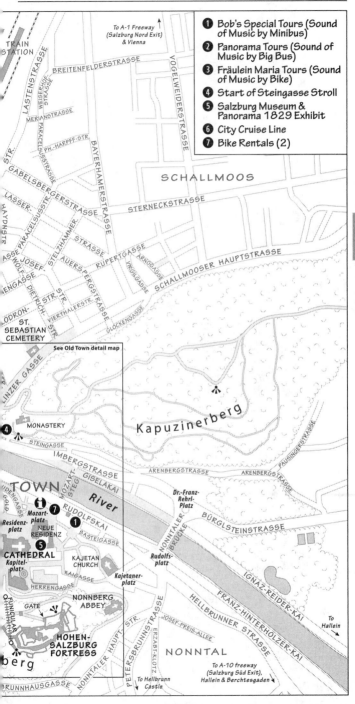

SALZBURG & BERCHTESGADEN

1. Bob's Special Tours (Sound of Music by Minibus)
2. Panorama Tours (Sound of Music by Big Bus)
3. Fräulein Maria Tours (Sound of Music by Bike)
4. Start of Steingasse Stroll
5. Salzburg Museum & Panorama 1829 Exhibit
6. City Cruise Line
7. Bike Rentals (2)

town are through the Mirabell Gardens along its riverbank pedestrian lanes.

Updates to This Book: For news about changes to this book's coverage since it was published, see www.ricksteves.com/update.

Getting Around Salzburg

By Bus: Most visitors take at least a couple of rides on Salzburg's extensive bus system. At *Tabak/Trafik* shops and ticket machines, you can buy €1.90 single-ride tickets or a €4.20 day pass *(Tageskarte)* good for 24 hours (€2.30 and €5.20 from the driver, respectively). Many lines converge at Hanuschplatz, on the Old Town side of the river, in front of the recommended Fisch Krieg restaurant. To get from the Old Town to the train station, catch bus #1 from the inland side of Hanuschplatz. From the other side of the river, find the Makartplatz/Theatergasse stop and catch bus #1, #3, #5, or #6. Busy stops like Hanuschplatz and Mirabellplatz have several bus shelters; look for your bus number to double-check where exactly you should stand. Bus info: www.svv-info.at, tel. 0662/632-900.

By Bike: Salzburg is great fun for cyclists. The following two bike-rental shops offer 20 percent off to anyone with this book—ask for it: **Top Bike** rents bikes on the river next to the Staatsbrücke (€6/2 hours, €10/4 hours, €15/24 hours, usually daily April-June and Sept-Oct 10:00-17:00, July-Aug 9:00-19:00, closed Nov-March, easy return available 24/7, free helmets with this book, mobile 0676-476-7259, www.topbike.at, Sabine). **A'Velo Radladen** rents bikes in the Old Town, just outside the TI on Mozartplatz (€4.50/1 hour, €10/4 hours, €16/24 hours, more for electric or mountain bikes; daily 9:00-18:00, until 19:00 July-Aug, but hours unreliable, shorter hours off-season and in bad weather; passport number for security deposit, mobile 0676-435-5950, www.a-velo.at). Some of my recommended hotels and pensions also rent bikes, and several of the B&Bs on Moosstrasse have free loaner bikes for guests.

By Funicular and Elevator: The Old Town is connected to the top of the Mönchsberg mountain (and great views) via funicular and elevator. The **funicular** *(Festungsbahn)* whisks you up into the imposing Hohensalzburg Fortress (included in castle admission, goes every few minutes). The **elevator** (Mönchsberg Aufzug) on the west side of the Old Town lifts you to the recommended Gasthaus Stadtalm café and hostel, the Museum of Modern Art and its chic café, wooded paths, and more great views (€2.10 one-way, €3.40 round-trip, normally Mon 8:00-19:00, Tue-Sun 8:00-24:00).

By Buggy: The horse buggies *(Fiaker)* that congregate at Residenzplatz charge €40 for a 25-minute trot around the Old Town (www.fiaker-salzburg.at).

Tours in Salzburg

Walking Tours
Any day of the week, you can take a one-hour guided walk of the Old Town without a reservation—just show up at the TI on Mozartplatz and pay the guide. The tours are informative. While generally in English only, on slow days you may be listening to everything in both German and English (€9, daily at 12:15, Mon-Sat also at 14:00, tel. 0662/8898-7330). To save money, you can easily do it on your own using this chapter's self-guided walk.

Local Guides
Salzburg is home to over a hundred licensed guides. I have worked with three who are art historians and well worth recommending: **Christiana Schneeweiss** ("Snow White") has been instrumental in both my guidebook research and my TV production in Salzburg, and has her own minibus for private tours outside of town (on foot: €135/2 hours, €165/3 hours; with minibus: €240/4 hours, €350-450/day, up to 6 people; mobile 0664-340-1757, other options explained at www.kultur-tourismus.com, info@kultur-tourismus.com). Two other excellent guides, both a joy to learn from, are **Sabine Rath** (€150/2 hours, €190/4 hours, €280/8 hours, mobile 0664-201-6492, www.tourguide-salzburg.com, info@tourguide-salzburg.com) and **Anna Stellnberger** (€145/2 hours, €185/4 hours, €275/8 hours, mobile 0664-787-5177, anna.stellnberger@aon.at). Salzburg has many other good guides (to book, call 0662/840-406).

Boat Tours
City Cruise Line (a.k.a. Stadt Schiff-Fahrt) runs a basic 40-minute round-trip river cruise with recorded commentary (€15, 9/day July-Aug, 7/day May-June, fewer Sept-Oct and March-April, no boats Nov-Feb). For a longer cruise, ride to Hellbrunn and return by bus (€18, 1-2/day April-Oct). Boats leave from the Old Town side of the river just downstream of the Makartsteg bridge (tel. 0662/825-858, www.salzburghighlights.at). While views can be cramped, passengers are treated to a fun finale just before docking, when the captain twirls a fun "waltz."

▲▲*The Sound of Music* Tours
I took a *S.O.M.* tour skeptically (as part of my research)—and had a great time. The bus tour version includes a quick but good general city tour, hits the *S.O.M.* spots (including the stately home used in the movie, flirtatious gazebo, and grand wedding church), and shows you a lovely stretch of the Salzkammergut Lake District. This is worthwhile for *S.O.M.* fans and those who won't otherwise be going into the Salzkammergut. Warning: Many

think rolling through the Austrian countryside with 30 Americans singing "Doe, a deer..." is pretty schmaltzy. Local Austrians don't understand all the commotion.

You have plenty of *S.O.M.* options: big buses (heavy on the  countryside around Salzburg, cannot go into Old Town), minibuses (a mix of town and countryside), and bike (best for the town and meadows nearby but doesn't get you into the foothills of the Alps). Guides are generally native English-speakers—young, fun-loving, and entertaining. Tourists are generally Japanese and American.

Of the many companies doing the tour by bus, consider Bob's Special Tours (usually uses a minibus) and Panorama Tours (big 50-seat bus). Each one provides essentially the same tour (in English with a live guide, 4 hours); with Bob's you pay a little more for being in a smaller group, while Panorama offers a more predictable, professional experience. You'll get a €5 discount from either if you book direct, mention Rick Steves, pay cash, and bring this book along (you'll need to show them this book to get the deal). Getting a spot is simple—just call and make a reservation. Note: Your hotel will be eager to call to reserve for you—to get their commission—but if you let them do it, you won't get the discount I've negotiated.

Minibus Option: Most of **Bob's Special Tours** use an eight-seat minibus (and occasionally a 20-seat bus) and therefore have good access to Old Town sights, promote a more casual feel, and spend less time waiting to load and unload. As it's a smaller operation, the quality of guides can be mixed (my readers have found some of their guides gruff or rude), and they may cancel with short notice if the tour doesn't fill up. Conversely, during busy times it can fill up early—reserving in advance increases your chances of getting a seat, but online bookings close three days prior to the tour date (€45 for adults, €5 discount with this book if you pay cash and book direct, €40 for kids over age 6 and students with ID, €35 for kids ages 0-6—includes required car seat but must reserve in advance; daily at 9:00 and 14:00 year-round, they'll pick you up at your hotel for the morning tour, afternoon tours leave from Bob's office along the river just east of Mozartplatz at Rudolfskai 38, tel. 0662/849-511, mobile 0664-541-7492, www.bobstours.com). Nearly all of Bob's tours stop for a fun luge ride when the weather is dry (mountain bobsled-€4.50 extra, generally April-Oct, confirm beforehand). While the afternoon tour leaves promptly, you'll waste up to 30 minutes on the morning tour doing the hotel pick-ups.

For a private minibus tour consider **Christina Schneeweiss**, who does an *S.O.M.* tour with more history and fewer jokes (€240, up to 6 people, see "Local Guides," earlier).

Big-Bus Option: Panorama Tours depart from their smart kiosk at Mirabellplatz daily at 9:30 and 14:00 year-round (€40, €5 discount for *S.O.M.* tours with this book if you book by phone and pay in cash, book by calling 0662/874-029 or 0662/883-2110, discount not valid for online reservations, www.panoramatours.com). Many travelers appreciate their more businesslike feel, roomier buses, and higher vantage point. As they do not pick up at hotels, you won't waste any time making the rounds before starting the tour.

Bike Tours by "Fräulein Maria": For some exercise with your *S.O.M.* tour, you can meet your guide (likely a man) at the Mirabell Gardens (at Mirabellplatz 4, 50 yards to the left of palace entry). The main attractions that you'll pass during the eight-mile pedal include the Mirabell Gardens, the horse pond, St. Peter's Cemetery, Nonnberg Abbey, Leopoldskron Palace, and, of course, the gazebo. The tour is very family-friendly, and you'll get lots of stops for goofy photo ops (€26 includes bike, €18 for kids ages 13-18, €12 for kids under age 13, €2 discount for adults and kids with this book, daily May-Sept at 9:30, June-Aug also at 16:30, allow 3.5 hours, reservations required for afternoon tours and recommended for morning tours, tel. 0650/342-6297, www.mariasbicycletours.com). For €8 extra (€20 per family), you're welcome to keep the bike all day.

Beyond Salzburg

Both Bob's and Panorama Tours also offer an extensive array of other day trips from Salzburg (e.g., Berchtesgaden/Eagle's Nest, salt mines, Hallstatt, and Salzkammergut lakes and mountains).

Bob's Special Tours offers two particularly well-designed day tours (both depart daily at 9:00; either one costs €90 with a €10 discount if you show this book and book direct, does not include entrance fees). Their *Sound of Music*/**Hallstatt Tour** first covers everything in the standard four-hour *Sound of Music* tour, then continues for a four-hour look at the scenic, lake-speckled Salzkammergut (with free time to explore charming Hallstatt). Bob's **Bavarian Mountain Tour** covers the main things you'd want to do in and around Berchtesgaden (Königssee cruise, Eagle's Nest, documentation center, salt mine tour). Although you can do all the top Berchtesgaden sights on your own with the information I've provided later in this chapter, Bob's makes it easy for those without a car to see these sights in one busy day.

Salzburg at a Glance

▲▲▲**Salzburg's Old Town Walk** Old Town's best sights in handy orientation walk. **Hours:** Always open. See page 172.

▲▲**Salzburg Cathedral** Glorious, harmonious Baroque main church of Salzburg. **Hours:** May-Sept Mon-Sat 9:00-19:00, Sun 13:00-19:00; March-April, Oct, and Dec closes at 18:00; Jan-Feb and Nov closes at 17:00. See page 177.

▲▲**Getreidegasse** Picturesque old shopping lane with characteristic wrought-iron signs. **Hours:** Always open. See page 182.

▲▲**Hohensalzburg Fortress** Imposing castle capping the mountain overlooking town, with tourable grounds, several mini-museums, commanding views, and good evening concerts. **Hours:** Fortress museums open daily May-Sept 9:00-19:00, Oct-April 9:30-17:00. Concerts nearly nightly. See page 186.

▲▲**Salzburg Museum** Best place to learn more about the city's history. **Hours:** Tue-Sun 9:00-17:00, closed Mon. See page 184.

▲▲***The Sound of Music* Tour** Cheesy but fun tour through the S.O.M. sights of Salzburg and the surrounding Salzkammergut Lake District, by minibus, big bus, or bike. **Hours:** Various options daily at 9:00, 9:30, 14:00, and 16:30. See page 169.

▲▲**Mozart's Birthplace** House where Mozart was born in 1756, featuring his instruments and other exhibits. **Hours:** Daily 9:00-17:30, July-Aug until 20:00. See page 185.

▲**Old Residenz** Prince Archbishop Wolf Dietrich's palace, with ornate rooms and good included audioguide. **Hours:** Daily 10:00-17:00. See page 176.

▲**Salzburg Panorama 1829** A vivid peek at the city in 1829. **Hours:** Daily 9:00-17:00. See page 185.

Self-Guided Walk

▲▲▲Salzburg's Old Town

I've linked the best sights in the Old Town into this handy self-guided orientation walk.

• *Begin in the heart of town, just up from the river, near the TI on...*

❶ Mozartplatz

All the happy tourists around you probably wouldn't be here if not

▲**Mozart's Residence** Restored house where the composer lived. **Hours:** Daily 9:00-17:30, July-Aug until 20:00. See page 193.

▲**Mönchsberg Walk** "The hills are alive" stroll you can enjoy right in downtown Salzburg. **Hours:** Doable anytime during daylight hours. See page 191.

▲**Mirabell Gardens and Palace** Beautiful palace complex with fine views, Salzburg's best concert venue, and *Sound of Music* memories. **Hours:** Gardens—always open; concerts—free in the park May-Aug Sun at 10:30, in the palace nearly nightly. See page 192.

▲**Steingasse** Historic cobbled lane with trendy pubs—a tranquil, tourist-free section of old Salzburg. **Hours:** Always open. See page 194.

▲**St. Sebastian Cemetery** Baroque cemetery with graves of Mozart's wife and father, and other Salzburg VIPs. **Hours:** Daily April-Oct 9:00-18:00, Nov-March 9:00-16:00. See page 195.

▲▲**Hellbrunn Palace** Lavish palace on the outskirts of town featuring gardens with trick fountains. **Hours:** Daily May-Sept 9:00-17:30, July-Aug until 21:00, April and Oct 9:00-16:30, closed Nov-March. See page 196.

St. Peter's Cemetery Atmospheric old cemetery with mini-gardens overlooked by cliff face with monks' caves. **Hours:** Cemetery—daily June-Aug 6:30-21:30, April-May 6:30-20:00, Sept 6:30-19:00, Oct-March 6:30-18:00. See page 180.

St. Peter's Church Romanesque church with Rococo decor. **Hours:** Daily April-Oct 8:00-21:00, Nov-March 8:00-19:00. See page 180.

for the man honored by this statue—Wolfgang Amadeus Mozart. (Many consider this to be a terrible likeness.) The statue was erected in 1842 on the 50th anniversary of Mozart's death, during a music festival that included his two sons (making this event, in a sense, the first Salzburg Festival). Mozart spent much of his first 25 years (1756-1777) in Salzburg, the greatest Baroque city north of the Alps. But the city itself is much older: The Mozart statue sits on bits of Roman Salzburg, and the pink Church of St. Michael that overlooks the square dates from A.D. 800. The first Salzburgers settled right around here. Near you is the TI (with a concert box office), and just around the downhill corner is a pedestrian bridge leading over the Salzach River to the quiet and most medieval street in town, Steingasse.

You may see lots of conservative Muslim families vacationing here. While there are plenty of Muslims in Austria, most of the conservatively dressed women you'll see here are generally from the United Arab Emirates. Lots of wealthy families from the Middle East come here in the summer to escape the heat back home, to enjoy a break from their very controlled societies, or for medical treatment. Nearby Munich is a popular destination for hospital visits, and the entire family usually joins in for sightseeing and shopping.

• *Walk toward the cathedral and into the big square with the huge fountain.*

❷ Residenzplatz

Important buildings have long ringed this square. Salzburg's energetic Prince Archbishop Wolf Dietrich von Raitenau (who ruled 1587-1612) was raised in Rome, was a cousin of the influential Florentine Medici family, and had grandiose Italian ambitions for Salzburg. After a convenient fire destroyed the town's cathedral, Wolf Dietrich set about building the "Rome of the North." This square, with his new cathedral and palace, was the centerpiece of his Baroque dream city. A series of interconnecting squares—like you'll see nowhere else—make a grand processional way, leading from here through the Old Town. As we stroll through this heart and soul of historic Salzburg, notice how easily we slip from noisy commercial streets to peaceful, reflective courtyards. Also notice the two dominant kinds of stone around town: a creamy red marble and a chunky conglomerate (see the cathedral's exterior wall). The conglomerate was cheap—actually cut right out of the town's little mountain. As you wander, enjoy the pedestrian-friendly peace and quiet. After 11:00 each morning, barrier stumps go up around the perimeter of the Old Town, keeping traffic out.

For centuries, Salzburg's leaders were both important church officials *and* princes of the Holy Roman Empire, hence the title "prince archbishop"—mixing sacred and secular authority. But Wolf Dietrich misplayed his hand, losing power and spending his last five years imprisoned in the Hohensalzburg Fortress. (It's a complicated story—basically, the pope counted on Salzburg to hold the line against the Protestants for several generations following the Refor-

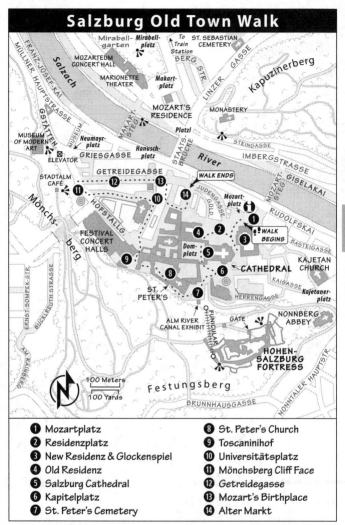

Salzburg Old Town Walk

1 Mozartplatz
2 Residenzplatz
3 New Residenz & Glockenspiel
4 Old Residenz
5 Salzburg Cathedral
6 Kapitelplatz
7 St. Peter's Cemetery

8 St. Peter's Church
9 Toscaninihof
10 Universitätsplatz
11 Mönchsberg Cliff Face
12 Getreidegasse
13 Mozart's Birthplace
14 Alter Markt

SALZBURG & BERCHTESGADEN

mation. Wolf Dietrich was a good Catholic, as were most Salzburgers. But the town's important businessmen and the region's salt miners were Protestant, and for Salzburg's financial good, Wolf Dietrich dealt with them in a tolerant and pragmatic way. So the pope—who allowed zero tolerance for Protestants in those heady Counter-Reformation days—had Wolf Dietrich locked up and replaced.)

The fountain (completed in 1661) is as Italian as can be, with a Triton matching Bernini's famous Triton Fountain in Rome. During the Baroque era, skilled Italian artists and architects were in high demand in central European cities such as Salzburg and

Prague. Local artists even Italianized their names in order to raise their rates.

• *Along the left side of Residenzplatz (as you face the cathedral) is the...*

❸ New (Neue) Residenz and Glockenspiel

This former palace, long a government administration building, now houses the central post office, the **Heimatwerk** (a fine shop showing off all the best local handi-crafts, Mon-Sat 9:00-18:00, closed Sun), and two worthwhile sights: the fascinating **Salzburg Panorama 1829** exhibit; and the **Salzburg Museum,** which offers the best peek at the history of this one-of-a-kind city (both sights described later).

The famous **glockenspiel** rings atop the New Residenz. This bell tower has a carillon of 35 17th-century bells (cast in Antwerp) that chimes throughout the day and plays tunes (appropriate to the month) at 7:00, 11:00, and 18:00. A big barrel with adjustable tabs turns like a giant music-box mechanism, pulling the right bells in the appropriate rhythm. Notice the ornamental top: an upside-down heart in flames surrounding the solar system (symbolizing that God loves all of creation). Twice-weekly tours let you get up close to watch the glockenspiel action (€3, April-Oct Thu at 17:30 and Fri at 10:30, no tours Nov-March, meet in Salzburg Panorama 1829, just show up).

Look back, past Mozart's statue, to the 4,220-foot-high **Gais-berg**—the forested hill with the television tower. A road leads to the top for a commanding view. Its summit is a favorite destination for local nature-lovers and strong bikers.

• *Head to the opposite end of the square. This building is the...*

❹ Old (Alte) Residenz

Across from the New Residenz is Wolf Dietrich's palace, the Old Residenz (rated ▲), which is connected to the cathedral by an arched bridge. Its series of ornately decorated "stately rooms" *(Prunkräume)* is well-described in an included audioguide, which gives you a good feel for the wealth and power of the prince arch-bishop. Walking through 15 fancy rooms (all on one floor), you'll see Renaissance, Baroque, and Classicist styles—200 years of let-them-eat-cake splendor.

Cost and Hours: €9, daily 10:00-17:00, tel. 0662/8042-2690, www.residenz-salzburg.at.

• *Walk under the prince archbishop's skyway and step into Domplatz (Cathedral Square), where you'll find...*

❺ Salzburg Cathedral (Salzburger Dom)

This cathedral, rated ▲▲, was one of the first Baroque buildings north of the Alps. It was consecrated in 1628, during the Thirty Years' War. (Pitting Roman Catholics against Protestants, this war devastated much of Europe and brought most grand construction projects to a halt.) Experts differ on what motivated the determined builders: emphasizing Salzburg's commitment to the Roman Catholic cause and the power of the Church here, or showing that there could be a peaceful alternative to the religious strife that was racking Europe at the time. Salzburg's archbishop was technically the top papal official north of the Alps, but the city managed to steer clear of the war. With its rich salt production, it had enough money to stay out of the conflict and carefully maintain its independence from the warring sides, earning it the nickname "Fortified Island of Peace."

Domplatz, the square in front of the cathedral, is surrounded by the prince archbishop's secular administration buildings. The **statue of Mary** (from 1771) is looking away from the church, welcoming visitors. If you stand in the rear of the square, immediately under the middle arch, you'll see that she's positioned to be crowned by the two angels on the church facade.

The dates on the cathedral's iron gates refer to milestones in the church's history: In 774, the previous church (long since destroyed) was founded by St. Virgil, to be replaced in 1628 by the church you see today. In 1959, a partial reconstruction was completed, made necessary by a WWII bomb that had blown through the dome.

Cost and Hours: Free, but donation prominently requested; May-Sept Mon-Sat 9:00-19:00, Sun 13:00-19:00; March-April, Oct, and Dec closes at 18:00; Jan-Feb and Nov closes at 17:00; www.salzburger-dom.at.

Visiting the Cathedral: Enter the cathedral as if part of a festival procession—drawn toward the resurrected Christ by the brightly lit area under the dome, and cheered on by ceiling paintings of the Passion.

Built in just 14 years (1614-1628), the church boasts harmonious architecture. When Pope John Paul II visited in 1998, some 5,000 people filled

the cathedral (330 feet long and 230 feet tall). The baptismal font (dark bronze, left of the entry) is from the previous cathedral (basin from about 1320, although the lid is modern). Mozart was baptized here (Amadeus means "beloved by God"). Concert and Mass schedules are posted at the entrance; the Sunday Mass at 10:00 is famous for its music (usually choral; more info at www.kirchen.net/dommusik).

The **paintings** lining the nave, showing events leading up to Christ's death, are relatively dark. But the Old Testament themes that foreshadow Jesus' resurrection, and the Resurrection scene painted at the altar, are well-lit. The church has never had stained glass—just clear windows to let light power the message.

The stucco, by a Milanese artist, is exceptional. Sit under the **dome**—surrounded by the tombs of 10 archbishops from the 17th century—and imagine all four organs playing, each balcony filled with musicians...glorious surround-sound. Mozart, who was the organist here for two years, would advise you that the acoustics are best in pews immediately under the dome. Study the symbolism of the decor all around you—intellectual, complex, and cohesive. Think of the altar in Baroque terms, as the center of a stage, with sunrays as spotlights in this dramatic and sacred theater.

In the left transept, stairs lead down into the **crypt** *(Krypta)*, where you can see foundations of the earlier church, more tombs, and a tourist-free chapel (reserved for prayer) directly under the dome.

Other Cathedral Sights: In July and August only, the **Cathedral Excavations Museum** (Domgrabungsmuseum, outside the church on Residenzplatz and down the stairs) offers a chance to see the foundations of the medieval church, some Roman engineering, and a few Roman mosaics from (Roman) street level. It has the charm of an old basement garage; unless you've never seen anything Roman, I'd skip it (€2.50, July-Aug daily 10:00-17:00, closed Sept-June, www.salzburgmuseum.at).

The **Cathedral Museum** (Dom Museum) has a rich collection of church art (entry at portico, €5, mid-May-Oct and Dec Mon-Sat 10:00-17:00, Sun 11:00-18:00, closed Nov and Jan-mid-May, tel. 0662/8047-1870), www.kirchen.net/dommuseum.

• *From the cathedral, exit left and walk toward the fortress into the next square.*

❻ Kapitelplatz

Head past the underground public WCs (€0.50) to the giant **chessboard.** It's just under the golden orb topped by a man gazing up at

the castle, trying to decide whether to walk up or shell out €11 for the funicular. Every year since 2002, a foundation has commissioned a different artist to create a new work of public art somewhere in the city; this is the piece from 2007.

Detour across the square to the fountain. This was a **horse bath,** the 18th-century equivalent of a car wash. Notice the puzzle above it—the artist wove the date of the structure into a phrase. It says, "Leopold the Prince Built Me," using the letters LLDVICMXVXI, which total 1732 (add it up...it works)—the year it was built. Return to the chessboard and face away from the cathedral. Look for the arrow pointing to the *Stieglkeller;* here a small road leads uphill to the fortress (and fortress funicular). To the right is a gate with a sign that reads *zum Peterskeller.* Walk through this gate, which leads to a waterwheel and St. Peter's Cemetery.

It's fair to say that Salzburg is glorious in great part because of its clever use of its water. The **waterwheel** is part of a canal system that has brought water into Salzburg from Berchtesgaden, 15 miles away, since the 13th century. Climb up the steps to watch the inflow and imagine the thrill felt by medieval engineers harnessing this raw power. The stream was divided into smaller canals and channeled through town to provide fire protection, to flush out the streets (Thursday morning was flood-the-streets day), and to power factories. As late as the 19th century there were still more than 100 watermill-powered firms in Salzburg. Because of its water-powered hygiene (relatively good for the standards of the time), Salzburg never suffered from a plague—it's probably the only Austrian town you'll see with no plague monument. For more on the canal system, check out the **Alm River Canal exhibit** (at the exit of the funicular).

Before leaving, drop into the fragrant and traditional **bakery** at the waterfall, which sells various fresh rolls—both sweet and not, explained on the wall—for less than €1 (Mon-Tue 8:00-17:30, Thu-Fri 7:00-17:30, Sat 7:00-13:00, closed Wed and Sun). From here there's a good view of the funicular climbing up to the castle.

• *Now find the* Katakomben *sign and step into...*

❼ St. Peter's Cemetery

This collection of lovingly tended mini-gardens abuts the Mönchberg's rock wall.

Cost and Hours: Cemetery—free, silence is requested, daily June-Aug 6:30-21:30, April-May 6:30-20:00, Sept 6:30-19:00, Oct-March 6:30-18:00; www.stift-stpeter.at.

Visiting the Cemetery: Walk in about 50 yards to the intersection of lanes at the base of the cliff marked by a stone ball. You're surrounded by three churches, each founded in the early Middle Ages atop a pagan Celtic holy site. St. Peter's Church is closest to the stone ball. Notice the fine Romanesque stonework on the apse of the chapel nearest you, and the rich guys' fancy Renaissance-style tombs decorating its walls. Wealthy as those guys were, they ran out of caring relatives. The graves surrounding you are tended by descendants of the deceased. In Austria, gravesites are rented, not owned. Rent bills are sent out every 10 years. If no one cares enough to make the payment, your tombstone is removed.

While the cemetery where the Von Trapp family hid out in *The Sound of Music* was a Hollywood set, it was inspired by this one. Look up the cliff. Legendary medieval hermit monks are said to have lived in the hillside—but "catacombs" they're not. You can climb lots of steps to see a few old caves, a chapel, and some fine views (€1.50, entrance at far end of cemetery, visit takes 10 minutes; May-Sept Tue-Sun 10:30-17:00, closed Mon; Oct-April Wed-Sun 10:30-15:30, closed Mon-Tue).

Stroll past the stark Gothic funeral chapel (c. 1491) to the uphill corner of the cemetery, and follow the high lane back to see the finer tombs in the arcade. Tomb #XXXI belongs to the cathedral's architect—forever facing his creation. Tomb #LIV, at the catacomb entry, is a chapel carved into the hillside, holding the tombs of Mozart's sister and Joseph Haydn's younger brother Michael, also a composer of note.

• *Continue downhill through the cemetery and out the opposite end. Just outside, hook right and drop into...*

❽ St. Peter's Church (Stiftskirche St. Peter)

Just inside, enjoy a carved Romanesque welcome. Over the inner doorway, a fine tympanum shows Jesus on a rainbow flanked by Peter and Paul over a stylized Tree of Life and under a Latin inscription reading, "I am the door to life, and only through me can you find eternal life." Enter the nave and notice how the once purely Romanesque vaulting has since been iced with a sugary Rococo finish. Salzburg's only Rococo interior feels Bavarian (because it is—the fancy stucco work was done by Bavarian artists). Up the right side aisle is the tomb of St. Rupert, with a painting showing Salzburg in 1750 (one bridge, salt ships sailing the river, and angels hoisting barrels of salt to heaven as St. Rupert prays for his city). Salt was Salzburg's white gold, granting the city enough wealth to maintain its independence as a prince-archbishopric for an entire millennium (798-1803). On pillars farther up the aisle are faded bits of 13th-century Romanesque frescoes. Similar frescoes hide under Rococo whitewash throughout the church.

Cost and Hours: Free, daily April-Oct 8:00-21:00, Nov-March 8:00-19:00, www.stift-stpeter.at.

• *Leaving the church, notice on the left the **Stiftskeller St. Peter** restaurant—known for its Mozart Dinner Concert. Charlemagne ate here in the year 803, allowing locals to claim that it's the oldest restaurant in Europe. Walk to the opposite end of the square from where you entered and look through the arch to see St. Rupert holding his staff and beckoning you into the next square. Once there, you're surrounded by early 20th-century Bauhaus-style dorms for student monks. Notice the modern crucifix (1926) painted on the far wall. Here's a good place to see the two locally quarried stones (marble and conglomerate) so prevalent in all the town's buildings.*

Walk through the archway under the crucifix into...

❾ Toscaninihof

This small courtyard is wedged behind the 1925 **Festival Hall.** The hall's three theaters seat 5,000 (see a photo of the main theater ahead on the wall, at the base of the stairs). This is where, in *The Sound of Music,* Captain von Trapp waits nervously before walking onstage to sing "Edelweiss," just before he escapes with his family. On the left is an entrance to the city's 1,500-space, inside-the-mountain parking lot; ahead, behind the *Felsenkeller* sign, is a tunnel (generally closed) leading to the actual concert hall; and to the right is the backstage of a smaller hall where carpenters are often building stage sets (door open on hot days). The stairway leads a few flights up to a picnic perch with a fine view, and then up to the top of the cliff and the recommended Gasthaus Stadtalm café and hostel.

Walk downhill through the archway onto **Max-Reinhardt-Platz.** Pause here to survey the line of Salzburg Festival concert halls to your left. As the festival was started in the austere 1920s, the city remodeled existing buildings (e.g., the prince archbishop's stables and riding school) for venues.

• *Continue straight—passing the big church on your left, along with popular wurst stands and a public WC—into...*

❿ Universitätsplatz

This square hosts an **open-air produce market**—Salzburg's liveliest, though it's pricey (mornings Mon-Sat, best on Sat). The market really bustles on Saturday mornings, when the farmers are in town.

Public marketplaces have fountains for washing fruit and vegetables. Bear left around the church and you'll find the one here—a part of the medieval water system. The sundial (over the fountain's drain) is accurate (except for the daylight savings hour) and two-dimensional, showing both the time (obvious) and the date (less obvious). The fanciest facade overlooking the square (the yellow one) is the backside of Mozart's Birthplace (we'll see the front soon).

• *Continue past the fountain to the far end of the square. Most of the houses on your right have nicely arcaded medieval passages that connect the square to Getreidegasse, which runs parallel to Universitätsplatz. Just for fun, you could weave between this street and Getreidegasse several times, following these "through houses" as you work your way toward the cliff face ahead.*

⓫ Mönchsberg Cliff Face

Look up—200 feet above you is the Mönchsberg, Salzburg's mountain. Today you see the remains of an aborted attempt in the 1600s to cut through the Mönchsberg. It proved too big a job, and when new tunneling technology arrived, the project was abandoned. The stones cut did serve as a quarry for the city's 17th-century growth spurt—the bulk of the cathedral, for example, is built of this economical and local conglomerate stone.

Early one morning in 1669, a huge landslide killed more than 200 townspeople who lived close to where the elevator is now (to the right). Since then the cliffs have been carefully checked each spring and fall. Even today, you might see crews on the cliff, monitoring its stability.

Across the busy road are giant horse troughs. Cross the street (looking left at the string of Salzburg Festival halls again) for a closer look. Paintings show the various breeds and temperaments of horses in the prince's stable. Like Vienna, Salzburg had a passion for the equestrian arts.

• *Turn right (passing a courtyard on your left that once housed a hospital for the poor, and now houses a toy museum and a museum of historic musical instruments), and then right again, which brings you to the start of a long and colorful pedestrian street. (At this point you could take a short side-trip up the mountain via the elevator—Mönchsberg Aufzug.)*

⓬ Getreidegasse

This street, rated ▲▲, was old Salzburg's busy, colorful main drag. It's been a center of trade since Roman times (third century). It's lined with *Schmuck* (jewelry) shops and other businesses. This is the burgher's (secular) Salzburg. The buildings, most of which date from the 15th century, are tall for that age, and narrow, and densely packed. Space was tight here because such little land was available between the natural fortifications provided by the mountain and the river, and so much of what was available was used up by the Church. Famous for its old wrought-iron signs, the architecture on the street still looks much as it did in Mozart's day—though much of its former elegance is now gone, replaced by chain outlets.

As you walk away from the cliffs, look up and enjoy the traditional signs indicating what each shop made or sold: Watch for spirits, bookmakers, a horn (indicating a place for the postal coach), brewery (the star for the name of the beer, Sternbräu—"Star Brew"), glazier (window-maker), locksmith, hamburgers, pastries, tailor, baker (the pretzel), pharmacy, and a hatter.

On the right at #39, **Sporer** serves up homemade spirits (€1.60/shot, Mon-Fri 9:30-19:00, Sat 8:30-17:00, closed Sun). This has been a family-run show for a century—fun-loving, proud, and English-speaking. *Nuss* is nut, *Marille* is apricot (typical of this region), the *Kletzen* cocktail is like a super-thick Baileys with pear, and *Edle Brande* are the stronger schnapps. The many homemade firewaters are in jugs at the end of the bar.

After noticing the building's old doorbells—one per floor—continue down Getreidegasse. At #40, **Eisgrotte** serves good ice cream (€1/scoop). Across from Eisgrotte, a tunnel leads to the recommended **Balkan Grill** (signed as *Bosna Grill*), the local choice for the very best wurst in town. At #28, Herr Wieber, the iron- and locksmith, welcomes the curious. Farther along, you'll pass McDonald's (required to keep its arches Baroque and low-key).

The knot of excited tourists and salesmen hawking goofy gimmicks by #9 marks the home of Salzburg's most famous resident: **⓭ Mozart's Birthplace** *(Geburtshaus)*—the house where Mozart was born, and where he composed many of his early works.

At #3, dip into the passage and walk under a whalebone, likely once used to advertise the wares of an exotic import shop. Look up at the arcaded interior. On the right, at the venerable **Schatz Konditorei,** you can enjoy coffee under the vaults with your choice of top-end cakes and pastries.

With your back to the pastry shop, go straight ahead through the passage to Sigmund-Haffner-Gasse. Before heading right, look left to see the tower of the old City Hall at the end. The blue-and-white ball halfway up is an 18th-century moon clock. It still tells the phase of the moon.

• *Go right, then take your first left to....*

⑩ Alter Markt

Here in Salzburg's old marketplace, you'll find the recommended **Café Tomaselli.** On the other side of the fountain, look for the fun **Josef Holzermayr candy shop,** and, next door, the beautifully old-fashioned **Alte F.E. Hofapotheke** pharmacy—duck in discreetly to peek at the Baroque shelves and containers (be polite—the people in line are here for medicine; no photography). Even in our fast-changing, modern age, the traditional soul of Salzburg—embraced by its citizens—lives on.

• *Our walk is finished. From here, you can circle back to some of the Old Town sights (such as those in the New Residenz, described next); head up to the Hohensalzburg Fortress on the cliffs over the Old Town; or continue to some of the sights across the river. To reach those New Town sights, head for the river, jog left (past the fast-food fish restaurant and free WCs), climb to the top of the Makartsteg pedestrian bridge, and follow my walking directions.*

Sights in Salzburg

In the Old Town

In the New (Neue) Residenz

▲▲Salzburg Museum

This two-floor exhibit is the best in town for history. The included audioguide wonderfully describes the great artifacts in the lavish prince archbishop's residence.

Cost and Hours: €7, €8.50 combo-ticket with Salzburg Panorama, includes audioguide, Tue-Sun 9:00-17:00, closed Mon, tel. 0662/620-8080, www.salzburgmuseum.at.

Visiting the Museum: The Salzburg Personalities exhibit fills the first floor with a charming look at Salzburg's greatest historic characters—mostly artists, scientists, musicians, and writers who would otherwise be forgotten. And upstairs is the real reason to come: lavish ceremonial rooms filled with an exhibit called The Salzburg Myth, which traces the city's proud history, art, and culture since early modern times. The focus is on its quirky absolutist prince archbishop and its long-standing reputation as a fairy-tale "Alpine Arcadia." The *Kunsthalle* in the basement shows off special exhibits.

From the Salzburg Museum, the Panorama Passage (clearly marked from the entry) leads underground to the Salzburg Panorama (described next). This passage is lined with archaeological finds (Roman and early medieval), helping you trace the development of Salzburg from its Roman roots until today.

▲Salzburg Panorama 1829

In the early 19th century, before the advent of photography, 360-degree "panorama" paintings of great cities or events were popular. These creations were even taken on extended road trips. When this one was created, the 1815 Treaty of Vienna had just divvied up post-Napoleonic Europe, and Salzburg had become part of the Habsburg realm. This photo-realistic painting served as a town portrait done at the emperor's request. The circular view, painted by Johann Michael Sattler, shows the city as seen from the top of its castle. When complete, it spent 10 years touring the great cities of Europe, showing off Salzburg's breathtaking setting.

Today, the exquisitely restored painting, hung in a circular room, offers a fascinating look at the city as it was in 1829. The river was slower and had beaches. The Old Town looks essentially as it does today, and Moosstrasse still leads into idyllic farm country. Your ticket also lets you see the temporary exhibitions in the room that surrounds the Panorama, which is part of the Salzburg Museum, but with a separate entrance and ticket counter.

Cost and Hours: €3, €8.50 combo-ticket with Salzburg Museum, open daily 9:00-17:00, Residenzplatz 9, tel. 0662/620-808-730, www.salzburgmuseum.at.

▲▲Mozart's Birthplace (Geburtshaus)

The Mozart family lived here for 26 years. Of the seven Mozart children born here, two survived. Wolfgang was born here in 1756. It was in this building that he composed most of his boy-genius works. Today it's the most popular Mozart sight in town—for fans, it's almost a pilgrimage. Shuffling through with all the crowds, you'll peruse three floors of rooms with exhibits displaying paintings, letters, personal items, and lots of facsimiles, all attempting to bring life to the Mozart story. There's no audioguide, but everything's described in English.

Cost and Hours: €10, €17 combo-ticket with Mozart's Residence in New Town, daily 9:00-17:30, July-Aug until 20:00, Getreidegasse 9, tel. 0662/844-313, www.mozarteum.at.

Visiting Mozart's Birthplace: Start by walking to the top

floor, where you enter the Mozart family apartment—furnished only with the violin given to him at age six. This section introduces Mozart's family, shows you the room where he was born, tells of his wife's and children's fates after his death, and tries to explain his enduring fame. Next is an exhibition on his life in Vienna, and a room of computer terminals with a wonderful program allowing you to see his handwritten scores and hear them performed at the same time (Mozart's Residence, across town, has the same terminals). The middle floor includes a room of dioramas showing stage sets for Mozart's operas and an old clavichord he supposedly composed on. (A predecessor of the more complicated piano, the clavichord's keys hit the strings with a simple teeter-totter motion that allows you to play very softly—ideal for composers living in tight apartment quarters.) The lower-floor exhibit takes you on the road with the child prodigy, and gives a slice-of-life portrait of Salzburg during Mozart's time, including a bourgeois living room furnished much as the Mozart family's would have been.

If I had to choose between Mozart's birthplace *(Geburtshaus)* and his residence *(Wohnhaus)*, I'd go with the birthplace, since its exhibits are more extensive and educational. If you're truly interested in Mozart and his times, take advantage of the combi-ticket and see both. If Mozart isn't important to you, skip both museums and concentrate on the city's other sights and glorious natural surroundings.

Atop the Cliffs Above the Old Town

Atop the Mönchsberg—the mini-mountain that rises behind the Old Town—is a tangle of paved walking paths with great views, a hostel with a pleasant café/restaurant, a modern art museum, a neighborhood of very fancy homes, and one major sight (the Hohensalzburg Fortress, perched on the Festungsberg, the Mönchsberg's southern arm). You can walk up from several points in town, including Festungsgasse (behind the cathedral), Toscaninihof, and the Augustiner Bräustübl beer garden. At the west end of the Old Town, the Mönchsberg elevator whisks you up to the top for a couple euros. The funicular directly up to the fortress is expensive, and worthwhile only if you plan to visit the fortress, which is included in the funicular ticket.

▲▲Hohensalzburg Fortress (Festung)

Construction of Hohensalzburg Fortress was begun by Archbishop Gebhard of Salzburg as a show of the Catholic Church's power (see sidebar). Built on a rock (called Festungsberg) 400 feet above the Salzach River, this fortress was never really used. That was the idea. It was a good investment—so foreboding, nobody attacked the town for nearly a thousand years. The city was never taken by force, but when Napoleon stopped by, Salzburg wisely surrendered. After a stint as a military barracks,

Battlefield Salzburg: Popes vs. Emperors

Salzburg is so architecturally impressive today to a great degree because of the Roman Catholic Church. This town was on the frontline of a centuries-long power struggle between Church and emperor. The town's mighty Hohensalzburg Fortress—a symbol of the Church's determination to assert its power here—was built around 1100, just as the conflict was heating up.

The medieval church-state argument, called the "Lay Investiture Controversy," was a classic tug-of-war between a series of popes and Holy Roman Emperors. The prize: the right to appoint (or "invest") church officials in the Holy Roman Emperor's domain. (Although called "Holy," the empire was headed not by priests, but by secular—or "lay"—rulers.)

The Church impinged on the power of secular leaders in several ways: Their subjects' generous tithes went to Rome, leaving less for the emperor to tax. In many areas, the Church was the biggest landowner (people willed their land to the Church in return for prayers for their salvation). And the pope's appointees weren't subject to secular local laws. Holy Roman Emperors were plenty powerful, but not as powerful as the Church.

In 1075, Emperor Henry IV bucked the system, appointing his own set of church officials and boldly renouncing Gregory VII as pope. In retaliation, Gregory excommunicated both Henry and the bishops he'd appointed. One of Henry's chief detractors was Salzburg's pope-appointed archbishop, Gebhard, who started construction of Hohensalzburg Fortress in a face-off with the defiant emperor.

The German nobility seized on the conflict as an opportunity to rebel, seizing royal property and threatening to elect a new emperor. To placate the nobles, Henry sought to regain the Church's favor. In January of 1077, Henry traveled south to Italy—supposedly crossing the Alps barefoot and in a monk's hair-shirt—to Canossa, where the pope was holed up. The emperor knelt in the snow outside the castle gate for three days, begging the pope's forgiveness. (To this day, the phrase "go to Canossa" is used to refer to any act of humility.)

But the German princes continued their revolt, electing their own king (Henry's brother-in-law, Rudolf of Rheinfelden). Henry's reconciliation with the Church was brief: In short order he named an antipope (Clement III), killed Rudolf in battle, and invaded Rome. Archbishop Gebhard was forced out of Salzburg and spent a decade in exile, raising forces against Henry in an attempt to reclaim the Salzburg archdiocese.

The back-and-forth continued until 1122, when a power-sharing accord was finally reached between Henry's son, Emperor Henry V, and Pope Calistus II.

SALZBURG & BERCHTESGADEN

the fortress was opened to the public in the 1860s by Habsburg Emperor Franz Josef. Today, it remains one of Europe's mightiest castles, dominating Salzburg's skyline and offering incredible views, as well as a couple mediocre museums.

Cost: You'll pay to enter the castle, whether on foot (the walk is easier than it looks), or, for a couple euros more, by funicular.

On Foot: If you walk up to the fortress (or walk over from the Mönchsberg, reachable either by stairs from Toscaninihof or the elevator from the west end of Griesgasse/southern end of Gstättengasse), you'll pay €7.80 to enter (at the fortress gate), which includes entry to the fortress grounds, all the museums inside, and your funicular ride down—whether you want it or not. Within one hour of the museums' closing time, the entry price is reduced to €4. After the museums close, you can't enter on foot, but you can exit (the door will lock behind you) and walk down. To visit the fortress in the evening for a concert, you'll need to take the funicular.

Via Funicular: Most visitors enter the fortress by taking a one-minute trip on the funicular *(Festungsbahn)*. The lower station is on Festungsgasse, which is just off Kapitelplatz, behind Salzburg's cathedral. The top end of the funicular is inside the fortress complex. Your round-trip funicular ticket includes admission to the fortress grounds and all the museums inside—whether you want to see them or not (€11, €25.50 family ticket). If you board the funicular within one hour of the museums' closing time (i.e., May-Sept after 18:00 or Oct-April after 16:00), you pay only €8, or €6.50 if you don't want to take the funicular down; this is a good deal if you only want a glimpse of the museums. After the museums have closed, the funicular continues to run until about 21:30 (later if there's a concert) and costs €4 round-trip, or €2.50 one-way.

Hours: The museums in the fortress are open daily year-round (May-Sept 9:00-19:00, Oct-April 9:30-17:00, tel. 0662/8424-3011). The grounds of the fortress stay open and the funicular continues to run even after the museums close—usually until about 21:30 or 22:00, especially when there's a concert (300 nights a year).

Concerts: The fortress serves as a venue for evening concerts (the Festungskonzerte), which are held in the old banquet rooms on the upper floor of the palace museum. A concert is a good way to see the fortress without noisy crowds.

Café: The cafés to either side of the upper funicular station are a great place to nibble on apple strudel while taking in the jaw-dropping view.

Orientation: Inside the fortress, your ticket lets you into two exhibits, labeled #1 and #2: The first is a tour of the fortifications, while the second is a historical museum inside the "palace" in the fortress courtyard. The courtyards themselves offer a few other things to see, as well as great views in several directions.

Ø Self-Guided Tour: At the top of the funicular, most visitors turn left. Instead, head right and down the stairs to bask in the **view** to the south (away from town) toward the Alps, either from the café or the view terrace a little farther along. (You'll enjoy superb city views later on this tour.)

• *Once you're done snapping photos, walk through the arches into the fortress courtyard and go left (uphill). From here, you'll make a clockwise circuit around the courtyard. The first sight you'll come to, labeled #1, is the...*

Fortress Interior: Here you get to see a few rooms in the outer fortifications. Only 40 people are allowed in at a time, usually with an escort who gives a 30-minute commentary. While the interior furnishings are mostly gone—taken by Napoleon—the rooms themselves survived fairly well (no one wanted to live here after 1500, so the building was never modernized). Your tour includes a room dedicated to the art of "enhanced interrogation" (to use American military jargon)—filled with tools of that gruesome trade. The highlight is the commanding city view from the top of a tower. In summer, there can be a long wait to get in.

• *Continue uphill to sight #2—the fortress's "palace" (labeled* Inneres Schloss). *Immediately inside, visit the...*

Marionette Exhibit: Two fun rooms show off this local tradition. Three videos play continuously: two with peeks at Salzburg's ever-enchanting Marionette Theater performances of Mozart classics (described under "Music in Salzburg," later) and one with a behind-the-scenes look at the action. Give the hands-on marionette a whirl.

• *Head down the hall and up the stairs following* Festungsmuseum *signs to the...*

Fortress Museum (Festungsmuseum): The lower floor of this spacious museum has exhibits on the history of the fortress, from music to torture. One room explains how they got all this stuff up here, while another has copies of the pencil sketches for the Salzburg Panorama (described earlier). On the top floor are three pretty ceremonial rooms, including the one where the evening concerts are held. (Check out the colorfully painted tile stove in the far room.) The rest of the top floor is given over to the Rainer Regiments Museum, dedicated to the Salzburg soldiers who fought mountain-to-mountain on the Italian front during World War I.

• *Exit the museum and continue on out into the...*

Fortress Courtyard: The courtyard was the main square for the medieval fortress's 1,000-some residents, who could be self-sufficient when necessary. The square was ringed by the shops of craftsmen, blacksmiths, bakers, and so on. The well dipped into a rain-fed cistern. As you enter, look to your left to see the well-described remains of a recently excavated Romanesque chapel. The current church is dedicated to St. George, the protector of horses (logical for an army church) and decorated by fine red marble reliefs (c. 1502). Behind the church is the top of the old lift (still in use) that helped supply the fortress. Under the archway next to it are the steps that lead back into the city, or to the paths across the Mönchsberg.

• *Near the chapel, turn left into the Kuenburg Bastion (once a garden) for fine city views.*

Kuenburg Bastion: Notice how the fortress has three parts: the original section inside the courtyard, the vast whitewashed walls (built when the fortress was a residence), and the lower, beefed-up fortifications (added for extra defense against the expected Ottoman invasion). Survey Salzburg from here and think about fortifying an important city by using nature. The Mönchsberg (the cliffs to the left) and Festungsberg (the little

mountain you're on) naturally cradle the Old Town, with just a small gate between the ridge and the river needed to bottle up the place. The New Town across the river needed a bit of a wall arcing from the river to its hill. Back then, only one bridge crossed the Salzach into town, and it had a fortified gate.

• *Go back inside the fortress courtyard. Our tour is over. Either circle back to where you entered and ride the funicular down, or go through the archway and down the stairs if you prefer to hike back to town or along the top of the Mönchsberg (see "Mönchsberg Walk," below). If you take the funicular down, don't miss (at the bottom of the lift) the...*

Alm River Canal Exhibit: At the base of the funicular, below the fortress, is this fine little exhibit on how the river was broken into five smaller streams—powering the city until steam took up the energy-supply baton. Pretend it's the year 1200 and follow (by video) the flow of the water from the river through the canals, into the mills, and as it's finally dumped into the Salzach River. (The exhibit technically requires a funicular ticket—but you can see it unofficially by slipping through the exit at the back of the amber shop, next door to the funicular terminal.)

Mönchsberg Sights
▲Mönchsberg Walk

The paved, wooded walking path between the Mönchsberg elevator and the fortress is less than a mile long and makes for a great 30-minute hike. The mountain is small, and frequent signposts direct you between all the key points, so it's hard to get lost. The views of Salzburg are the main draw, but there's also a modern art museum, mansions to ogle, and a couple of places to eat or enjoy a scenic drink.

You can do this walk in either direction. (To save a few euros—and the climb—visit the fortress last: Take the Mönchsberg elevator, walk across to the fortress, pay the reduced entry price at the fortress gate, see the fortress, then take the funicular down—included in your fortress ticket.) The Mönchsberg **elevator** *(Aufzug)* starts from Gstättengasse/Griesgasse on the west side of the Old Town (€2.10 one-way, €3.40 round-trip, normally Mon 8:00-19:00, Tue-Sun 8:00-24:00).

You can also **climb** up and down under your own power; this saves a few more euros (no matter which direction you go). Paths or stairs lead up from the Augustiner beer hall, Toscaninihof (near the Salzburg Festival concert halls), and Festungsgasse (at the base of the fortress).

Cafés: The elevator deposits you right at Mönchsberg 32, a sleek modern café/bar/restaurant adjacent to the modern art museum and a fine place for a drink or splurge meal (they serve breakfast until 16:00). From there, it's a five-minute walk to the rustic Gasthaus Stadtalm café, with wooden picnic tables and a one-with-nature allure. Next to the Stadtalm is a surviving section of Salzburg's medieval wall; pass under the wall and walk left along it to a tableau showing how the wall once looked.

Museum of Modern Art on Mönchsberg

The modern-art museum, which features temporary exhibits, is right at the top of the Mönchsberg elevator.

Cost and Hours: €8, Tue-Sun 10:00-18:00, Wed until 20:00, closed Mon.

In the New Town, North of the River

The following sights are across the river from the Old Town. I've connected them with walking instructions.

• *Begin at the Makartsteg pedestrian bridge, where you can survey the...*

Salzach River

Salzburg's river is called "salt river" not because it's salty, but because of the precious cargo it once carried—the salt mines of Hallein are just nine miles upstream. Salt could be transported from here all the way to the Danube, and on to the Mediterranean via the Black Sea. The riverbanks and roads were built when the river was regulated in the 1850s. Before that, the Salzach was much wider and slower moving. Houses opposite the Old Town fronted the river with docks and "garages" for boats. The grand buildings just past the bridge (with their elegant promenades and cafés) were built on reclaimed land in the late 19th century.

Scan the cityscape. Notice all the churches. Salzburg, nick-named the "Rome of the North," has 38 Catholic churches (plus two Protestant churches and a synagogue). Find the five streams gushing into the river. These date from the 13th century, when the river was split into five canals running through the town to power its mills. The Stein Hotel (upstream, just left of next bridge) has a popular roof-terrace café. Downstream, notice the Museum of Modern Art atop the Mönchsberg, with a view restaurant and a faux castle (actually a water reservoir). The Romanesque bell tower with the green copper dome in the distance is the Augus-tine church, site of the best beer hall in town (the Augustiner Bräustübl).

• Cross the bridge, pass the recommended Café Bazar (a fine place for a drink), walk two blocks inland, and take a left past the heroic statues into...

▲Mirabell Gardens and Palace (Schloss)

These bubbly gardens, laid out in 1730 for the prince archbishop, have been open to the public since 1850 (thanks to Emperor Franz

Josef, who was rattled by the popular revolutions of 1848). The gardens are free and open until dusk. The palace is open only as a concert venue (ex-plained later). The statues and the arbor (far left) were featured in *The Sound of Music*.

Walk through the gardens to the palace and find the statue of the horse (on the river side of the palace). Look back, enjoy the garden/cathedral/castle view, and imagine how the prince archbishop must have reveled in a vista that reminded him of all his secular and religious power.

The rearing **Pegasus statue** (rare and very well-balanced) is the site of a famous *Sound of Music* scene where the kids all danced before lining up on the stairs with Maria (30 yards farther along). The steps lead to a small mound in the park (made of rubble from a former theater).

Nearest the horse, stairs lead between two lions to a pair of tough dwarfs (early volleyball players with spiked mittens) welcom-ing you to Salzburg's **Dwarf Park.** Cross the elevated walk (noticing the city's fortified walls) to meet statues of a dozen dwarfs who served the prince archbishop—modeled after real people with real fashions in about 1600. This was Mannerist art, from the hyper-realistic age that followed the Renaissance.

There's plenty of **music** here, both in the park and in the palace. A brass band plays free park concerts (May-Aug Sun at 10:30). To properly enjoy the lavish Mirabell Palace—once the prince archbishop's summer palace and now the seat of the mayor—get a ticket to a Schlosskonzerte (my favorite venue for a classical concert).

• *Now go a long block southeast to Makartplatz, where, opposite the big and bright Hotel Bristol, you'll find...*

▲Mozart's Residence (Wohnhaus)

Mozart's second home (his family moved here when he was 17) is less interesting than the house where he was born, but it's also roomier, less crowded, and comes with an informative audioguide and a 30-minute narrated slideshow. The building, bombed in World War II, is a reconstruction.

Cost and Hours: €10, €17 combo-ticket with Mozart's Birthplace in Old Town, daily 9:00-17:30, July-Aug until 20:00, allow at least an hour for visit, Makartplatz 8, tel. 0662/8742-2740, www.mozarteum.at. Behind the ticket desk is the free Ton und Filmsammlung, an archive of historic concerts on video (Mon-Tue and Fri 9:00-13:00, Wed-Thu 13:00-17:00, closed Sat-Sun).

Visiting Mozart's Residence: The exhibit—seven rooms on one floor—starts in the main hall, which was used by the Mo-

zarts to entertain Salzburg's high society. Here, you can see the museum's prize possession, Mozart's very own piano. Notice the family portrait (c. 1780) on the wall, showing Mozart with his sister Nannerl, their father, and their mother—who'd died two years earlier in Paris. Mozart also had silly crude bull's-eyes made for the pop-gun game popular at the time (licking an "arse," Wolfgang showed his disdain for the rigors of high society). The rest of the seven rooms feature real artifacts that explore his loves, his intellectual pursuits, his travels, and his family life. At the end, the 30-minute slideshow runs twice an hour, with alternating German/English narration (confirm times when you enter, English usually starts around :40 after the hour).

This museum offers the same computer program as Mozart's

Birthplace does, allowing you to see handwritten scores scroll along while actually listening to the same music.

• *From here, you can walk a few blocks back to the main bridge (Staatsbrücke), where you'll find the Platzl, a square once used as a hay market. Pause to enjoy the kid-pleasing little fountain. Near the fountain (with your back to the river), Steingasse leads darkly to the right.*

▲Steingasse Stroll

This street, a block in from the river, is wonderfully tranquil and free of Salzburg's touristy crush. Inviting cocktail bars along here come alive at night.

The kid-pleasing fountain where Linzergasse meets Steingasse marks an important intersection: where the road to Vienna (Linzergasse) hit the road to Italy (Steingasse). From here, traders and pilgrims would look across the river and see the impressive domed University Church (modeled after Vienna's Karlskirche) and know they were entering an important place. Heading up dank, narrow Steingasse, you get a rare glimpse of medieval Salzburg. It's not the church's Salzburg of grand squares and Baroque facades, but the people's Salzburg, of cramped quarters and humble cobbled lanes.

Stop at #9 and look across the river into the Old Town; this is where the city's original bridge once connected Salzburg's two halves. According to the plaque (of questionable veracity) at #9, this is where Joseph Mohr, who wrote the words to "Silent Night," was born—poor and illegitimate—in 1792. There is no doubt, however, that the popular Christmas carol was composed and first sung in the village of Oberndorf, just outside of Salzburg, in 1818. Stairs lead from near here up to a 17th-century Capuchin monastery.

On the next corner, the wall is gouged out. This scar was left even after the building was restored, to serve as a reminder of the American GI who tried to get a tank down this road during a visit to the town brothel—two blocks farther up Steingasse. Within steps of here is the art cinema (showing movies in their original language) and four recommended bars.

At #19, find the carvings on the old door. Some say these are notices from beggars to the begging community (more numerous after post-Reformation religious wars, which forced many people out of their homes and towns)—a kind of "hobo code" indicating whether the residents would give or not. Trace the wires of the old-fashioned doorbells to the highest floors.

Farther on, you step through the old fortified gate (at #20) and find a commanding Salzburg view across the river. Notice the red dome marking the oldest nunnery in the German-speaking world (established in 712) under the fortress and to the left. The real Maria, who inspired *The Sound of Music,* taught in this nunnery's school. In 1927, she and Captain von Trapp were married in the church you see here (not the church filmed in the movie). He was 47. She was 22. Hmmmm.

From here look back, above the arch you just passed through, and up at part of the town's medieval fortification. The coat of arms on the arch is of the prince archbishop who paid Bavaria a huge ransom to stay out of the Thirty Years' War (smart move). He then built this fortification (in 1634) in anticipation of rampaging armies from both sides.

Today, this street is for making love, not war. The Maison de Plaisir (a few doors down, at #24) has for centuries been a Salzburg brothel. But the climax of this walk is more touristic.

• *For a grand view, head back to the Platzl and the bridge, enter the Stein Hotel (left corner, overlooking the river), and ride the elevator to…*

Stein Terrasse

This café offers one of the best views in town. Hidden from the tourist crush, it's a trendy, professional, local scene. You can discreetly peek at the view, enjoy a drink or light meal, or come back later to gaze into the eyes of your travel partner as you sip a nightcap (small snacks, indoor/outdoor seating, daily 9:00-24:00).

• *Back at the Platzl and the bridge, you can head straight up Linzergasse (away from the river) into a neighborhood packed with recommended accommodations, as well as our final New Town sight, the…*

▲St. Sebastian Cemetery

Wander through this quiet oasis. Mozart is buried in Vienna, his mom's in Paris, and his sister is in Salzburg's Old Town (St. Peter's)—but Wolfgang's wife Constanze ("Constantia") and his father Leopold are buried here (from the black iron gate entrance on Linzergasse, walk 19 paces and look left). When Prince Archbishop Wolf Dietrich had the cemetery moved from around the cathedral and put here, across the river, people didn't like it. To help popularize it, he had his own mausoleum built as its centerpiece.

Continue straight past the Mozart tomb to this circular building (English description at door). In the corner to the left of the entrance is the tomb of the Renaissance scientist and physician Paracelsus, best known for developing laudanum as a painkiller.

Cost and Hours: Free, daily April-Oct 9:00-18:00, Nov-March 9:00-16:00, entry at Linzergasse 43 in summer; in winter go around the corner to the right, through the arch at #37, and around the building to the doorway under the blue seal.

Near Salzburg

▲▲Hellbrunn Palace and Gardens

In about 1610, Prince Archbishop Sittikus decided he needed a lavish palace with a vast and ornate garden purely for pleasure (I imagine after meditating on stewardship and Christ-like values). He built this summer palace and hunting lodge, and just loved inviting his VIP guests from throughout Europe for fun with his trick fountains. Today, Hellbrunn is a popular sight for its formal garden (one of the oldest in Europe, with a gazebo made famous by *The Sound of Music*), amazing fountains, palace exhibits, and the excuse it offers to simply get out of the city.

Cost and Hours: €10.50 ticket includes fountain tour and palace audioguide, daily May-Sept 9:00-17:30, July-Aug until 21:00—but tours from 18:00 on don't include the castle (which closes in the evening), April and Oct 9:00-16:30, these are last tour times, closed Nov-March, tel. 0662/820-3720, www.hellbrunn.at.

Getting There: Hellbrunn is nearly four miles south of Salzburg.

By Bus: Take bus #25 from the train station or the Rathaus stop by the Staatsbrücke bridge (2-3/hour, 20 minutes). Get off at the Schloss Hellbrunn stop.

By Bike: In good weather, the trip out to Hellbrunn makes for a pleasant 30-minute bike excursion (see "Riverside or Meadow Bike Ride," later, and ask for a map when you rent your bike).

Visiting the Palace: Upon arrival, buy your **fountain tour** ticket and get a tour time. Tours generally go on the half-hour. The 40-minute English/German tours take you laughing and scrambling through a series of amazing 17th-century garden settings with lots of splashy fun and a guide who seems almost sadistic in the joy he has in soaking his group. (Hint: When you see a wet place, cover your camera.) If there's a wait until your tour, you can see the palace first.

With the help of the included audioguide, wander through the

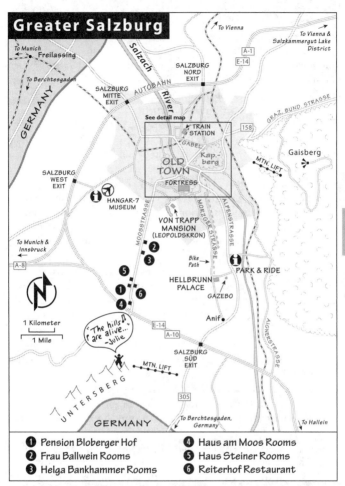

Greater Salzburg

To Munich — Freilassing

To Vienna

To Vienna & Salzkammergut Lake District

To Berchtesgaden

GERMANY

Salzach River

AUTOBAHN

SALZBURG MITTE EXIT

SALZBURG NORD EXIT

A-1
E-14

158

GRAZ. BUND. STRASSE

See detail map

TRAIN STATION

GABEL

Kapuberg

Gaisberg

MTN. LIFT

OLD TOWN

SALZBURG WEST EXIT

FORTRESS

HANGAR-7 MUSEUM

MOOSSTRASSE

MORZGER STRASSE

ALPENSTRASSE

VON TRAPP MANSION (LEOPOLDSKRON)

To Munich & Innsbruck

A-8

②

③

⑤

① ⑥

④

Bike Path

HELLBRUNN PALACE

GAZEBO

PARK & RIDE

AIGNERSTRASSE

1 Kilometer
1 Mile

"The hills are alive..." –Julie

E-14
A-10

Anif

UNTERSBERG

MTN. LIFT

SALZBURG SÜD EXIT

305

GERMANY

To Berchtesgaden, Germany

To Hallein

① Pension Bloberger Hof
② Frau Ballwein Rooms
③ Helga Bankhammer Rooms
④ Haus am Moos Rooms
⑤ Haus Steiner Rooms
⑥ Reiterhof Restaurant

SALZBURG & BERCHTESGADEN

modest **palace** exhibit to the sounds of shrieking fountain-taunted tourists below. The palace was built in a style inspired by the Venetian architect Palladio, who was particularly popular around 1600, and it quickly became a cultural destination. This was the era when the aristocratic ritual was to go hunting in the morning (hence the wildlife-themed decor) and enjoy an opera in the evening. The first opera north of the Alps, imported from Italy, was performed here. The decor is Mannerist (between Renaissance and Baroque), with faux antiquities and lots of surprising moments—intentional irregularities were in vogue after the strict logic, balance, and Greek-inspired symmetry of the Renaissance. (For example, the main hall is not in the palace's center, but at the far end.) The palace exhibit also explains the impressive 17th-century hydraulic engineering that let gravity power the intricate fountains.

After the fountain tour you're also free to wander the delightful **garden**. Pop out to see the **gazebo** made famous by the "Sixteen Going On Seventeen" song from *The Sound of Music* (relocated here in the 1990s; look for *Sound-of-Music Pavilion* signs).

▲▲Riverside or Meadow Bike Ride

The Salzach River has smooth, flat, and scenic bike lanes along each side (thanks to medieval tow paths—cargo boats would float downstream and be dragged back up by horses). On a sunny day, I can think of no more shout-worthy escape from the city.

Perhaps the most pristine, meadow-filled farm-country route is the nearly four-mile path along Hellbrunner Allee; it's an easy ride with a worthy destination (Hellbrunn Palace, listed above): From the middle of town, head along the river on Rudolfskai, with the river on your left and the fortress on your right. After passing the last bridge at the edge of the Old Town (Nonntaler Brücke), cut inland along Petersbrunnstrasse, until you reach the university and Akademiestrasse. Beyond it find the start of Freisaalweg, which becomes the delightful Hellbrunner Allee bike path...which leads directly to the palace (paralleling Morzgerstrasse). For a nine-mile ride, continue on to Hallein (where you can tour a salt mine—see next listing; if heading to Hallein directly from Salzburg, head out from the north bank of the river, i.e. the New Town side, which is more scenic).

Even a quickie ride across town is a great Salzburg experience. In the evening, the riverbanks are a world of floodlit spires. For bike rental information, see "Getting Around Salzburg—By Bike," earlier.

▲Hallein Bad Dürrnberg Salt Mine (Salzbergwerke)

You'll be pitched plenty of different salt-mine excursions from Salzburg, all of which cost substantial time and money. One's plenty.

This salt-mine tour (above the town of Hallein, 9 miles from Salzburg) is a good choice. Wearing white overalls and sliding down the sleek wooden chutes, you'll cross underground from Austria into Germany while learning about the old-time salt-mining process. The tour entails lots of time on your feet as you walk from cavern to cavern, learning the  history of the mine by watching a series of video skits with an actor channeling Prince Archbishop Wolf Dietrich. The visit also includes a "Celtic Village" open-air museum.

Cost and Hours: €19, €17 if purchased online, allow 2.5 hours for the visit, daily April-Oct 9:00-17:00, Nov-Dec and Feb-March 10:00-15:00—these are last tour times, closed Jan, English-speaking guides—but let your linguistic needs be known loud and clear, tel. 06132/200-8511, www.salzwelten.at.

Getting There: The convenient *Salz Erlebnis* ticket from Salzburg's train station covers your transport and admission in one money-saving round-trip ticket (€29, buy ticket at train station, no discount with railpass; covers train to Hallein, then 11-minute ride on bus #41 to salt mines in Bad Dürrnberg, runs hourly, check schedules when buying tickets).

Hangar-7

This purpose-built hangar at the Salzburg airport houses the car-and-aircraft collection of Dietrich Mateschitz, the flamboyant founder of the Red Bull energy-drink empire. Under the hangar's modern steel-and-glass dome are 20 or so glittering planes and racecars, plus several pretentious bars, cafés, and restaurants, all designed to brandish the Red Bull "culture." To learn about what's on display you can borrow an iPod Touch with English information, or get information on the iPads posted by each exhibit.

Mateschitz is Salzburg's big personality these days: He has a mysterious mansion at the edge of town, sponsors the local "Red Bull" soccer and hockey teams, owns several chic Salzburg eateries and cocktail bars, and employs 6,000 mostly good-looking people. He seems much like the energy drink that made him rich and powerful—a high-energy, anything's-possible cultural Terminator.

Cost and Hours: Free, daily 9:00-22:00, bus #8 from Hanuschplatz or #2 from Mirabellplatz to the Salzburg airport, tel. 0662/2197, www.hangar-7.com.

Eating: At the hangar, the Mayday Bar serves experimental food, and Restaurant Ikarus features a different well-known chef each month. (Mateschitz's recommended Carpe Diem cocktail bar, in the Old Town, is also Red Bullish.)

▲▲▲Hallstatt and Berchtesgaden

Rustic Hallstatt, crammed like a swallow's nest into the narrow shore between a lake and a steep mountainside, is a 2.5-hour bus or train ride from Salzburg. It's my favorite town in the scenic Salzkammergut Lake District. Berchtesgaden (covered later in this chapter) is equally scenic, and home to Hitler's Eagle's Nest and other interesting sights. Both of these towns make for busy but worthwhile side-trips from Salzburg, and both are easy enough to do on your own. But if you're on a quick schedule, taking an all-day bus tour to these places can be a good use of your time and money.

Music in Salzburg

▲▲Salzburg Festival (Salzburger Festspiele)

Each summer, from late July to the end of August, Salzburg hosts its famous Salzburg Festival, founded in 1920 to employ Vienna's musicians in the summer. This fun and festive time is crowded—a total of 200,000 tickets are sold to festival events annually—but there are usually plenty of beds (except for a few August weekends). Events take place primarily in three big halls: the Opera and Orchestra venues in the Festival House, and the Landes Theater, where German-language plays are performed. Tickets for the big festival events are generally expensive (€50-600) and sell out well in advance (bookable from January). Most tourists think they're "going to the Salzburg Festival" by seeing smaller non-festival events that go on during the festival weeks. For these lesser events, same-day tickets are normally available (the ticket office on Mozartplatz, in the TI, prints a daily list of concerts and charges a 30 percent fee to book them). For specifics on this year's festival schedule and tickets, visit www.salzburgfestival.at.

Music lovers in town during the festival who don't have tickets (or money) can still enjoy **Festival Nights,** a free series showing videos of previous festival performances, projected on a big screen on Kapitelplatz (behind the cathedral). It's a fun scene, with plenty of folding chairs and a food circus of temporary eateries; schedules are posted next to the screen.

▲▲Musical Events Year-Round

Salzburg is busy throughout the year, with 2,000 classical performances in its palaces and churches annually. Pick up the events calendar at the TI (free, bimonthly). I've never planned in advance, and I've enjoyed great concerts with every visit. Whenever you visit, you'll have a number of concerts (generally small chamber groups) to choose from. Here are some of the more accessible events:

Concerts at Hohensalzburg Fortress (Festungskonzerte)

Nearly nightly concerts—Mozart's greatest hits for beginners—are held atop Festungsberg, in the "prince's chamber" of the fortress, featuring small chamber groups (open seating after the first six more expensive rows, €32 or €39 plus €4 for the funicular; at 19:30, 20:00, or 20:30; doors open 30 minutes early, reserve at tel. 0662/825-858 or via www.salzburghighlights.at, pick up tickets at the door). The medieval-feeling chamber has windows overlooking the city, and the concert gives you a chance to enjoy the grand city view and a stroll through the castle courtyard. For €54, you can combine the concert with a four-course dinner (starts 2 hours before concert). The downside: Hearing Baroque music in an incongruously Gothic setting is not ideal.

Concerts at the Mirabell Palace (Schlosskonzerte)

The nearly nightly chamber music concerts at the Mirabell Palace are performed in a lavish Baroque setting. They come with more sophisticated programs and better musicians than the fortress concerts...and Baroque music flying around a Baroque hall is a happy bird in the right cage (open seating after the first five pricier rows, €31-37, usually at 20:00—but check flier for times, doors open one hour ahead, tel. 0662/848-586, www.salzburger-schlosskonzerte.at).

"Five O'Clock Concerts" (5-Uhr-Konzerte)

These concerts are cheaper, since they feature young artists. While the series is formally named after the brother of Joseph Haydn, it offers music from various masters. Performances are generally chamber music with a string trio playing original 18th-century instruments. Most are held in the Michael-Haydn-Museum next to St. Peter's Church in the Old Town (€12-15, June-Aug Tue and Thu at 17:00, no concerts in off-season, 45-60 minutes, tel. 0662/8445-7619, www.5-uhr-konzerte.com).

Mozart Piano Sonatas

St. Peter's Abbey hosts these concerts each weekend. This short (45-minute) and inexpensive concert is ideal for families (€18, €9 for children, €45 for a family of four, Fri and Sat at 19:00 year-round, in the abbey's Romanesque Hall—a.k.a. Romanischer Saal, mobile 0664-423-5645).

Marionette Theater

Salzburg's much-loved marionette theater offers operas with spellbinding marionettes and recorded music. A troupe of 10 puppeteers—actors themselves—brings to life the artfully created puppets at the end of their five-foot strings. The 180 performances a year alternate between *The Sound of Music* and various German-language operas (with handy superscripts in English). While the 300-plus-seat venue is forgettable, the art of the marionettes enchants adults and children alike (€18-35, kids-€14, May-Sept nearly nightly at 17:00 or 19:30, near Mozart's Residence at Schwarzstrasse 24, tel. 0662/872-406, www.marionetten.at). For a sneak preview, check out the videos playing at the marionette exhibit up in the fortress—and on their website.

Mozart Dinner Concert

For those who'd like some classical music but would rather not sit through a concert, the recommended Stiftskeller St. Peter restaurant offers a traditional candlelit meal with Mozart's greatest hits performed by a string quartet and singers in historic costumes gavotting among the tables. In this elegant Baroque setting, tourists clap between movements and get three courses of food (from Mozart-era recipes) mixed with three 20-minute courses of crowd-pleasing music—structured much as such evenings were

The Sound of Music Debunked

Rather than visit the real-life sights from the life of Maria von Trapp and family, most tourists want to see the places where Hollywood chose to film this fanciful story. Local guides are happy not to burst any *S.O.M.* pilgrim's bubble, but keep these points in mind:

- "Edelweiss" is not a cherished Austrian folk tune or national anthem. Like all the "Austrian" music in *The S.O.M.*, it was composed for Broadway by Rodgers and Hammerstein. It was the last composition that the famed team wrote together, as Hammerstein died in 1960—nine months after the musical opened.
- *The S.O.M.* implies that Maria was devoutly religious throughout her life, but Maria's foster parents raised her as a socialist and atheist. Maria discovered her religious calling while studying to be a teacher. After completing school, she joined the convent not as a nun, but as a novitiate (that is, she hadn't taken her vows yet).
- Maria's position was not as governess to all the children, as portrayed in the musical, but specifically as governess and teacher for the Captain's second-oldest daughter, also called Maria, who was bedridden with rheumatic fever.
- The Captain didn't run a tight domestic ship. In fact, his seven children were as unruly as most. But he did use a whistle to call them—each kid was trained to respond to a certain pitch.
- Though the von Trapp family did have seven children, the show changed all their names and even their genders. As an adult, Rupert, the eldest child, responded to the often-asked question, "Which one are you?" with a simple, "I'm Liesl!"
- The family didn't escape by hiking to Switzerland (which is a five-hour drive away). Rather, they pretended to go on one of their frequent mountain hikes. With only the possessions in their backpacks, they "hiked" all the way to the train station (it was at the edge of their estate) and took a train

in Baroque-era times (€54, €9 discount for Mozart-lovers who book direct with this book, music starts nightly at 20:00—arrive at 19:30, dress is "smart casual," call to reserve at 0662/828-695, www.mozartdinnerconcert.com).

Music at Mass

Each Sunday morning, three great churches offer a Mass, generally with glorious music. The **Salzburg Cathedral** is likely your best bet for fine music to worship by, and many Masses are followed by a free organ concert (10:00 Mass, music program at www.kirchen.net/dommusik). Nearby (just outside Domplatz, to Italy. The movie scene showing them climbing into Switzerland was actually filmed near Berchtesgaden, Germany... home to Hitler's Eagle's Nest, and certainly not a smart place to flee to.

- The actual von Trapp family house exists...but it's not the one in the film. The mansion in the movie is actually two different buildings—one used for the front, the other for the back. The interiors were all filmed on Hollywood sets.

- For the film, Boris Levin designed a reproduction of the Nonnberg Abbey courtyard so faithful to the original (down to its cobblestones and stained-glass windows) that many still believe the cloister scenes were really shot at the abbey. And no matter what you hear in Salzburg, the graveyard scene (in which the von Trapps hide from the Nazis) was also filmed on the Fox lot.

- In 1956, a German film producer offered Maria $10,000 for the rights to her book. She asked for royalties, too, and a share of the profits. The agent claimed that German law forbids film companies from paying royalties to foreigners (Maria had by then become a US citizen). She agreed to the contract and unknowingly signed away all film rights to her story. Only a few weeks later, he offered to pay immediately if she would accept $9,000 in cash. Because it was more money than the family had seen in all of their years of singing, she accepted the deal. Later, she discovered the agent had swindled them—no such law existed.

 Rodgers, Hammerstein, and other producers gave the von Trapps a percentage of the royalties, even though they weren't required to—but it was a fraction of what they otherwise would have earned. But Maria wasn't bitter. She said, "The great good the film and the play are doing to individual lives is far beyond money."

with the pointy green spire), the **Franciscan Church** is the locals' choice and is enthusiastic about its musical Masses (at 9:00, www.franziskanerkirche-salzburg.at—click on "Programm"). **St. Peter's Church** sometimes has music (at 10:15, www.stift-stpeter.at—click on "Kirchenmusik," then "Jahresprogramm"). For more, see the Salzburg events guide (available at TIs) for details.

Free Brass Band Concert

A traditional brass band plays in the Mirabell Gardens (May-Aug Sun at 10:30).

Sleeping in Salzburg

Finding a room in Salzburg, even during its music festival (mid-July-Aug), is usually easy. Rates always rise significantly (20-30 percent) during the music festival, during Advent (four weeks leading up to Christmas, when street markets are at full blast) and usually around Easter. Unless otherwise noted, these higher "festival" prices do not appear in the ranges I've listed. Many places charge 10 percent extra for a one-night stay. Remember, to call Salzburg from Germany, dial 00-43 and then the number (minus the initial zero).

In the New Town, North of the River

These listings cluster around Linzergasse, a lively pedestrian shopping street that's a 15-minute walk or quick bus ride from the train station (for directions, see "Arrival in Salzburg," earlier) and a 10-minute walk to the Old Town. If you're coming from the Old Town, simply cross the main bridge (Staatsbrücke). Linzergasse is straight ahead. If driving, exit the highway at Salzburg-Nord, follow Vogelweiderstrasse straight to its end, and turn right. Parking is easy at the nearby Mirabell-Congress garage (€15/day, your hotel may be able to get you a €1-2 discount, Mirabellplatz).

$$ Altstadthotel Wolf-Dietrich, around the corner from Linzergasse on pedestrians-only Wolf-Dietrich-Strasse, has 40 well-located, tastefully plush rooms (half of them overlook St. Sebastian Cemetery; a third are in an annex across the street). It projects a big-hotel feeling—prices include a huge breakfast spread and an afternoon *Kaffee-und-Kuchen* snack—but has small-hotel prices (roughly Sb-€80, Db-€120, Tb-€145, rates vary with demand, family deals, readers of this book get a 10 percent discount on prevailing price—insist on this discount deducted from whatever price is offered that day, non-smoking, elevator, free guest computer and Wi-Fi, annex rooms have air-con, pool with loaner swimsuits, sauna, free DVD library, Wolf-Dietrich-Strasse 7, tel. 0662/871-275, www.salzburg-hotel.at, office@salzburg-hotel.at).

$$ Hotel Trumer Stube, well-located three blocks from the river just off Linzergasse, has 20 small, attractive rooms (Sb-€72.50, Db-€120, Tb-€151, Qb-€177; for best prices, email and ask for the best Rick Steves cash-only rate, €7.50/person less if you skip breakfast; non-smoking, elevator, free Wi-Fi, look for the flower boxes at Bergstrasse 6, tel. 0662/874-776, www.trumer-stube.at, info@trumer-stube.at, Vivienne).

Sleep Code

(€1 = about $1.30, country code: 43, area code: 0662)
S = Single, **D** = Double/Twin, **T** = Triple, **Q** = Quad, **b** = bathroom, **s** = shower only. Unless otherwise noted, credit cards are accepted, breakfast is included, and hotel staff speaks basic English.

To help you sort easily through these listings, I've divided the accommodations into three categories, based on the price for a standard double room with bath during high season:

$$$ **Higher Priced**—Most rooms €125 or more.
$$ **Moderately Priced**—Most rooms between €75-125.
$ **Lower Priced**—Most rooms €75 or less.

Prices can change without notice; verify the hotel's current rates online or by email. For the best prices, always book direct.

$$ Hotel Krone 1512, about five blocks from the river, offers 23 decent, simply furnished rooms in a building that dates to medieval times. Back-facing rooms are quieter than the streetside ones, and the hotel encourages you to skip the expensive breakfast. Cheapskates can save by requesting the near-windowless "student" double. Stay a while in their pleasant cliffside garden (Sb-€78, Db-€107-122, Tb-€151, Qb-€198, €14/person less if you skip breakfast—bakeries and cafés nearby, guests with this book get about 8 percent off if you reserve direct, elevator, free guest computer and Wi-Fi, Linzergasse 48, tel. 0662/872-300, www.krone1512.at, hotel@krone1512.at, run by Ukrainian-Austrian-Canadian Niko).

$$ Hotel Schwarzes Rössl is a university dorm that becomes a student-run hotel each July, August, and September. The location couldn't be handier. It looks like a normal hotel from the outside, and its 56 rooms, while a bit spartan, are as comfortable as a hotel on the inside (S-€58, Sb-€68, D-€84, Db-€104, Tb-€135, ask for Rick Steves discount, good breakfast, free guest computer and Wi-Fi in common areas, no rooms rented Oct-June, just off Linzergasse at Priesterhausgasse 6, tel. 0662/874-426, www.academiahotels.at, schwarzes.roessl@academiahotels.at).

$ Institute St. Sebastian is in a somewhat sterile but very clean historic building next to St. Sebastian Cemetery. From October through June, the institute houses female students from various Salzburg colleges and also rents 40 beds for travelers (men and women). From July through September, the students are gone, and they rent all 100 beds (including 20 twin rooms) to travelers. The building has spacious public areas, a roof garden, a piano

Salzburg Hotels

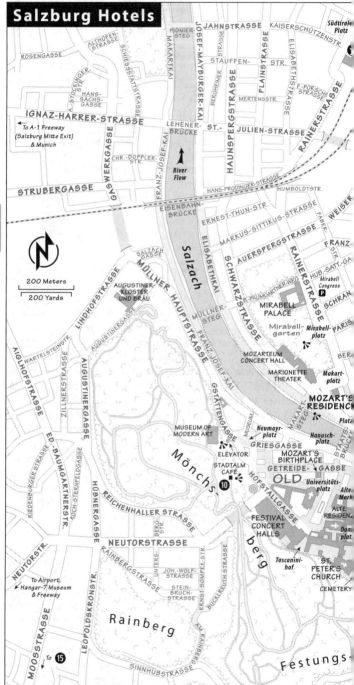

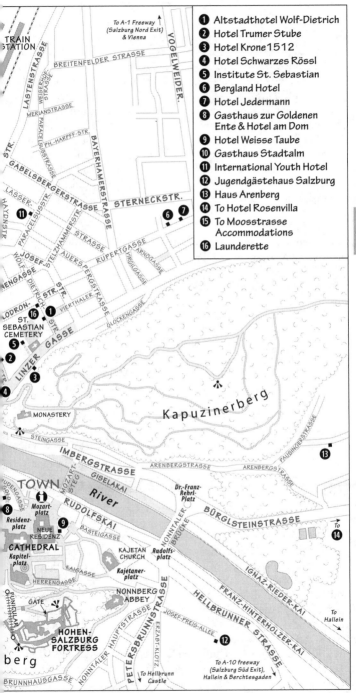

1 Altstadthotel Wolf-Dietrich
2 Hotel Trumer Stube
3 Hotel Krone 1512
4 Hotel Schwarzes Rössl
5 Institute St. Sebastian
6 Bergland Hotel
7 Hotel Jedermann
8 Gasthaus zur Goldenen Ente & Hotel am Dom
9 Hotel Weisse Taube
10 Gasthaus Stadtalm
11 International Youth Hotel
12 Jugendgästehaus Salzburg
13 Haus Arenberg
14 To Hotel Rosenvilla
15 To Moosstrasse Accommodations
16 Launderette

SALZBURG & BERCHTESGADEN

that guests are welcome to play, and some of the best rooms and dorm beds in town for the money. The immaculate doubles come with modern baths and head-to-toe twin beds (S-€38.50, Sb-€47, D-€60, Db-€75, Tb-€90, Qb-€102, €2/person extra for one-night stays, includes simple breakfast, elevator, non-smoking, pay cable Internet in rooms, pay Wi-Fi in common areas, self-service laundry-€4/load; reception is closed after 21:00 or in the afternoon off-season; Linzergasse 41, enter through arch at #37, tel. 0662/871-386, www.st-sebastian-salzburg.at, office@st-sebastian-salzburg.at). Students like the €22 bunks in 4- to 10-bed dorms (€2 less if you have sheets, no lockout, free lockers). You'll find self-service kitchens on each floor (fridge space is free; request a key). If you need parking, request it well in advance.

On Rupertgasse

These two similar hotels are about five blocks farther from the river on Rupertgasse—a breeze for drivers but with more street noise than the places on Linzergasse. They're both modern and well-run, with free on-site parking, making them good values if you don't mind being a 15-20-minute walk or quick bus ride from the Old Town. From the station, take bus #2 to the Vogelweiderstrasse stop.

$$ Bergland Hotel is charming and classy, with 18 comfortable neo-rustic rooms. It's a modern building, spacious and solid (Sb-€65, Db-€95-105 depending on size, big Db suites-€130, non-smoking, elevator, free guest computer and Wi-Fi, Rupertgasse 15, tel. 0662/872-318, www.berglandhotel.at, office@berglandhotel.at, Kuhn family).

$$ Hotel Jedermann, a few doors down, is simpler and larger. It's tastefully done and comfortable, with an artsy painted-concrete ambience, a backyard garden, and 30 rooms (Sb-€75, Db-€95, Tb-€120, Qb-€160, non-smoking, elevator, cable Internet in rooms, Wi-Fi in common areas, free guest computer, Rupertgasse 25, tel. 0662/873-2410, www.hotel-jedermann.com, office@hotel-jedermann.com, Herr und Frau Gmachl).

In the Old Town

These three hotels are perfectly located near Residenzplatz. While this area is car-restricted, your hotel can give you a code that lets you drive in to unload, pick up a map and parking instructions, and head for the €18-per-day garage in the mountain (punch the code into the gate near Mozartplatz). You can't actually drive into the narrow Goldgasse, but you can park to unload at the end of the street.

$$$ Gasthaus zur Goldenen Ente is in a 600-year-old building with medieval stone arches and narrow stairs on a pedestrian street in old Salzburg. Located above a good restaurant, most of its

22 rooms are modern and newly renovated—ask for one when you book. Ulrike, Franziska, and Anita run a tight ship for the absentee owners (Sb-€100, Db-€125; festival rates Sb-€125, Db-€180; extra person-€40, non-smoking, elevator, free guest computer and Wi-Fi in common areas, Goldgasse 10, tel. 0662/845-622, www.ente.at, hotel@ente.at).

$$$ Hotel am Dom, across from the Goldenen Ente, offers 15 chic, upscale rooms, some with their original wood-beam ceilings. Manager Josef promises his best rates to readers of this book who reserve direct and pay cash (Sb-€110-170, standard Db-€140-240, "superior" Db-€160-260, rates vary with demand, air-con, non-smoking, elevator; free guest computer, cable Internet, and Wi-Fi; Goldgasse 17, tel. 0662/842-765, www.hotelamdom.at, office@hotelamdom.at).

$$ Hotel Weisse Taube has 30 comfortable rooms in a quiet dark-wood 14th-century building, well-located about a block off Mozartplatz (Sb-€72-94, Db with shower-€109-145, bigger Db with bath-€129-192, extra bed-€30-35, higher prices are during festival, 10 percent discount with this book if you reserve direct and pay cash, elevator, pay guest computer and Wi-Fi, tel. 0662/842-404, Kaigasse 9, www.weissetaube.at, hotel@weissetaube.at).

Hostels

The Institute St. Sebastian, listed earlier, also has cheap dorm beds.

$ Gasthaus Stadtalm (a.k.a. the *Naturfreundehaus*) is a local version of a mountaineers' hut and a fun budget alternative. Snuggled in a forest on the remains of a 15th-century castle wall atop the little mountain overlooking Salzburg, it has magnificent town and mountain views. While the 22 beds are designed-for-backpackers basic (and getting up here with luggage is a bother), the price and view are the best in town—with the right attitude, it's a fine experience (€19/person in 4- and 6-bed dorms, one double-bedded D-€43; includes breakfast and sheets; non-smoking, free Wi-Fi, recommended café, lockers, 5-minute walk from top of Mönchsberg elevator, Mönchsberg 19C, tel. 0662/841-729, www.stadtalm. at, info@diestadtalm.com, Peter). Once you've dropped your bags here, it's a five-minute walk down the cliffside stairs into Toscaninihof, in the middle of the Old Town (path always lit).

$ International Youth Hotel, a.k.a. the "Yo-Ho," is the most lively, handy, and American of Salzburg's hostels. This backpacker haven is a youthful and easygoing place that speaks English first; has cheap meals, 186 beds, lockers, tour discounts, and no curfew; plays *The Sound of Music* free daily at 19:00; runs a lively bar; and welcomes anyone of any age. The noisy atmosphere and lack of a curfew can make it hard to sleep (€18-21/person in 4- to 8-bed dorms, €21-22 in dorms with bathrooms, S-€35, D-€55, Ds-€60-

65, T-€60, Q-€72, Qs-€81, includes sheets, breakfast-€3.50, pay guest computer, free Wi-Fi, laundry-€4/load, 6 blocks from station toward Linzergasse and 6 blocks from river at Paracelsusstrasse 9, tel. 0662/879-649, www.yoho.at, office@yoho.at).

$ Jugendgästehaus Salzburg, quietly set amidst modern university buildings a short walk from the Old Town, is an upscale, privately run "hostel" that actually has mostly double and quad rooms with very spartan furnishings. It has pleasant public spaces and offers lots of extras—including Ping-Pong, foosball, and a cafeteria with inexpensive meals—but the rooms can cost as much as at a hotel (bed in 8-person dorm-€21-35, Db-€80-120, Qb-€150-190, higher prices are during festival, includes breakfast and sheets, free guest computer and Wi-Fi in common areas, *The Sound of Music* plays daily, bike rental-€10/day or €6/half-day, laundry-€5/load, limited parking-€5/day, just around the east side of the castle hill at Josef-Preis-Allee 18; from train station, take bus #5 or #25 to the Justizgebäude stop, then continue one block past the bushy wall, cross Petersbrunnstrasse, find shady Josef-Preis-Allee, and walk a few minutes to the end—the hostel is the big orange/green building on the right; tel. 05/708-3613, www.jufa.eu/en, salzburg@jufa.eu).

Four-Star Hotels in Residential Neighborhoods away from the Center

If you want to pay a little extra for plush furnishings, spacious public spaces, generous balconies, gardens, and free parking—and don't mind a longish walk or bus ride to the Old Town—consider the following places. These two modern hotels are set near each other in a residential area. While not ideal for train travelers, drivers in need of no-stress comfort for a home base should consider these.

$$$ Haus Arenberg rents 17 big, breezy rooms—most with generous balconies—in a modern, ranch-style mansion with a quiet garden. It's a long walk from the Old Town, or take bus #7 or #10 to the Volksgarten stop and hike five minutes uphill (Sb-€85-104, Db-€135-159, Tb-€159-175, Qb-€165-185, higher prices are during festival, no elevator, free Wi-Fi, library, electric bikes-€12/day, Blumensteinstrasse 8, tel. 0662/640-097, www.arenberg-salzburg.at, info@arenberg-salzburg.at, family Leobacher).

$$$ Hotel Rosenvilla, farther out than Haus Arenberg, offers 15 rooms with bright furnishings, surrounded by a leafy garden (Sb-€79-

108, Db-€135-165, bigger Db-€145-199, Db suite-€168-255, higher prices are during festival, no elevator, free Wi-Fi, electric bikes-€12/day, Höfelgasse 4, tel. 0662/621-765, www.rosenvilla. com, hotel@rosenvilla.com, take bus #7 to the Finanzamt stop).

Pensions on Moosstrasse

These are generally roomy and comfortable, and come with a good breakfast, free parking, farm-fresh scents, and mountains in the distance. They offer more for your money than lodgings in town, and off-season, competition softens prices. Each is mere steps from a bus stop and the ride from town is easy: with a €4.20 transit day pass *(Tageskarte)* and the frequent service, it shouldn't keep you away. Most places will do laundry for a small fee for those staying at least two nights. I've listed prices for two nights or more—if staying only one night, expect a 10 percent surcharge. Most push tours and concerts to make money on the side. As they are earning a commission, if you go through them, you'll probably lose the discount I've negotiated for my readers who go direct.

Moosstrasse runs southwest from the Old Town (behind the Mönchsberg). It was laid out a century ago through reclaimed marshland and lined with farm lots on each side. Some farm families continue to work the land, while others concentrate on offering rooms.

Handy bus #21 connects Moosstrasse to the center frequently (Mon-Fri 4/hour until 19:00, Sat 4/hour until 17:00, evenings and Sun 2/hour, 20 minutes). To get to these pensions from the train station, take any bus heading toward the center to Makartplatz, where you'll change to #21. If you're coming from the Old Town, catch bus #21 from Hanuschplatz, just downstream of the Staatsbrücke bridge near the *Tabak* kiosk. Buy a €1.90 *Einzelkarte-Kernzone* ticket (for one trip) or a €4.20 *Tageskarte* (day pass, good for 24 hours) from the streetside machine and punch it when you board the bus. The bus stop you use for each place is included in the following listings. Follow along with the stops on the map in the bus and press the button as soon as you hear yours announced—the bus only stops when requested.

If you're driving from the center, go through the tunnel, continue straight on Neutorstrasse, and take the fourth left onto Moosstrasse. Drivers exit the autobahn at *Süd* and then head in the direction of *Grodig*.

Each place can recommend a favorite Moosstrasse eatery (Reiterhof, at #151 by the Hammerauer Strasse bus stop, is particularly popular).

$$ Pension Bloberger Hof, while more a hotel than a pension, is comfortable and friendly, with a peaceful, rural location and

20 farmer-plush, good-value rooms. Inge and her daughter Sylvia offer a 10 percent discount to those who have this book, reserve direct, and pay cash (Sb-€60-75, Db-€80-85, big new Db with balcony-€105-115, Db suite-€130-140, higher prices are during festival, extra bed-€20, 10 percent extra for one-night stays, dinner for guests available Mon-Sat 18:00-21:00, no dinner on Sun, family apartment with kitchen, non-smoking, free guest computer and Wi-Fi, free loaner bikes, free station pickup if staying 3 nights, Hammerauer Strasse 4, bus stop: Hammerauer Strasse, tel. 0662/830-227, www.blobergerhof.at, office@blobergerhof.at).

$ Frau Ballwein offers eleven cozy, charming, and fresh rooms in a delightful, family-friendly farmhouse. Some rooms have balconies with an intoxicating view (Sb-€38-45, Db-€55-65, Tb-€75-85, Qb-€85-95, 2-bedroom apartment for up to 5 people-€95-115, higher prices are during festival, no surcharge for one-night stays, free station pickup if staying 3 nights, cash only, farm-fresh breakfasts amid her hanging teapot collection, non-smoking, free Wi-Fi, 2 free loaner bikes, Moosstrasse 69a, bus stop: Gsengerweg, tel. 0662/824-029, www.haus-ballwein.at, haus.ballwein@gmx.net).

$ Helga Bankhammer rents four inexpensive, nondescript rooms in a farmhouse, with a real dairy farm out back (D-€50, Db-€53, no surcharge for one-night stays, family deals, non-smoking, Wi-Fi, laundry-about €7/load, Moosstrasse 77, bus stop: Marienbad, tel. 0662/830-067, www.privatzimmer.at/helga.bankhammer, bankhammer@aon.at).

$ Haus am Moos has nine nicely furnished rooms in a relaxed country atmosphere, with a garden, swimming pool, breakfast buffet with mountain views, and a tiny private chapel (Sb-€32, Db-€60, extra bed-€15, family rooms, no surcharge for one-night stays, non-smoking, free guest computer and Wi-Fi, Moosstrasse 186a, bus stop: Lehrbauhof, tel. 0662/824-921, www.ammoos.at, ammoos186a@yahoo.de, Strasser family).

$ Haus Steiner's six rooms are straightforward, with older modern furnishings; there's a minimum two-night stay (Sb-€35, Db-€58, Tb-€87, non-smoking, free guest computer and Wi-Fi, Moosstrasse 156c, bus stop: Hammerauer Strasse, tel. 0662/830-031, www.haussteiner.com, info@haussteiner.com, Rosemarie Steiner).

More Hotels in Salzburg

Here are other hotels to consider:

$$$ Star Inn Gablerbrau, a chain hotel with rare air-conditioning, has a great location just off the Linzergasse (Db-€89-189, Richard Mayr Gasse 2, tel. 0662/879-662, www.starinnhotels.com, salzburg.gablerbraeu@starinnhotels.com).

$$$ Goldenes Theaterhotel, popular with groups, has comfortable rooms and an impersonal staff (Db-€85-172, Schallmooser Hauptstrasse 13, tel. 0662/881-681, www.gt-hotel-salzburg.com, info@gthotelsalzburg.com).

$$$ Altstadthotel Kasererbraeu is an odd combination hotel/cinema (though all films are screened in German), with 45 alpine-cozy rooms buried deep in Salzburg's Old Town (Db-€89-229, Kaigasse 33, tel. 0662/8424-4551, www.kasererbraeu.at, info@kasererbraeu.at).

Eating in Salzburg

In the Old Town
Salzburg boasts many inexpensive, fun, and atmospheric eateries. Most of these restaurants are centrally located in the Old Town, famous with visitors but also enjoyed by locals.

Gasthaus zum Wilden Mann is *the* place if the weather's bad and you're in the mood for a hearty, cheap meal at a shared table in one well-antlered (and non-smoking) room. Notice the century-old flood photos on the wall. For a quick lunch, get the *Bauernschmaus*, a mountain of dumplings, kraut, and peasant's meats (€12.50). While they have a few outdoor tables, the atmosphere is all indoors, and the menu is more geared to cold weather. Owner Robert—who runs the restaurant with Schwarzenegger-like energy—enjoys fostering a convivial ambience and encouraging strangers to share tables. I simply love this place (€8.50 two-course lunch specials, €9-15 daily specials posted on the wall, kitchen open Mon-Sat 11:00-21:00, closed Sun, 2 minutes from Mozart's Birthplace, enter from Getreidegasse 22 or Griesgasse 17, tel. 0662/841-787).

Stiftskeller St. Peter has been in business for more than 1,000 years—it was mentioned in the biography of Charlemagne. It's classy and high-end touristy, serving uninspired traditional Austrian cuisine (€18-27 main courses, daily 11:30-22:30, indoor/outdoor seating, next to St. Peter's Church at foot of Mönchsberg, tel. 0662/841-268). They host the Mozart Dinner Concert.

St. Paul's Stub'n Beer Garden is tucked secretly away under the fortress with a decidedly untouristy atmosphere. The food is better than at beer halls, and a young, bohemian-chic clientele fills its two troll-like rooms and its idyllic tree-shaded garden. *Kasnock'n* is a tasty dish of *Spätzle* with cheese served in an iron pan. It includes a side salad for €9 (€10 with ham)—it's enough for two. Reservations are smart (€9-17 main courses, Mon-Sat 17:00-22:00, open later for drinks only, closed Sun, Herrengasse 16, tel. 0662/843-220, Bernard).

Zirkelwirt serves cheese dumplings and modern Mediterranean, Italian, and Austrian dishes, and always has a daily special (chalked on the board). It's an old *Gasthaus* dining room with a medieval tiki-hut terrace a block off Mozartplatz, yet a world away from the tourism of the Old Town. While the waitstaff, music, and vibe feel young, it attracts Salzburgers of all ages (€10-15 main courses, Mon-Sat 17:00-24:00, closed Sun, Pfeifergasse 14, tel. 0662/843-472).

Café Tomaselli (with its Kiosk annex and terrace seating across the way) has long been Salzburg's top place to see and be seen. While pricey, it is good for lingering and people-watching. Tomaselli serves light meals and lots of drinks, keeps long hours daily, and has fine seating on the square, a view terrace upstairs, and indoor tables. Despite its fancy inlaid wood paneling, 19th-century portraits, and chandeliers, it's surprisingly low-key (€4-8 light meals, daily 7:00-20:00, until 22:00 during music festival, Alter Markt 9, tel. 0662/844-488, www.tomaselli.at).

Saran Essbar is the product of hardworking Mr. Saran (from the Punjab), who cooks and serves with his heart. This delightful little eatery casts a rich orange glow under medieval vaults. Its fun menu is small (Mr. Saran is committed to both freshness and value), mixing Austrian (great schnitzel and strudel), Italian, and Asian vegetarian, and always offering salads (€10-16 main courses, daily 11:00-15:00 & 17:00-22:00, longer hours during festival, a block off Mozartplatz at Judengasse 10, tel. 0662/846-628).

Vietnam Pho 18, fragrant with fresh cilantro, is where the Nguyen family dishes up Vietnamese noodle soups and other Asian standards in a six-table restaurant a long block from the cathedral (€8 main courses, eat in or take out, Sat-Thu 11:30-15:00 & 17:00-20:00, Fri 11:30-15:00, Kapitelgasse 11, mobile 0660-257-5588).

Youthful Cafés at the West End of the Old Town

Bar Club Café Republic, a hip hangout for local young people opposite the base of the Mönchsberg elevator, feels like a theater lobby during intermission. It serves good food both outdoors and in (with both smoking- and non-smoking rooms inside). It's ideal if you want something mod, untouristy, and un-wursty (Asian and international menu, €10-16 main courses, lots of hard drinks, open daily 8:00-late, trendy breakfasts served 8:00-18:00, Sun brunch with live music 10:00-13:00, music with a DJ Fri and Sat from 23:00, salsa dance club Tue night from 21:00—no cover, Anton Neumayr Platz 2, tel. 0662/841-613, www.republic-cafe.at).

Afro Cafe, between Getreidegasse and the Mönchsberg elevator, is a hit with local students. Its agenda: to put a fun spin on African cuisine (adapted to European tastes). It serves tea, coffee, cocktails, and tasty food with a dose of '70s funk and a healthy sense of humor. The menu includes pan-African specialties—try the spicy chicken couscous—as well as standard salads (€7.20 weekday lunch specials, €11-15 main courses, Mon-Sat 9:00-24:00, closed Sun, between Getreidegasse and cliff face at Bürgerspitalplatz 5, tel. 0662/844-888).

Carpe Diem is a project by the local Donald Trump, Red Bull tycoon Dietrich Mateschitz. Salzburg's beautiful people, fueled by Red Bull, present themselves here in the chic ground-floor café and trendy "lifestyle bar," which serves quality cocktails and fine finger food in cones (café open daily 8:30-24:00). Upstairs is an expensive restaurant boasting a Michelin star (€25-35 main courses, €4.50 cover charge, €19.50 lunch special, restaurant open Mon-Sat 12:00-14:00 and 18:00-22:00, closed Sun; Getreidegasse 50, tel. 0662/848-800, www.carpediemfinestfingerfood.com).

On the Cliffs Above the Old Town
Riding the Mönchsberg elevator from the west end of the Old Town up to the clifftop deposits you near two very different eateries: the chic Mönchsberg 32 at the modern art museum, and the Gasthaus Stadtalm Café at the funky old mountaineers' hut—each with commanding city views.

Mönchsberg 32 is a sleek, modern café/bar/restaurant overlooking Salzburg from the top of the Mönchsberg elevator. Even if you're not hiking anywhere, this makes for a great place to enjoy a drink and the view (€22-32 main courses, €3 cover charge, €14 lunch special, Tue-Sun 9:00-24:00, closed Mon except during festival, popular breakfasts served until 16:00, buy a one-way elevator ticket—they give customers a free pass to descend, tel. 0662/841-000. www.m32.at).

Gasthaus Stadtalm Café, in Salzburg's mountaineers' hut, sits high above the Old Town on the edge of the cliff with cheap prices, good traditional food, and great views. If hiking across the Mönchsberg, make this a stop (€10-12 main dishes, €9-10 salads, cliff-side garden seating or cozy-mountain-hut indoor seating—one indoor view table is booked for a decade of New Year's celebrations, daily May-Sept 10:00-22:00, Oct-April 10:00-18:00, hours are weather-dependent, 5 minutes from top of Mönchsberg elevator, also reachable by stairs from Toscaninihof, Mönchsberg 19C, tel. 0662/841-729, Peter).

Eating Cheaply in the Old Town
Fisch Krieg Restaurant, on the river where the fishermen used to sell their catch, is a great value. They serve fast, fresh, and inexpensive fish in a casual dining room—where trees grow through the ceiling—as well as great riverside seating (€2.50-€3 fishwiches to go, €8 self-serve main courses, salad bar, Mon-Fri 8:30-18:30, Sat 8:30-13:00, closed Sun, Hanuschplatz 4, tel. 0662/843-732).

Salzburg Restaurants

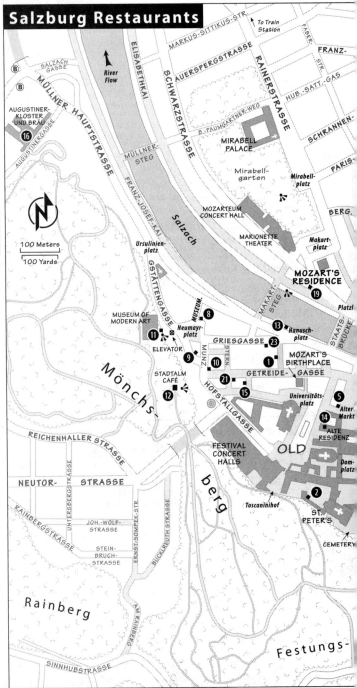

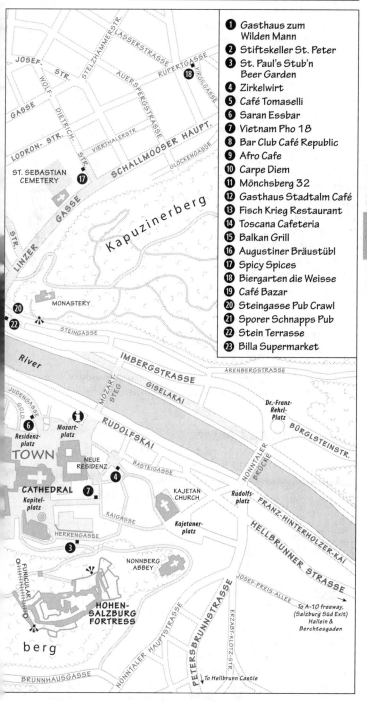

1. Gasthaus zum Wilden Mann
2. Stiftskeller St. Peter
3. St. Paul's Stub'n Beer Garden
4. Zirkelwirt
5. Café Tomaselli
6. Saran Essbar
7. Vietnam Pho 18
8. Bar Club Café Republic
9. Afro Cafe
10. Carpe Diem
11. Mönchsberg 32
12. Gasthaus Stadtalm Café
13. Fisch Krieg Restaurant
14. Toscana Cafeteria
15. Balkan Grill
16. Augustiner Bräustübl
17. Spicy Spices
18. Biergarten die Weisse
19. Café Bazar
20. Steingasse Pub Crawl
21. Sporer Schnapps Pub
22. Stein Terrasse
23. Billa Supermarket

Toscana Cafeteria Mensa is the university lunch canteen, fast and cheap—with indoor seating and a great courtyard for sitting outside with students and teachers instead of tourists. Choose between two daily soup- and main-course specials, each around €5 (Mon-Thu 7:00-16:30, Fri 7:00-15:00, hot meals served 11:00-14:00 only, closed Sat-Sun, behind the Old Residenz, in the courtyard opposite Sigmund-Haffner-Gasse 16).

Sausage stands *(Würstelstände)* serve the town's favorite "fast food." The best stands (like those on Universitätsplatz) use the same boiling water all day, which gives the weenies more flavor. The 60-year-old **Balkan Grill,** run by chatty Frau Ebner, is a Salzburg institution, selling just one type of spicy sausage—*Bosna*—with your choice of toppings (€3.30; survey the five options—described in English—and choose a number; takeout only, steady and sturdy local crowd, Mon-Sat 11:00-19:00, Sun 15:00-19:00, hours vary with demand, Jan-Feb closed Sun, hiding down the tunnel at Getreidegasse 33 across from Eisgrotte).

Picnics: Picnickers will appreciate the well-stocked **Billa supermarket** at Griesgasse 19a, just across the street from the recommended Fisch Krieg Restaurant (Mon-Fri 7:15-19:30, Sat 7:15-18:00, closed Sun). The bustling morning **produce market** (Mon-Sat, closed Sun) on Universitätsplatz, behind Mozart's Birthplace, is fun, but expensive.

Away from the Center

Augustiner Bräustübl, a huge 1,000-seat beer garden within a monk-run brewery in the Kloster Mülln, is rustic and raw. On busy

nights, it's like a Munich beer hall with no music but the volume turned up. When it's cool outside, enjoy a historic indoor setting in any of several beer-sloshed and smoke-stained halls (one of which is still for smokers). On balmy evenings, it's like a Renoir painting—but with beer breath and cigarette smoke—outdoors under chestnut trees. Local students mix with tourists eating hearty slabs of grilled meat with their fingers or cold meals from the self-serve picnic counter, while children frolic on the playground kegs. For your beer: Pick up a half-liter or full-liter mug, pay the lady (*schank* means self-serve price, *bedienung* is the price with waiter service), wash your mug, give Mr. Keg your receipt and empty mug, and you will be made happy. Waiters only bring beer; they don't bring food—instead, go up the stairs, survey the hallway of deli counters, grab a tray, and assemble your own meal (or, as long as you buy a drink, you can bring in a picnic). Classic pretzels from the bakery and spiraled, salty radishes make great beer even better. Stick with the freshly cooked meat dishes: I made the mistake of choosing schnitzel which was reheated in the microwave. For dessert—after a visit to the strudel kiosk—enjoy the incomparable floodlit view of old Salzburg from the nearby Müllnersteg pedestrian bridge and a riverside stroll home (open daily 15:00-23:00, Augustinergasse 4, tel. 0662/431-246).

Getting There: It's about a 15-minute walk along the river (with the river on your right) from the Old Town side of the Staatsbrücke bridge. After passing the Müllnersteg pedestrian bridge, just after Café am Kai, follow the stairs up to a busy street, and cross it. From here, either continue up more stairs into the trees and around the small church (for a scenic approach to the monastery), or stick to the sidewalk as it curves around to Augustinergasse. Either way, your goal is the huge yellow building. Don't be fooled by second-rate gardens serving the same beer nearby. You can also take a bus from Hanuschplatz (#7, #8, #21, #24, #27, or #28) two stops to the Landeskrankenhaus stop, right in front of the beer garden.

North of the River, near Recommended Linzergasse Hotels

Spicy Spices is a trippy vegetarian-Indian restaurant where Suresh Syal (a.k.a. "Mr. Spicy") serves tasty curry and rice, samosas, organic salads, vegan soups, and fresh juices. It's a *namaste* kind of place, where everything's proudly organic (€7 specials served all day, €8.50 with soup or salad, €0.50 extra for takeout, Mon-Fri 10:30-21:30, Sat-Sun 12:00-21:30, Wolf-Dietrich-Strasse 1, tel. 0662/870-712).

Biergarten die Weisse, close to the hotels on Rupertgasse and away from the tourists, is a longtime hit with the natives. If a beer hall can be happening, this one—modern yet with antlers—is it. Their famously good beer is made right there; favorites include their fizzy wheat beer *(Weisse)* and their seasonal beers (on request). Enjoy the beer with their good, cheap traditional food in the great garden seating, or in the wide variety of indoor rooms—sports bar, young and noisy, or older and more elegant (€10-13 main courses, Mon-Sat 10:00-24:00, closed Sun, Rupertgasse 10, east of Bayerhamerstrasse, tel. 0662/872-246).

Café Bazar, overlooking the river between the Mirabell Gardens and the Staatsbrücke bridge, is as close as you'll get to a Vienna coffee house in Salzburg. Their outdoor terrace is a venerable spot for a classy drink with an Old-Town-and-castle view (reasonable prices, light meals, Mon-Sat 7:30-23:00, Sun 9:00-18:00, closes Mon-Sat at 19:30 in off-season, Schwarzstrasse 3, tel. 0662/874-278).

Steingasse Pub Crawl

For a fun post-concert activity, drop in on a couple of atmospheric bars along medieval Steingasse. This is a local and hip scene—yet is accessible to older tourists: dark bars filled with well-dressed Salzburgers lazily smoking cigarettes and talking philosophy to laid-back tunes (no hip-hop). These four places are all within about 100 yards of each other. Start at the Linzergasse end of Steingasse. As they are quite different, survey all before choosing your spot (all open until the wee hours). Most don't serve food, but there's a convenient pizzeria and Döner Kebab shop near these hot spots.

Pepe Cocktail Bar, with Mexican decor and Latin music, serves cocktails and nachos (nightly 19:00-3:00 in the morning, live DJs Fri-Sat from 19:00, Steingasse 3, tel. 0662/873-662).

Saiten Sprung wins the "Best Atmosphere" award. The door is kept closed to keep out the crude and rowdy. Just ring the bell and enter its hellish interior—lots of stone and red decor, with mountains of melted wax beneath age-old candlesticks and an ambience of classic '70s and '80s music. Stelios, who speaks English with Greek charm, serves cocktails and fine wine, though no food (Mon-Sat 21:00-4:00 in the morning, closed Sun, Steingasse 11, tel. 0662/881-377).

Fridrich, two doors down, is an intimate little place under an 11th-century vault, with lots of mirrors and a silver ceiling fan. Bernd Fridrich is famous for his martinis and passionate about Austrian wines, and has a tattered collection of vinyl that seems hell-bent on keeping the 1970s alive. Their Yolanda cocktail (grapefruit and vodka) is a favorite. He and his partner Ferdinand serve little dishes designed to complement the focus on socializing and drinking, though their €13 "little of everything dish" can be a meal for two (€6-13 appetizers, Thu-Tue from 18:00, closed Wed, Steingasse 15, tel. 0662/876-218).

Selim's Bar, with cozy seating both inside and out, has a cool, conversation-friendly atmosphere with mellow music (no food, Mon-Sat 18:00-late, also open Sun in summer and during festival, across street from cinema at Steingasse 10, mobile 0664-433-844).

Salzburg Connections

By train, Salzburg is the first stop over the German-Austrian border. This means that if Salzburg is your only stop in Austria, and you're using a railpass that covers Germany (including the Bayern-Ticket) but not Austria, you don't have to pay extra or add Austria to your pass to get here. Deutsche Bahn (German Railway) ticket machines at the Salzburg train station make it easy to buy tickets to German destinations.

From Salzburg by Train to: Berchtesgaden (roughly hourly, 1-1.5 hours, change in Freilassing, faster and prettier by bus—see "Getting There" in the Berchtesgaden section), **Munich** (2/hour, 1.5-2 hours), **Füssen** (roughly hourly, 4 hours, 1-2 changes), **Reutte,** Austria (hourly, 4.5-5.5 hours, change in Augsburg and Kempten or Munich and Garmisch), **Nürnberg** (hourly with change in Munich, 3 hours), **Hallstatt,** Austria (hourly, 50 minutes to Attnang-Puchheim, 20-minute wait, then 1.5 hours to Hallstatt; also works well by bus—see below), **Innsbruck,** Austria (hourly, direct, 2 hours), **Vienna,** Austria (3/hour, 2.75-3 hours), **Ljubljana,** Slovenia (6/day, 4.25-5 hours, some with change in Villach), **Prague,** Czech Republic (8/day, 6.5-7.5 hours, 1-2 changes, no decent overnight connection), **Interlaken,** Switzerland (9/day, 7.5-8 hours, 2-3 changes), **Florence,** Italy (4/day, 8.5-9 hours, 2 changes, overnight options), **Venice,** Italy (7/day, 7-8 hours, 2-3 changes). Austrian train info: Austrian tel. 051-717 (to get an operator, dial 2, then 2), from Germany call 00-43-51-717, www.oebb.at. German train info: tel. 0180-599-6633, from Austria call 00-49-180-599-6633, www.bahn.com.

From Salzburg by Bus to: Hallstatt, Austria (bus #150 to Bad Ischl—Mon-Fri nearly hourly at :15 past the hour, fewer buses Sat-Sun, 1.5 hours, leaves from platform F outside Salzburg train station, also stops at Mirabellplatz and Hofwirt, Austrian tel. 0810-222-333, from Germany call 00-43-1-71101, www.postbus.at; at Bad Ischl station, change to the train—25-minute ride to Hallstatt, then ride the boat across the lake—or continue by bus to the Lahn section of Hallstatt with a change in Gosaumühle). Reaching Hallstatt via the bus to Bad Ischl is cheaper, more scenic (with views of Wolfgangsee lake), and no slower than the train via Attnang-Puchheim—but the bus trip isn't covered by railpasses.

Berchtesgaden

This alpine ski region, just across the border from Salzburg in a finger of German territory that pokes south into Austria, is famous for its fjord-like lake and its mountaintop Nazi retreat. Long before its association with Hitler, Berchtesgaden (BERKH-tehs-gah-dehn) was one of the classic Romantic corners of Germany. In fact, Hitler's propagandists capitalized on the Führer's love of this region to establish the notion that the native Austrian was truly German at heart. Today visitors cruise up the romantic Königssee to get in touch with the soul of Bavarian Romanticism; ride a bus up to Hitler's mountain retreat (5,500 feet); see the remains of the Nazis' elaborate last-ditch bunkers; ride an old miners' train into the mountain to learn all about salt mining; and hike along a secluded gorge to a high waterfall.

Remote little Berchtesgaden (pop. 7,500) can be inundated with Germans during peak season, when you may find yourself in a traffic jam of tourists desperately trying to turn their money into fun.

Getting There

Berchtesgaden is only 15 miles from Salzburg. The quickest way there **from Salzburg** is by bus #840 from the Salzburg train station (runs about hourly Mon-Fri, 6-8/day Sat-Sun, usually at :15 past the hour, 45 minutes, buy tickets from driver, €9.50 *Tageskarte* day pass covers your round trip plus most local buses in Berchtesgaden—except bus #849 up to the Eagle's Nest, last bus back leaves Berchtesgaden at 18:15; check schedules at www.svv-info.at—click "Timetables," then under "Find a timetable" select "Timetable book page," then enter "840"). On my last visit, bus #840 left from platform G across the street from the Salzburg train station (beyond the bike racks). You can also catch bus #840 from the middle of Salzburg—after leaving the station, it stops a few minutes later on Mirabellplatz, and then in Salzburg's Old Town (on Rudolfskai, near Mozartplatz).

Coming **from Munich,** it's simplest to reach Berchtesgaden by train (almost hourly, 2.5-3 hours, change in Freilassing). You can also get to Berchtesgaden from Salzburg by train via Freilassing, but it takes twice as long as the bus and isn't as scenic. The train is an option, though, if you need to get between Salzburg and Berchtesgaden in the evening or early morning, when no buses run.

Planning Your Time

The Nazi and Hitler-related sites outside Berchtesgaden are the town's main draw and need a half-day to see. David and Christine Harper's tour of the sites is a good value and worth planning around (afternoons only, see "Tours in Berchtesgaden"), but you can also get to the main Nazi sites on your own by bus.

If you have more time, Berchtesgaden also has tourable salt mines (similar to the ones at Hallein) and a romantic, pristine lake called Königssee (extremely popular with less-adventurous Germans). Visiting either can take up to another half-day. While combining either of these with the Nazi sights is easy for drivers, it's challenging for those coming by public transport. Bus travelers wanting to fill up the rest of the day might be happier spending an hour walking through Berchtesgaden's Old Town, or going for a short hike in the Almbach Gorge (described later). If you're visiting Berchtesgaden on your way between Salzburg and points in Germany, you can leave luggage in lockers at the Berchtesgaden train station during your visit.

Orientation to Berchtesgaden

Berchtesgaden's train station is worth a stop for its luggage lockers (along the train platform), WC (free, also near platform), and history (specifically, its vintage 1937 Nazi architecture and the murals in the main hall). The oversized station was built to accommodate (and intimidate) the hordes of Hitler fans who flocked here in hopes of seeing the Führer. The building next to the station, just beyond the round tower, was Hitler's own V.I.P. reception area.

Berchtesgaden's bus terminal (ZOB) is just in front of the train station. There are bakeries and a few forgettable restaurants nearby (consider bringing a picnic). The old center of Berchtesgaden, bypassed by most tourists, is up the hill behind the station (use the bridge over the tracks).

Tourist Information

The TI is on the other side of the roundabout from the train station, in the yellow building with green shutters (mid-June-Sept Mon-Fri 8:30-18:00, Sat 9:00-17:00, Sun 9:00-15:00; Oct-mid-June Mon-Fri 8:30-17:00, Sat 9:00-12:00, closed Sun; German tel. 08652/9670, from Austria call 00-49-8652-9670, www.berchtesgadener-land.info). Pick up a local map, and consider the 30-page local-bus schedule *(Fahrplan,* €0.30) if you'll be hopping more than one bus.

Getting Around Berchtesgaden

None of the sights I list are within easy walking distance from the station, but they're all connected by convenient local buses, which use the station as a hub (all these buses—except the special bus #849 between the Obersalzberg Documentation Center and the

Eagle's Nest chalet—are free with the *Tageskarte* day pass from Salzburg; timetables at www.rvo-bus.de, or call 08652/94480). You'll want to note departure times and frequencies while still at the station, or pick up a schedule at the TI.

From the train station, buses #840 (the same line as the bus from Salzburg) and #837 go to the salt mines (a 20-minute walk otherwise). Bus #840 also goes to the Almbach Gorge. Bus #838 goes to the Obersalzberg Documentation Center, and bus #841 goes to the Königssee.

Tours in Berchtesgaden

Eagle's Nest Historical Tours

For 20 years, David and Christine Harper—who rightly consider this visit more an educational opportunity than simple sightseeing—have organized thoughtful tours of the Hitler-related sites near Berchtesgaden. Their bus tours, usually led by native English speakers, depart from the TI, opposite the Berchtesgaden train station. Tours start by driving through the remains of the Nazis' Obersalzberg complex, then visit the bunkers underneath the Documentation Center, and end with a guided visit to the Eagle's Nest (€50/person, €1 discount with this book, English only, daily at 13:15 mid-May-late Oct, 4 hours, 30 people maximum, reservations strongly recommended, private tours available, German tel. 08652/64971, from Austria call 00-49-8652-64971, www.eagles-nest-tours.com). While the price is €50, your actual cost for the guiding is only about €23, as the tour takes care of your transport and admissions, not to mention relieving you of having to figure out the local buses up to Obersalzberg. Coming from Salzburg, you can take the 10:15 or 11:15 bus to Berchtesgaden, eat a picnic lunch, take the tour, then return on the 18:15 bus from Berchtesgaden, which gets you back to Salzburg 45 minutes later. If you're visiting near the beginning or end of the season, be aware that tours will be cancelled if it's snowing at the Eagle's Nest (as that makes the twisty, precipitous mountain roads too dangerous to drive). David and Christine also arrange off-season tours, though the Eagle's Nest isn't open for visitors in winter (€120/up to 4 people; see website for details).

Bus Tours from Salzburg

Bob's Special Tours, based in Salzburg, bring you to (but not into) most of the sights described here (Eagle's Nest, Obersalzberg Documentation Center, salt mines, and Königssee if you insist) on one busy full-day trip in a minibus (€90, doesn't include €16.10 bus up to the Eagle's Nest, €10 discount with this book, half-day Eagle's Nest-only options available, tel. 0662/849-511, mobile 0664-541-7492, www.bobstours.com). **Panorama Tours,**

which usually runs larger buses, also offers half-day excursions to the Eagle's Nest (€53, €5.50 discount with this book, tel. 0662/874-029 or 0662/883-2110, www.panoramatours.com). While these tours offer all-in-one convenience, the experience is more rushed than you would be on your own, and they don't visit the bunkers.

Sights in Berchtesgaden

▲▲▲Nazi Sites near Berchtesgaden

Early in his career as a wannabe tyrant, Adolf Hitler had a radical friend who liked to vacation in Berchtesgaden, and through him

Hitler came to know and love this dramatic corner of Bavaria. Berchtesgaden's part-Bavarian, part-Austrian character held a special appeal to the Austrian-German Hitler. In the 1920s, just out of prison, he checked into an alpine hotel in Obersalzberg, three miles uphill from Berchtesgaden, to finish work on his memoir and Nazi primer, *Mein Kampf*. Because it was here that he claimed to be inspired and laid out his vision, some call Obersalzberg the "cradle of the Third Reich."

In the 1930s, after becoming the German Chancellor, Hitler chose Obersalzberg to build his mountain retreat, a supersized alpine farmhouse called the Berghof. His handlers crafted Hitler's image here—surrounded by nature, gently receiving alpine flowers from adoring little children, lounging around with farmers in lederhosen...no modern arms industry, no big-time industrialists, no ugly extermination camps. In reality, Obersalzberg was home to much more than Hitler's alpine chalet. It was a huge compound of 80 buildings—fenced off from the public after 1936—where the major decisions leading up to World War II were hatched. Hitler himself spent about a third of his time at the Berghof, hosted world leaders in the compound, and later had it prepared for his last stand.

Some mistakenly call the entire area "Hitler's Eagle's Nest." But that name actually belongs only to the Kehlsteinhaus, a small mountaintop chalet on a 6,000-foot peak that juts up two miles south of Obersalzberg. (A visiting diplomat humorously dubbed it the "Eagle's Nest," and the name stuck.) In 1939, it was given to the Führer for his 50th birthday. While a fortune was spent building this perch and the road up to it, Hitler, who was afraid of heights, visited only 14 times. Hitler's mistress, Eva Braun, though, liked to hike up to the Eagle's Nest to sunbathe.

Near Berchtesgaden

In April of 1945, Britain's Royal Air Force bombed the Obersalzberg compound nearly flat, but missed the difficult-to-target Eagle's Nest entirely. Almost all of what survived the bombing at Obersalzberg was blown up in 1952 by the Allies—who wanted to leave nothing as a magnet for future neo-Nazi pilgrims—before they turned the site over to the German government. The most extensive surviving remains are of the Nazis' bunker system, intended to serve as a last resort for the regime as the Allies closed in. In the 1990s, a museum, the Obersalzberg Documentation Center, was built on top of one of the bunkers. The museum and bunker, plus the never-destroyed Eagle's Nest, are the two Nazi sites worth seeing near Berchtesgaden.

Obersalzberg Documentation Center and Bunker

To reach the most interesting part of this site, walk through the museum and down the stairs into the vast and complex bunker system. Construction began in 1943, after the Battle of Stalingrad ended the Nazi aura of invincibility. This is a professionally engineered underground town, which held meeting rooms, offices, archives for the government, and lavish living quarters for Hitler—all connected by

four miles of tunnels cut through solid rock by slave labor. You can't visit all of it, and what you can see was stripped and looted bare after the war. But enough is left that you can wander among the concrete and marvel at megalomania gone mad.

The museum above, which has almost no actual artifacts, is designed primarily for German students and others who want to learn and understand their still-recent history. There's little English, but you can rent the €2 English audioguide.

Cost and Hours: €3 covers both museum and bunker; April-Oct daily 9:00-17:00; Nov-March Tue-Sun 10:00-15:00, closed Mon; last entry one hour before closing, allow 1.5 hours for visit, German tel. 08652/947-960, from Austria tel. 00-49-8652-947-960, www.obersalzberg.de.

Getting There: Hop on bus #838 from Berchtesgaden's train station (Mon-Fri almost hourly, Sat-Sun 10/day, 12 minutes, 5-minute walk from Obersalzberg stop).

Eagle's Nest (Kehlsteinhaus)

Today, the chalet that Hitler ignored is basically a three-room, reasonably priced restaurant with a scenic terrace, 100 yards

below the summit of a mountain. You could say it's like any alpine hiking hut, just more massively built. On a nice day, the views are magnificent. If it's fogged in (which it often is), most people won't find it worth coming up here (except on David and Christine Harper's tours—described earlier—which can make the building come to life even without a view). Bring a jacket, and prepare for crowds in summer (less crowded if you go early or late in the day).

From the upper bus stop, a finely crafted tunnel (which will have you humming the *Get Smart* TV theme song) leads to the original polished-brass elevator, which takes you the last 400 feet up to the Eagle's Nest. Wander into the fancy back dining room (the best-preserved from Hitler's time), where you can see the once-sleek marble fireplace chipped up by souvenir-seeking troops in 1945.

Cost and Hours: Free, generally open mid-May-late Oct, snowfall sometimes forces a later opening or earlier closing.

Getting There: The only way to reach the Eagle's Nest—even if you have your own car—is by specially equipped bus #849, which leaves from the Documentation Center and climbs steeply up the one-way, private road—Germany's highest (every 25 minutes, 15 minutes, €16.10 round-trip, *Tageskarte* day passes not valid, buy ticket from windows, last bus up 16:00, last bus down 16:25, free parking at Documentation Center).

▲Salt Mines (Salzbergwerk Berchtesgaden)

At the Berchtesgaden salt mines, you put on traditional miners' outfits, get on funny little trains, and zip deep into the mountain. For two hours (which includes time to get into and back out of your miner's gear), you'll cruise subterranean lakes; slide speedily down two long, slick, wooden banisters; and learn how they mined salt so long ago. Call ahead for crowd-avoidance advice; when the weather gets bad, this place is mobbed with a two-hour wait for the next open tour. Tours are in German, but English-speakers get audioguides.

Cost and Hours: €15.50, daily May-Oct 9:00-17:00, Nov-April 11:00-15:00—these are last-entry times, German tel. 08652/600-20, from Austria dial 00-49-8652-600-20, www.salzzeitreise.de.

Getting There: The mines are a 20-minute walk or quick bus ride (#837 or #840) from the Berchtesgaden station; ask the driver to let you off at the Salzbergwerk stop. (Since buses coming from Salzburg pass here on the way into Berchtesgaden, you can also simply hop off at the mines before getting into town, instead of backtracking from the station.) If you have extra time, you can take a longer, more interesting 35-minute walk from the station to the mines through Berchtesgaden's Old Town.

▲Königssee

Three miles south of Berchtesgaden, the idyllic Königssee stretches like a fjord through pristine mountain scenery to the dramatically situated Church of St. Bartholomä and beyond. To get to the lake from Berchtesgaden, hop on bus #841 (about hourly from train station to boat dock, 10 minutes), or take the scenically woodsy, reasonably flat 1.25-hour walk (well-signed). Drivers pay €4 to park.

Most visitors simply glide scenically for 35 minutes on the silent, electronically propelled **boat** to the church, enjoy that peaceful setting, then glide back. Boats, going at a sedate Bavarian speed and filled with Germans chuckling at the captain's commentary, leave with demand—generally 2-4 per hour (late April-mid-Oct, no boats off-season, €13.30 round-trip, German tel. 08652/96360, from Austria dial 00-49-8652-96360, www.seenschifffahrt.de). At a rock cliff midway through the journey, your captain stops, and the first mate pulls out a trumpet to demonstrate the fine echo.

The remote, red-onion-domed **Church of St. Bartholomä** (once home of a monastery, then a hunting lodge of the Bavarian royal family) is surrounded by a fine beer garden, rustic fishermen's pub, and inviting lakeside trails. The family next to St. Bartholomä's lives in the middle of this national park and has a license to fish—so very fresh trout is the lunchtime favorite.

While the Königssee is lovely once you're on the water, all the preliminaries are a bit tedious. The bus from Berchtesgaden drops you next to a complex with WCs, ATMs, and a TI; across the parking lot rise the golden arches of McDonald's. From there, a brick path leads five minutes downhill to the lakeshore through a thicket of souvenir stores selling marmot-fat ointment, quartz chunks, carved birdhouses, and "superpretzels." At the ticket windows, you'll get a set departure time (expect a wait, as boats fill up). Rowboat rental is also an option (€7-10/hour), but the church is too far up the lake to reach easily by muscle power alone.

Almbach Gorge (Almbachklamm)

This short, popular hike is a good option for nature-lovers who come to see Berchtesgaden's Nazi sights, then want to fill up the rest of the day hiking along a stream-filled gorge with a minimum of fuss and crowds. Though not a world-class attraction (and not for children, due to drop-offs), it can easily make for an enjoyable two or three hours. Most visitors do it as roughly a four-mile roundtrip, though you can go farther if you wish.

Leave bus #840 at the Kugelmühle stop (12 minutes towards Salzburg from Berchtesgaden) and check the next bus times—two hours between buses is enough for a quick visit, three hours for a leisurely one. Walk five minutes along Kugelmühlweg (following the *Almbachklamm* signs) to the trailhead. First you'll see the **Gasthaus zur Kugelmühle,** which serves reasonably priced meals (daily 11:30-19:30, tel. 08650/461, from Austria dial 00-49-8650-461). In front of the restaurant is an old wooden apparatus for shaping marble blocks into round toy spheres (hence the name—*Kugel* means ball, *Mühle* means mill). Just beyond is a gate where you pay €3 to enter the gorge; pick up a map and get hiking advice here (daily May-Oct 9:00-18:00; gorge closed in winter).

A rushing stream cascades through the gorge, which the trail crosses and recrosses on numbered steel bridges. The trail is well-maintained and exciting, and accessible to anyone who is reasonably fit, sure-footed, and wearing sturdy shoes. However, it's not safe or appropriate for young children because the path has some steep, unguarded drop-offs that could land kids into the cold water. Expect some narrow and slippery parts, but there are handrails and benches along the way. You can just walk up as far as you have time for, but the high Sulzer waterfall by bridge #19 is a traditional turn-around point. The walk there and back can be done in two hours at a good clip, but allowing three makes for a more pleasant visit.

PRACTICALITIES

This section covers just the basics on traveling in this region (for much more information, see *Rick Steves' Germany*). Unless otherwise noted, you can assume that the information about Germany in this section also applies to Austria (the city of Salzburg and the region of Tirol). You'll find free advice on specific topics at www.ricksteves.com/tips.

Money

Germany and Austria use the euro currency: 1 euro (€) = about $1.30. To convert prices in euros to dollars, add about 30 percent: €20 = about $26, €50 = about $65. (Check www.oanda.com for the latest exchange rates.)

The standard way for travelers to get euros is to withdraw money from ATMs (which locals call a *Geldautomat* in Germany, or *Bankomat* in Austria) using a debit card, ideally with a Visa or MasterCard logo. Before departing, call your bank or credit-card company: Confirm that your card(s) will work overseas, ask about international transaction fees, and alert them that you'll be making withdrawals in Europe. Also ask for the PIN number for your credit card in case it'll help you use Europe's "chip-and-PIN" payment machines (see below); allow time for your bank to mail your PIN to you. To keep your valuables safe, wear a money belt.

Dealing with "Chip and PIN": Much of Europe—including Germany and Austria—is adopting a "chip-and-PIN" system for credit cards, and some merchants rely on it exclusively. European chip-and-PIN cards are embedded with an electronic chip, in addition to the magnetic stripe used on our American-style cards. This means that your credit (and debit) card might not work at payment machines, such as those at train and subway stations, toll roads, parking garages, luggage lockers, and self-serve gas pumps.

Memorizing your credit card's PIN lets you use it at some chip-and-PIN machines—just enter your PIN when prompted. If a payment machine won't take your card, look for a machine that takes cash or see if there's a cashier nearby who can process your transaction. Often the easiest solution is to pay for your purchases with cash you've withdrawn from an ATM using your debit card (Europe's ATMs still accept magnetic-stripe cards).

Phoning

Smart travelers use the telephone to reserve or reconfirm rooms, reserve restaurants, get directions, research transportation connections, confirm tour times, phone home, and lots more.

To call Germany from the US or Canada: Dial 011-49 and then the area code (minus its initial zero) and local number. (The 011 is our international access code, and 49 is Germany's country code.)

To call Germany from a European country: Dial 00-49 followed by the area code (minus its initial zero) and local number. (The 00 is Europe's international access code.)

To call Austria: Follow the same directions above, but use Austria's country code: 43.

To call within Germany or Austria: If you're dialing within an area code, just dial the local number; but if you're calling outside your area code, you have to dial both the area code (which starts with a 0) and the local number.

To call from Germany or Austria to another country: Dial 00 followed by the country code (for example, 1 for the US or Canada), then the area code and number. If you're calling European countries whose phone numbers begin with 0, you'll usually have to omit that 0 when you dial.

Tips on Phoning: Local phone numbers in Germany and Austria can have different numbers of digits within the same city or even the same business.

A mobile phone—whether an American one that works in Germany and Austria, or a European one you buy when you arrive—is handy, but can be pricey. If traveling with a smartphone, switch off data-roaming until you have free Wi-Fi. With Wi-Fi, you can use your smartphone to make free or inexpensive domestic and international calls by taking advantage of a calling app such as Skype or FaceTime.

To make cheap international calls from any phone (even your hotel-room phone), you can buy an international phone card. These work with a scratch-to-reveal PIN code at any phone, allow you to call home to the US for pennies a minute, and also work for domestic calls. In Germany, avoid using international phone cards at pay phones. Because the German phone company slaps on

From:	rick@ricksteves.com
Sent:	Today
To:	info@hotelcentral.com
Subject:	Reservation request for 19-22 July

Dear Hotel Central,

I would like to reserve a room for 2 people for 3 nights, arriving 19 July and departing 22 July. If possible, I would like a quiet room with a double bed and a bathroom inside the room.

Please let me know if you have a room available and the price.

Thank you!
Rick Steves

hefty surcharges, you'll get far fewer minutes for your money (for example, 10 minutes instead of 100 on a €5 card) than if you call from your hotel room. Certain international phone cards work in multiple countries—if traveling to both Germany and Austria, try to buy a card that will work in both places.

Another option is buying an insertable phone card. These are usable only at pay phones, are reasonable for making calls within the country, and work for international calls as well (though not as cheaply as the international phone cards). Note that insertable phone cards work only in the country where you buy them.

Calling from your hotel-room phone is usually expensive, unless you use an international phone card. For much more on phoning, see www.ricksteves.com/phoning.

Making Hotel Reservations

To ensure the best value, I recommend reserving rooms in advance, particularly during peak season. Email the hotelier with the following key pieces of information: number and type of rooms; number of nights; date of arrival; date of departure; and any special requests. (For a sample form, see the sidebar.) Use the European style for writing dates: day/month/year. Hoteliers typically ask for your credit-card number as a deposit.

Given the economic downturn, hoteliers may be willing to make a deal—try emailing several hotels to ask for their best price. In general, hotel prices can soften if you do any of the following: offer to pay cash, stay at least three nights, or travel off-season.

Eating

At mealtime, there are many options beyond restaurants. For hearty, stick-to-the-ribs meals—and plenty of beer—look for a beer hall *(Bräuhaus)* or beer garden *(Biergarten)*. *Gasthaus, Gasthof, Gaststätte,* and *Gaststube* all loosely describe an informal, inn-type eatery. A *Kneipe* is a bar, a *Weinstub* is a wine bar, and a *Keller* (or *Ratskeller*) is a restaurant or tavern located in a cellar. A *Schnell Imbiss* is a small fast-food take-away stand. Department store cafeterias are also common and handy.

The classic Germanic dish is sausage *(Wurst)*. The hundreds of varieties are usually served with mustard *(Senf)*, a roll *(Semmel)* or pretzel *(Breze)*, and sauerkraut. The various types of Bratwurst are grilled *(gebraten)*. To enjoy a *Weisswurst*—a boiled white Bavarian sausage made of veal—peel off the skin and eat it with sweet mustard. *Currywurst* comes with a delicious curry-infused ketchup. Particularly in Austria, the traditional favorite is Wiener schnitzel (breaded veal cutlet).

If you prefer smaller portions in this land of heavy cuisine, order from the *kleine Hunger* ("small hunger") section of the menu. Salads are big, leafy, and good; a *Salatteller* is a meal-sized salad. Europeans are passionate about choosing organic products—look for *Bio*.

Ethnic eateries—Turkish, Greek, Italian, and Asian—offer a good value and a welcome break from Germanic fare. Shops and stands selling Turkish-style *Döner Kebab* (gyro-like, pita-wrapped rotisserie meat) are also common.

This region has both great wine *(Wein)* and beer *(Bier)*. Order wine *süss* (sweet), *halb trocken* (medium), or *trocken* (dry). For beer, *dunkles* is dark, *helles* or *Lager* is light, *Flaschenbier* is bottled, and *vom Fass* is on tap. *Pils* is barley-based, and *Weizen, Hefeweizen,* or *Weissbier* is yeasty and wheat-based. When you order beer, ask for *eine Halbe* for a half-liter (though it's not always available) or *eine Mass* for a whole liter (about a quart).

Service: Good service is relaxed (slow to an American). When you want the bill, say, *"Rechnung* (REHKH-noong), *bitte."* To tip for good service, it's customary to round up around 10 percent. Rather than leave coins on the table, do as the locals do: When you pay, tell the waiter how much you want him to keep, including his tip. For example, for a €10 meal, you can hand over a €20 bill and say *"Elf Euro"*—"Eleven euros"—to include a €1 tip and get €9 change.

Transportation

By Train: Europe's trains—speedy, comfortable, non-smoking, and fairly punctual—cover cities and small towns well. Faster trains (such as the high-speed ICE) are more expensive than slower "regional" trains. To see if a railpass could save you money—which is often the case in Germany and Austria—check www.ricksteves.com/rail. If buying point-to-point tickets, note that prices can fluctuate (you can usually save money by booking more expensive train journeys online; tickets are sold up to three months in advance). To research train schedules and fares, visit Germany's excellent all-Europe timetable: www.bahn.com.

By Car: It's cheaper to arrange most car rentals from the US. For tips on your insurance options, see www.ricksteves.com/cdw, and for route planning, consult www.viamichelin.com. Bring your driver's license. Germany's toll-free autobahn (freeway) system lets you zip around the country in a snap. While there's often no official speed limit, going above the posted recommended speed invalidates your insurance. Many German cities—including Munich, Freiburg, Frankfurt, Köln, Dresden, Leipzig, and Berlin—require drivers to buy a special sticker *(Umweltplakette)* to drive in the city center. These already come standard with most German rental cars; ask when you pick up your car. A car is a worthless headache in any big city—park it safely (get tips from your hotelier).

If you're driving in Austria, you're technically required to have an International Driving Permit, which is a translation of your driver's license (sold at your local AAA office for $15 plus the cost of two passport-type photos; see www.aaa.com). Note that to drive on Austria's freeways, you're required to buy a toll sticker (Vignette, €8.30/10 days, €24.20/2 months, sold at gas stations). Unlike Germany, Austria enforces a speed limit on its freeways.

Local road etiquette is similar to that in the US. Ask your car-rental company about the rules of the road, or check the US State Department website (www.travel.state.gov, click on "International Travel," then specify your country of choice and click "Traffic Safety and Road Conditions").

Helpful Hints

Emergency Help: To summon the **police** or an **ambulance,** call 112. For passport problems, call the **US Embassy** in Germany (in Berlin: tel. 030/83050; consular services tel. 030/8305-1200—Mon–Thu 14:00–16:00 only, http://germany.usembassy.gov) or in Austria (in Vienna: tel. 01/313-390; consular services tel. 01/313-397-535—Mon-Fri 8:00–11:30, www.usembassy.at). For other concerns, get advice from your hotel.

Theft or Loss: To replace a passport, you'll need to go in person to an embassy (see above). Cancel and replace your credit and debit cards by calling these 24-hour US numbers collect: Visa—tel. 303/967-1096, MasterCard—tel. 636/722-7111, American Express—tel. 336/393-1111. File a police report either on the spot or within a day or two; you'll need it to submit an insurance claim for lost or stolen railpasses or travel gear, and it can help with replacing your passport or credit and debit cards. Precautionary measures can minimize the effects of loss—back up your digital photos and other files frequently. For more information, see www.ricksteves.com/help.

Time: Europe uses the 24-hour clock. It's the same through 12:00 noon, then keep going: 13:00, 14:00, and so on. Germany and Austria, like most of continental Europe, are six/nine hours ahead of the East/West Coasts of the US.

Business Hours: In Germany and Austria, most shops are open from about 9:00 until 18:00 to 20:00 on weekdays, but close early on Saturday (generally between 12:00 and 17:00, depending on whether you're in a town or a big city). In small towns, a few shops may take a mid-afternoon break on weekdays (roughly between 12:00 and 14:00 or 15:00). Most shops close entirely on Sundays.

Holidays and Festivals: Europe celebrates many holidays, which can close sights and attract crowds (book hotel rooms ahead). For more on holidays and festivals, check the national websites: www.germany.travel and www.austria.info. For a simple list showing major—though not all—events, see www.ricksteves.com/festivals.

Numbers and Stumblers: What Americans call the second floor of a building is the first floor in Europe. Europeans write dates as day/month/year. Commas are decimal points and vice versa—a dollar and a half is 1,50, and there are 5.280 feet in a mile. Europe uses the metric system: A kilogram is 2.2 pounds; a liter is about a quart; and a kilometer is six-tenths of a mile.

Resources from Rick Steves

This Snapshot guide is excerpted from my latest edition of *Rick Steves' Germany*, which is one of more than 30 titles in my series of guidebooks on European travel. I also produce a public television series, *Rick Steves' Europe*, and a public radio show, *Travel with Rick Steves*. My website, www.ricksteves.com, offers free travel information, a forum for travelers' comments, guidebook updates, my travel blog, an online travel store, and information on European railpasses and our tours of Europe. If you're bringing a mobile device on your trip, you can download free information from Rick Steves Audio Europe, featuring podcasts of my radio shows, free audio tours of major sights in Europe, and travel interviews about Germany and Austria (via www.ricksteves.com/audioeurope, iTunes, Google Play, or the Rick Steves Audio Europe free smartphone app). You can follow me on Facebook and Twitter.

Additional Resources

Tourist Information: www.germany.travel and www.austria.info
Passports and Red Tape: www.travel.state.gov
Packing List: www.ricksteves.com/packlist
Travel Insurance: www.ricksteves.com/insurance
Cheap Flights: www.kayak.com
Airplane Carry-on Restrictions: www.tsa.gov/travelers
Updates for This Book: www.ricksteves.com/update

How Was Your Trip?

If you'd like to share your tips, concerns, and discoveries after using this book, please fill out the survey at www.ricksteves.com/feedback. Thanks in advance—it helps a lot.

German Survival Phrases

In the phonetics, ī sounds like the long i in "light," and bolded syllables are stressed.

English	German	Pronunciation
Good day.	Guten Tag.	**goo**-tehn tahg
Do you speak English?	Sprechen Sie Englisch?	**shprehkh**-ehn zee **ehgn**-lish
Yes. / No.	Ja. / Nein.	yah / nīn
I (don't) understand.	Ich verstehe (nicht).	ikh fehr-**shtay**-heh (nikht)
Please.	Bitte.	**bit**-teh
Thank you.	Danke.	**dahng**-keh
I'm sorry.	Es tut mir leid.	ehs toot meer līt
Excuse me.	Entschuldigung.	ehnt-**shool**-dig-oong
(No) problem.	(Kein) Problem.	(kīn) proh-**blaym**
(Very) good.	(Sehr) gut.	(zehr) goot
Goodbye.	Auf Wiedersehen.	owf **vee**-der-zayn
one / two	eins / zwei	īns / tsvī
three / four	drei / vier	drī / feer
five / six	fünf / sechs	fewnf / zehkhs
seven / eight	sieben / acht	**zee**-behn / ahkht
nine / ten	neun / zehn	noyn / tsayn
How much is it?	Wieviel kostet das?	**vee**-feel **kohs**-teht dahs
Write it?	Schreiben?	**shrī**-behn
Is it free?	Ist es umsonst?	ist ehs oom-**zohnst**
Included?	Inklusive?	in-kloo-**zee**-veh
Where can I buy / find...?	Wo kann ich kaufen / finden...?	voh kahn ikh **kow**-fehn / **fin**-dehn
I'd like / We'd like...	Ich hätte gern / Wir hätten gern...	ikh **heh**-teh gehrn / veer **heh**-tehn gehrn
...a room.	...ein Zimmer.	īn **tsim**-mer
...a ticket to ____.	...eine Fahrkarte nach ____.	ī-neh **far**-kar-teh nahkh
Is it possible?	Ist es möglich?	ist ehs **mur**-glikh
Where is...?	Wo ist...?	voh ist
...the train station	...der Bahnhof	dehr **bahn**-hohf
...the bus station	...der Busbahnhof	dehr **boos**-bahn-hohf
...the tourist information office	...das Touristen-informations-büro	dahs too-**ris**-tehn-in-for-maht-see-**ohns**-bew-roh
...toilet	...die Toilette	dee toh-**leh**-teh
men	Herren	**hehr**-rehn
women	Damen	**dah**-mehn
left / right	links / rechts	links / rehkhts
straight	geradeaus	geh-**rah**-deh-**ows**
When is this...	Um wieviel Uhr ist hier...	oom **vee**-feel oor ist heer
...open / closed?	...geöffnet / geschlossen?	geh-**urf**-neht / geh-**shloh**-sehn
At what time?	Um wieviel Uhr?	oom **vee**-feel oor
Just a moment.	Moment.	moh-**mehnt**
now / soon / later	jetzt / bald / später	yehtst / bahld / **shpay**-ter
today / tomorrow	heute / morgen	**hoy**-teh / **mor**-gehn

In the Restaurant

English	German	Pronunciation
I'd like / We'd like...	Ich hätte gern / Wir hätten gern...	ikh **heh**-teh gehrn / veer **heh**-tehn gehrn
...a reservation for...	...eine Reservierung für...	ī-neh rehr-zer-**feer**-oong fewr
...a table for one / two.	...einen Tisch für eine Person / zwei Personen.	ī-nehn tish fewr ī-neh pehr-**zohn** / tsvī pehr-**zoh**-nehn
Non-smoking.	Nichtraucher.	**nikht**-rowkh-er
Is this seat free?	Ist hier frei?	ist heer frī
Menu (in English), please.	Speisekarte (auf Englisch), bitte.	**shpī**-zeh-kar-teh (owf **ehng**-lish) **bit**-teh
service (not) included	Trinkgeld (nicht) inklusive	**trink**-gehlt (nikht) in-kloo-**zee**-veh
cover charge	Eintritt	**īn**-trit
to go	zum Mitnehmen	tsoom **mit**-nay-mehn
with / without	mit / ohne	mit / **oh**-neh
and / or	und / oder	oont / **oh**-der
menu (of the day)	(Tages-) Karte	(**tah**-gehs-) **kar**-teh
set meal for tourists	Touristenmenü	too-**ris**-tehn-meh-new
specialty of the house	Spezialität des Hauses	shpayt-see-ah-lee-**tayt** dehs **how**-zehs
appetizers	Vorspeise	**for**-shpī-zeh
bread / cheese	Brot / Käse	broht / **kay**-zeh
sandwich	Sandwich	**zahnd**-vich
soup	Suppe	**zup**-peh
salad	Salat	zah-**laht**
meat	Fleisch	flīsh
poultry	Geflügel	geh-**flew**-gehl
fish	Fisch	fish
seafood	Meeresfrüchte	**meh**-rehs-frewkh-teh
fruit	Obst	ohpst
vegetables	Gemüse	geh-**mew**-zeh
dessert	Nachspeise	**nahkh**-shpī-zeh
mineral water	Mineralwasser	min-eh-**rahl**-vah-ser
tap water	Leitungswasser	**lī**-toongs-vah-ser
milk	Milch	milkh
(orange) juice	(Orangen-) Saft	(oh-**rahn**-zhehn-) zahft
coffee / tea	Kaffee / Tee	kah-**fay** / tay
wine	Wein	vīn
red / white	rot / weiß	roht / vīs
glass / bottle	Glas / Flasche	glahs / **flah**-sheh
beer	Bier	beer
Cheers!	Prost!	prohst
More. / Another.	Mehr. / Noch eins.	mehr / nohkh īns
The same.	Das gleiche.	dahs **glīkh**-eh
Bill, please.	Rechnung, bitte.	**rehkh**-noong **bit**-teh
tip	Trinkgeld	**trink**-gehlt
Delicious!	Lecker!	**lehk**-er

For more user-friendly German phrases, check out *Rick Steves' German Phrase Book and Dictionary* or *Rick Steves' French, Italian & German Phrase Book.*

PRACTICALITIES

INDEX

INDEX

Rick's Free Travel App

Join a Rick Steves tour

Enjoy Europe's warmest welcome... with the flexibility and friendship of a small group getting to know Rick's favorite places and people. It all starts with our free tour catalog and DVD.

Great guides, small groups, no grumps.

▸ Explore Europe

Browse thousands of articles, video clips, photos and radio interviews, plus find a wealth of money-saving tips for planning your dream trip. You'll find up-to-date information on Europe's best destinations, packing smart, getting around, finding rooms, staying healthy, avoiding scams and more.

▸ Travel News

Subscribe to our free Travel News e-newsletter, and get monthly updates from Rick on what's happening in Europe!

▸ Travel Forums

Learn, ask, share—our online community of savvy travelers is a great resource for first-time travelers to Europe, as well as seasoned pros.

NOW AVAILABLE:
eBOOKS, DVD & BLU-RAY

TRAVEL CULTURE

Europe 101
European Christmas
Postcards from Europe
Travel as a Political Act

eBOOKS

Nearly all Rick Steves guides are available as eBooks. Check with your favorite bookseller.

RICK STEVES' EUROPE DVDs

11 New Shows 2013–2014
Austria & the Alps
Eastern Europe
England & Wales
European Christmas
European Travel Skills & Specials
France
Germany, BeNeLux & More
Greece, Turkey & Portugal
Iran
Ireland & Scotland
Italy's Cities
Italy's Countryside
Scandinavia
Spain
Travel Extras

BLU-RAY

Celtic Charms
Eastern Europe Favorites
European Christmas
Italy Through the Back Door
Mediterranean Mosaic
Surprising Cities of Europe

PHRASE BOOKS & DICTIONARIES

French
French, Italian & German
German
Italian
Portuguese
Spanish

JOURNALS

Rick Steves' Pocket Travel Journal
Rick Steves' Travel Journal

PLANNING MAPS

Britain, Ireland & London
Europe
France & Paris
Germany, Austria & Switzerland
Ireland
Italy
Spain & Portugal

Rick Steves

www.ricksteves.com

EUROPE GUIDES

Best of Europe
Eastern Europe
Europe Through the Back Door
Mediterranean Cruise Ports
Northern European Cruise Ports

COUNTRY GUIDES

Croatia & Slovenia
England
France
Germany
Great Britain
Ireland
Italy
Portugal
Scandinavia
Spain
Switzerland

CITY & REGIONAL GUIDES

Amsterdam, Bruges & Brussels
Barcelona
Budapest
Florence & Tuscany
Greece: Athens & the Peloponnese
Istanbul
London
Paris
Prague & the Czech Republic
Provence & the French Riviera
Rome
Venice
Vienna, Salzburg & Tirol

SNAPSHOT GUIDES

Berlin
Bruges & Brussels
Copenhagen & the Best of
   Denmark
Dublin
Dubrovnik
Hill Towns of Central Italy
Italy's Cinque Terre
Krakow, Warsaw & Gdansk
Lisbon
Madrid & Toledo
Milan & the Italian Lakes District
Munich, Bavaria & Salzburg
Naples & the Amalfi Coast
Northern Ireland
Norway
Scotland
Sevilla, Granada & Southern Spain
Stockholm

POCKET GUIDES

Athens
Barcelona
Florence
London
Paris
Rome
Venice

Rick Steves guidebooks are published by Avalon Travel, a member of the Perseus Books Group.

Avalon Travel
a member of the Perseus Books Group
1700 Fourth Street
Berkeley, CA 94710

Printed in Canada by Friesens. First printing January 2014.

ISBN 978-1-61238-693-5

For the latest on Rick's lectures, guidebooks, tours, public radio show, and public television series, contact Europe Through the Back Door, Box 2009, Edmonds, WA 98020, tel. 425/771-8303, fax 425/771-0833, www.ricksteves.com, rick@ricksteves.com.

Europe Through the Back Door

Managing Editor: Risa Laib
Editorial & Production Manager: Jennifer Madison Davis
Editors: Glenn Eriksen, Tom Griffin, Cameron Hewitt, Deb Jensen, Suzanne Kotz, Cathy Lu, John Pierce, Carrie Shepard
Editorial Assistant: Jessica Shaw
Editorial Intern: Zosha Millman
Researchers: Glenn Eriksen, Cameron Hewitt, Cary Walker, Ian Watson
Maps & Graphics: David C. Hoerlein, Sandra Hundacker, Lauren Mills, Mary Rostad, Laura VanDeventer

Avalon Travel

Senior Editor and Series Manager: Madhu Prasher
Editor: Jamie Andrade
Associate Editor: Annette Kohl
Assistant Editor: Maggie Ryan
Copy Editor: Suzie Nasol
Proofreader: Gayle Hart
Indexer: Stephen Callahan
Production & Typesetting: McGuire Barber Design
Cover Design: Kimberly Glyder Design
Maps & Graphics: Kat Bennett, Mike Morgenfeld

Front Cover Photo: Marienplatz in Munich © Hirotaka Ihara / 123rf.com
Title Page Photo: view over Munich © koi88/www.123rf.com
Page 1 Photo: Marienplatz © foottoo/www.123rf.com
Additional Photography: Dominic Bonuccelli, Lee Evans, Cameron Hewitt, David C. Hoerlein, Robyn Stencil, Rick Steves, Gretchen Strauch, Karoline Vass, Ian Watson

ABOUT THE AUTHOR

RICK STEVES

 Since 1973, Rick Steves has spent 100 days every year exploring Europe. Along with writing and researching a bestselling series of guidebooks, Rick produces a public television series *(Rick Steves' Europe)*, a public radio show *(Travel with Rick Steves)*, and an app and podcast *(Rick Steves Audio Europe)*; writes a nationally syndicated newspaper column; organizes guided tours that take over ten thousand travelers to Europe annually; and offers an information-packed website (www.ricksteves.com). With the help of his hardworking staff of 80 at Europe Through the Back Door—in Edmonds, Washington, just north of Seattle—Rick's mission is to make European travel fun, affordable, and culturally enlightening for Americans.

Connect with Rick:

More for your trip!
Maximize the experience with Rick Steves as your guide

Guidebooks
Switzerland, Vienna and Prague guid
make side-trips smooth and affordal

Phrase Books
Rely on Rick's
German Phrase Book
& Dictionary

Rick's DVDs and Blu-rays
Preview where you're
going with 4 shows
on Germany

Free! Rick's Audio Europe™ App
Hear free Germany travel tips from
Rick's radio shows

Small-Group Tours
Including the Best of Germany,
Austria and Switzerland